# STAR WALK

COVER
ILLUSTRATOR

SPOTLIGHT

## CHARLES A. CSURI

❖ Dr. Charles A. Csuri, whose computer-enhanced images make up the cover of *Star Walk*, is the director of Ohio State University's Advanced Computing Center for the Arts and Design. A pioneer in the field of computer graphics, Csuri says "I was serious about art when I was eleven years of age."

❖ Csuri creates his unique works of art by scanning photographs of his paintings and drawings into a computer. Then he uses the computer to manipulate the shapes and figures in the photographs. As *Star Walk*'s cover illustrates, the results are both original and engaging.

Acknowledgments appear on pages 414–415, which constitute an extension of this copyright page.

© 1993 Silver Burdett Ginn Inc.
Cover art © 1993 by Charles A. Csuri.

ISBN 0–663–54661–3

1 2 3 4 5 6 7 8 9 10 RRD 98 97 96 95 94 93 92

*New Dimensions*
IN THE
## WORLD OF READING

# STAR WALK

## PROGRAM AUTHORS

| | | |
|---|---|---|
| James F. Baumann | Roselmina Indrisano | P. David Pearson |
| Theodore Clymer | Dale D. Johnson | Taffy E. Raphael |
| Carl Grant | Connie Juel | Marian Davies Toth |
| Elfrieda H. Hiebert | Jeanne R. Paratore | Richard L. Venezky |

## SILVER BURDETT GINN

**NEEDHAM, MA    MORRISTOWN, NJ**
ATLANTA, GA    DALLAS, TX    DEERFIELD, IL    MENLO PARK, CA

# Unit 1 Theme
# *Turning Points*

# Unit 2 Theme
# Making Connections

# Unit 3 Theme

# On Dreamers' Wings

9

# Unit 4 Theme
# Whispers from the Past

# Turning Points

"*Each* person is a truth,"
a wise person once said.
How do stories help you know
what is true for you?

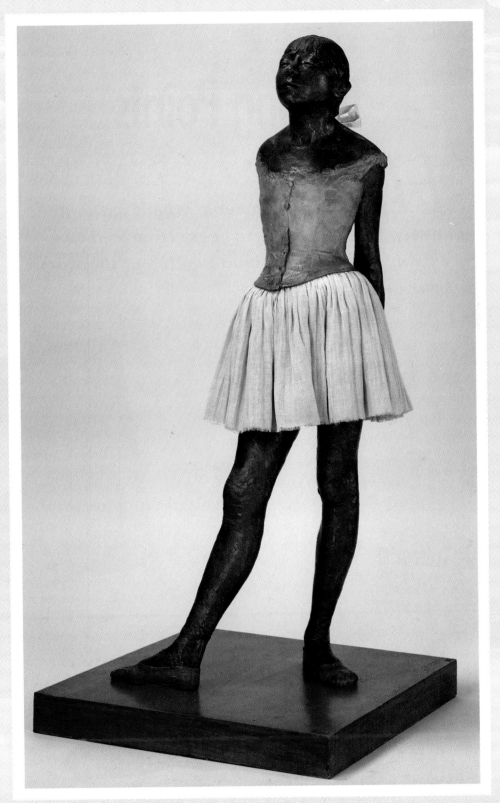

LITTLE FOURTEEN-YEAR-OLD DANCER, *bronze sculpture by Hilaire-Germain Edgar Degas (French, 1834-1917), Bronze, tulle skirt, and satin hair ribbon, 39" high, bequest of Mrs. H.O. Havemeyer, 1929, H.O. Havemeyer Collection. 29.100.370, © The Metropolitan Museum of Art, New York*

13

*Theme Books for*

# Turning Points

*H*ow well can we know others without knowing where they have been? How well can we know ourselves without looking at the story of our own lives?

❖ While the end of the world seems imminent, eighth-grader Tim Walden struggles to fulfill his most cherished wishes and demanding duties. William Corbin tells the story of what may be the last months of Tim's life in *Me and the End of the World*.

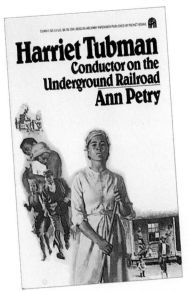

❖ Author Ann Petry's real-life hero is *Harriet Tubman: Conductor on the Underground Railroad*. A woman born into slavery, Tubman chose not only to make her own difficult and dangerous flight from bondage, but also to lead more than 300 other people to freedom.

14

✤ In Katherine Paterson's *The Sign of the Chrysanthemum*, young Muna struggles to come of age, searching for the father he never knew. Will Muna's father be the respected warrior of his dreams?

✤ Whenever temperamental Elaine gets into trouble, her frustrated family relies on thirteen-year-old Andrea in Stella Pevsner's *And You Give Me a Pain, Elaine*. But Andrea is not sure she likes being the reliable one—nor being taken for granted.

*More Books to Enjoy*

*Romeo and Juliet: Together (and Alive!) at Last* by Avi
*So Far from the Bamboo Grove* by Yoko Kawashima Watkins
*Dicey's Song* by Cynthia Voight
*Bill Cosby: Family Funny Man* by Larry Kettelkamp

# THE OBSIDIAN RING

**from *Rafael and the Raiders* by Hilary Beckett**

When Rafael's parents travel to Europe on a long business trip, they decide that Rafael should stay in New York City with his aunt and cousins. New York City is a long way from Rafael's home in Mexico, and on Monday Rafael must start at a new school.

"Rafael," she kept saying, trying to make me see it her way, "we'll only be gone for a few months. And all that time your father's business will keep us on the move. How can you go to school over there in Europe with all that moving? Besides, you will improve your English here in New York."

It was September. The idea was that I would start in Miguel's school while my parents were gone. I would be living with him and his five-year-old brother, Francisco, at Aunt Teresa's house.

"I still want to go with you," I kept insisting.

"Rafael, it is impossible! You cannot," she said. "But tell me what you want for your birthday," she went on. "It is coming in December. Tell me what you want. Then we'll bring you back a present from Europe."

I guess this was supposed to make me feel better, her remembering my birthday. And I knew she and my father would buy me a fantastic birthday present. Almost anything I asked for.

But they wouldn't do this *one* thing for me, now—take me with them on their trip—so I said to my mother (to show her how angry I still felt), "Get me anything. You pick it out. Get what you like." I shrugged.

"Go on! Please tell me what you want, *mi hijo*,"[1] my mother said. "Tell me before our flight is called."

We were in this crowded passenger lounge at Kennedy. I was standing with my mother near the exit door. My father was over by the checkout counter attending to last-minute details. Aunt Teresa and my cousins were looking out the big window at planes landing and taking off.

"Please, Rafael? Don't be childish about it. You're not a baby any more. You're almost thirteen, Rafael. Practically a man. Why, you are almost as tall as I am! If you grow any more while we are away, how will I recognize you when I come home?"

"You'll recognize me all right when you get home. But—" I was losing the fight. I looked down at the floor.

"Rafael, it's hard for us saying good-bye, too." My mother tilted my face up so that I would look at her. She stared straight into my eyes. "It's hard for you, I know—leaving Mexico and

[1]mi hijo (mē ē′ hō) my son

17

your friends."

"I wish at least I had something to give you to make you less homesick, a *recuerdo*[2] of Mexico." Her face brightened. She touched her middle right finger with the fingers of her left hand. "I know! Why don't you take the ring now, Rafaelito, the obsidian ring? Grandfather wanted you to have it some day. I think today is the perfect day!"

She pulled my grandfather's ring off her finger and folded it into my hand. "There. It's yours, Rafaelito. It will be a souvenir for you, a link to Mexico."

I looked at it. The shiny black stone was set in an old-fashioned silver band. Strong streaks of light ran through the dark obsidian as if the sun of Mexico was trapped in rich Mexican earth. Obsidian was "a jewel from a Mexican volcano." I remembered my grandfather telling me something like that when I was little.

"Take care of it, Rafael," said my mother. "And take care of yourself while we are away!" She hugged me.

I felt older because she'd given the ring to me, closer to being grown up. On the other hand, I knew I was still young enough to miss her very much while she was away. I rubbed the ring between my fingers.

"Thank you," I said. My eyes itched. But I didn't want her to think I was crying, so I didn't rub them.

Seconds later, it seemed, the plane departure was announced. The passengers in the lounge started collecting cameras, umbrellas, hand luggage, and began moving toward the exit. Friends and family saying good-bye to them pressed with them, as far as the gate and the big glass window. I held the ring tight as I kissed my parents good-bye. "*Adiós! Adiós!*"[3] we all said to each other.

Then the four of us (Aunt Teresa, my cousins, and I) stood waving at the big plane through the window after my parents boarded, although we couldn't really make out faces at the plane's tiny windows. It seemed to me that the smell of my mother's perfume still hung in the now almost empty passenger lounge.

"Come on, boys, let's go," said Aunt Teresa, gently putting an arm around my shoulders. "You won't be able to see the plane

18    [2]recuerdo (re kwer′ dō) momento; souvenir
[3]adiós (ä dyôs′) good-bye

once it's taxied down the field. Let's get the bus back home. You want sodas? Comic books?"

"I want a comic book!" Francisco jumped up and down with excitement.

"All right, *niños*.[4] Come on."

We picked out comic books and then climbed on a bus near the entrance to the airport. In the yellowish light inside the bus I showed my cousins the obsidian ring.

"Wow!" said Miguel. "The Aztecs used to have obsidian in ancient times in Mexico."

Francisco asked, "Is it worth a lot of money?"

"I don't think so."

"It's nice anyway," he told me. He touched the obsidian with his small finger. "Can I see Mexico some day, Mom?"

"You were born there, although you don't remember. Of course, you can see it again some day, Francisco," Aunt Teresa answered.

In half an hour we were in her neighborhood. She lived in Queens, and I knew it was not far from the airport. In fact, I'd been there earlier in the morning. But I didn't remember the neighborhood at all when we got off the bus.

How could I recognize anything I'd seen that day? We'd come in early, my parents and I, from Mexico—so early the sun hadn't yet risen. Then we'd dropped off my stuff at Aunt Teresa's. My parents wanted to sight-see in New York before they left for Europe, so the day (to me) was a jumble of Radio City, the Statue of Liberty, Central Park Zoo, the Empire State Building. It was like one of these round tubes you get for Christmas, that you look through and see jagged patterns of colored glass.

Aunt Teresa pointed down her street. "There's the apartment."

She lived in what she called "garden apartments," low two-story buildings with shrubs and trees around them. Above the trees, I saw the moon in the clear autumn sky. Near the stars I could make out the flickering lights of a plane. I wondered how near my parents' plane was to Europe. Francisco looked up, too.

[4]*niños* (nē nyōs) children

19

"That plane Aunt Maria and Uncle Emilio went away in, how big was it, Miguel?"

"As big as the Empire State Building," said Miguel.

"That big?"

"Maybe not quite . . ."

"Mom, can I stay up and talk with Rafe and Miguel? Rafe, are you going to stay with us a long time?"

"Right," I said in answer to Francisco's second question. I lifted him up on my shoulders. He grabbed onto my hair.

"Rafe, do they have TV in Mexico?"

"Sure."

"Comic books?"

"Sure."

"Baseball? Bubble gum? Ice cream?"

"Sure, Francisco. It's just like here."

Only it wasn't, of course. Mexico was my home.

"Time for bed, Francisco!" Aunt Teresa called.

I hugged him and put him down.

"Come on into my room, Rafe," Miguel said. I was going to sleep in the other bed, the bed Francisco usually had. For the time I was staying there he had a cot in Aunt Teresa's bedroom.

That morning I'd thrown my suitcases on the bed without really looking at the room. So I wasn't prepared, when Miguel turned on his light, for the sight of so many familiar things. Miguel and I had a lot of the same posters, the same books, the same records. I walked around the room touching his stuff, telling him, "I've got that in Mexico. And that. And that."

He grinned. "Don't you remember that the aunts and uncles always said we were like twins? That we looked alike and acted alike? And we always liked the same things? Do you think we look like brothers, now?"

I stood near him and we looked in the closet mirror. Miguel was taller. His hair was longer. But our eyes were alike—gray-green and deep-set. And we both were on the skinny side.

I was born five days before Miguel, and we had the same sign of the zodiac—Sagittarius.

"Aunt Luisa said Sagittarians were always close. Especially when they were relatives. Remember?" Miguel said. "You'll be here for your birthday, won't you, Rafe? Wow, that's the first time since before I left Mexico!"

"Can we have a party?"

"A super-party! *Una fiesta fantástica!*[5] Like no other party in the world!"

Miguel settled himself on his bed and stretched out with his hands under his head. "Hey, Rafe, do you remember the jokes we used to save for each other?"

Before Miguel had moved up to New York after his father died, he'd lived in Guadalajara[6]—just far enough away from Mexico City to mean we couldn't see each other every day. Or even every week. We'd gone through a stage where we'd done nothing but store up jokes between visits. Even after he'd come up to the States, we'd written jokes to each other in letters.

"Hey, Miguel," I said, "Where does a sheep go to get a haircut?"

[5]Una fiesta fantástica (oo′ nä fē es′ tä fän täs′ tē kä) a wonderful feast
[6]Guadalajara (gwä dä lä hä′ rä)

21

"To the baa-baa shop!" He started to laugh. "That was the summer we went up to Disneyland. We weren't much older than Francisco is now. Hey, Rafe, how does an elephant get down from a tree?"

"He sits in a tree and waits until fall!"

Laughing hysterically, we threw ourselves on the beds and muffled our giggles in pillows. We heard Aunt Teresa call to us. "Quiet, boys! Not so much noise. It's after Francisco's bedtime. You can laugh tomorrow."

"Tomorrow we'll explore the neighborhood!" Miguel whispered. "I'll take you to meet my friends."

That scared me. I wanted to think Miguel had no other friends but me in this strange neighborhood where everyone spoke English, where I was going to have to start a new school. I wanted to be his only friend, the way it had been when we'd been together during vacations when we were little kids.

We undressed and got ready for bed. After Miguel switched off the light, I reached back up to the table for my ring, my obsidian ring. I thought about Mexico. I'd be away from home, and from my own friends, for a long time. Suppose they forgot me? I decided to send them all post cards the next day.

But the next day Miguel had big plans. He was on the phone calling his friends before breakfast. "We've only got Saturday and Sunday before school starts. A lot of people to see."

Aunt Teresa and Francisco and I sat at the table in the dinette. She offered to put bread in the toaster for me. I said, "No thanks, Aunt Teresa. I'm not hungry."

She laughed. It was a nice laugh, not a teasing one.

"Thinking about Monday, about a new school and about meeting new people, Rafael?"

I shrugged. "I guess they'll laugh at my English."

I figured the English I'd learned as a kid growing up in Mexico was going to turn out to be about as much like the English kids spoke in Queens as apples are like oranges.

"Try speaking it more with us," she said. "You speak it already with Francisco."

It was true. He knew hardly any Spanish. I'd used English with him all the time. I guess I wasn't scared because he was so young. I didn't expect a *little* kid to laugh at me.

"I know how you feel about school, Rafael. I remember how I felt when we moved to a new city when I was a girl. *Dios mio,* nobody disliked school like I did, for a while. It was because I was afraid I'd be laughed at."

"How come, Aunt Teresa?"

"Would you believe it was because of a jar of preserves? Of jam? The lunch I took to the new school wasn't exactly like the other kids'." She laughed again. "It was—well, a little unusual. A little funny. All because *mamacita*[7] used to put in a little jar of jam my grandmother made. As a treat. None of the children had ever heard of taking jam to school in their lunch in a jar. They thought it was funny. They all enjoyed something to laugh at. *Me.* For a while I was the saddest child in the new school."

"What could you do about it, Aunt Teresa?"

"I came home in tears to my mother. And she told me that of course if I didn't want to take the jam, I didn't have to. But if I wanted it, I would have to stand up to the other children."

"What did you decide?"

"I decided there was a day now and then when I liked the jam and that I wouldn't be bullied into leaving it at home. I told the children to stop laughing."

"Did they?"

"Some did. Some didn't. But I didn't give anyone the satis-faction of seeing me cry any more. And after a while, the children respected me. Some of them even asked for a taste of the jam.

"It sounds scary."

"Oh, it was. But, you see, it was the only thing to do. Want some toast now, Rafael?"

"OK."

Miguel was still on the phone, his feet up and over one end of the sofa. How was he dressed? I looked carefully to see.

It was OK to listen to a grown-up person like Aunt Teresa tell me how brave she'd been about a jar of jam, but I still didn't

[7]mamacita (mä mä sē′ tä)                                                      23

intend to make any more mistakes than I had to, to stand out any more than I had to, in Queens.

I especially didn't intend to *look* funny. Whatever Miguel had on, I'd wear it, too.

Jeans?

I checked out mine.

He had on sneakers.

Right. I had mine on, too.

"What do you want to eat tonight, Rafael? *Comida mexicana*?"[8] Aunt Teresa asked. She was on her way to the shopping center.

"Something American . . ." I kept looking at Miguel's clothes.

"All right. American food it will be. So long, kids!"

She took Francisco with her, even though he wanted to stay with us, wanting to be in on any fun we might be having. "Have a good day!"

Miguel got off the phone. "What do you do in Mexico these days, on a Saturday? Or on a vacation day? I forget. It's been such a long time."

"See friends. Play ball."

Miguel grinned. "Exactly the same as in Queens! Let's go."

To look at, Queens wasn't too different from the part of Mexico City I lived in. I lived in a taller apartment building (we had an elevator). And we had a balcony, not a small backyard. Also, the trees are different in Mexico City (more tropical). But the highways, the traffic, the parks reminded me of home. Except that the signs here were all in English, not in Spanish.

"Any other new kids going to start school Monday besides me?" I asked. "Will I be the only one?"

"There are always a lot of kids coming and going." Miguel sighed. "Hey, I wish you'd stay the whole year, Rafe, not just one semester. Any chance? It would really be great to have you around!"

Wow, he was planning my entire year, and I wasn't even eager for the first day of school.

[8]comida mexicana (kô mē′ dä  me hē kä′ nä) Mexican food

"Thanks," I said, and meant it. As I said, Miguel was my favorite cousin.

Which made it all the harder meeting his friends.

Not only did I want him not to *have* friends—except for me—but I wanted to be cool. I wanted to be friendly, but I didn't want to open my mouth and sound foolish. Don't think it wasn't a strain.

Yet I really liked his friends, I decided, after we'd gone to visit some. We ended up in Josh's backyard. He was Miguel's closest friend. Josh, Karen (another friend), and Miguel and I sat in the sun on the edge of Josh's kid brother's sandbox. Like kids, we played with the sand while we talked.

"Hey, Rafe, are you hungry?" Miguel asked when the sun was directly over our heads.

"Let's go to Louie's for lunch," Josh suggested.

We called Aunt Teresa and told her we'd eat lunch out. Then we went to this special hamburger place.

Now, we have big fancy hamburger stands in Mexico, but I'd never seen one as big as this one. It had an arch over it that made it look about a mile high. And the big glass front looked about a mile wide. A million people seemed to be inching in, then inching out, with their arms full of paper bags.

"They've got thirty-one kinds of hamburgers," Miguel boasted. "Anything you want!"

I looked at the giant menu over the counter while we waited in line. "Hey, what's a Luau Burger?" I spelled it out.

"Hawaiian. It's got pineapple," Karen said.

"And a True Blue Burger?"

"Blue cheese on top," Josh said.

To be polite, the other kids pushed me ahead of them in the line. I was the visitor, the guest. It was hard making my mind up. I finally settled on a Chili Burger.

That was great. But why, oh, why, didn't I keep my mouth shut after that? The kids kept nudging me, asking me if I wanted potatoes, relish, catsup—

So I finally asked for "potato ships."

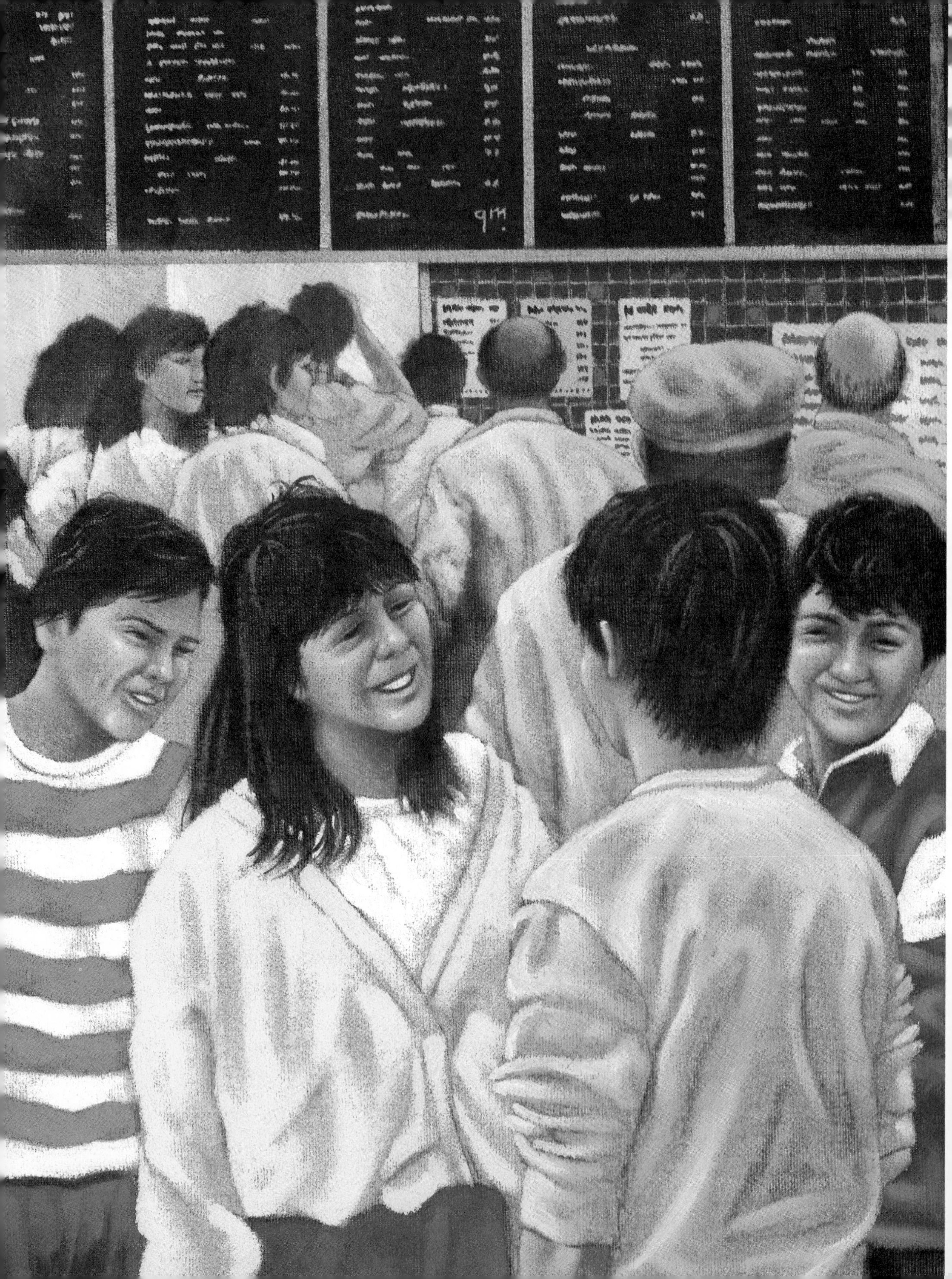

Or maybe I said "potato sheeps."

Whatever it was, the kids cracked up, laughing. I knew they didn't want to hurt my feelings, but they thought what I said was funny. And it really upset me. I hate being laughed at.

Which was why I spent the rest of the weekend dreaming of every possible way I could think of to make my parents come back and get me. Could I tell them I was dying of a mysterious disease, that they'd have to hurry back if they wanted to see me alive? No, they wouldn't really believe that. Nor would they believe the other phony excuses I thought up.

There really wasn't any reason, any way, I could get out of staying at Aunt Teresa's, and I knew it.

Sunday I was a miserable blob of homesickness. Only I didn't want Miguel to know that was the reason I was refusing to go out with him.

He knew, anyway. "Listen, Rafe, they laughed at my English too when I first came to Queens. There's no way to keep kids from laughing. But that doesn't mean they don't like you. Come on, let's go see Karen and Josh."

I let him drag me out of the house. But I didn't feel like talking much that day. I went to bed early, worrying about the next day.

"Are you sure school really starts today?" I asked Miguel in the morning.

"Sure. Come on and eat breakfast, Rafe."

Miguel sat there and calmly buttered his second piece of toast while elephants played soccer in my stomach. As much alike as we were, I remembered one of the main differences between Miguel and me.

When we were kids the relatives always called him "daring" and me "thoughtful." I think they meant I would think of all the scary sides to everything.

"Are you positive this isn't the wrong day?" I asked again.

"Today," Miguel insisted.

"Yeah, today." Francisco nodded vigorously. He stopped

listening to his cereal crackle in the milk long enough to say, "It's the first day of kindergarten, too. Maybe I can be milk monitor, like I was in nursery school." His brown eyes widened at the happy thought.

"Maybe this year you'll be late. Hurry up, Francisco!"

Aunt Teresa had to leave him at his school before she went to the office where she worked. "*Andale*,[9] Francisco!"

Miguel and I were the first ones out the door. Francisco and Aunt Teresa waved good-bye.

"Smell the fall leaves, Rafe!" Miguel said, happily shuffling his way to school through them.

"I don't feel like it," I said. The nearer we got to school the slower my steps got. Like I was walking through warm tar instead of through crisp leaves.

"I keep telling you, Rafe, you won't be the only new kid." Miguel dragged me up the front steps of the school.

"You naturally like people!" I said. "I'm afraid of them."

"But people like *you*, Rafe."

Everyone said hello to Miguel. He tried to introduce me to kids but I was afraid to start talking. I stood alone. Everyone else but me had someone to talk over the good times of summer with. I deliberately stood alone. I felt like I was watching a foreign movie with fuzzy subtitles.

When the bell rang, we pushed in. Miguel pointed out a line to me, a line in the front hall where new kids waited for their home-room assignments. I got on it automatically, like I was sleep-walking.

I began writing a letter (in my head) to my parents. "Dear Mother and Father, come to my rescue!" Then before I wrote much more, I found myself at the front of the line and I froze, remembering the "potato ships."

"Your name, please."

"Ortiz. Rafael Ortiz," I managed to say.

"Are you new?"

"Y-yes. My aunt t-telephoned about me." I took a deep breath and spoke slowly.

[9]ándale (än' dä le) walk

"Do you have a passport? Or other identification?"

Aunt Teresa had told me to bring my birth certificate. I handed it to the lady behind the desk.

She looked at it. Then she filled out a card with my name, a room number, the name of a teacher.

"Out that way." She pointed.

I found myself in the hall again. Every doorway looked exactly alike. There were miles of steel lockers. The number on the card was 243. Where was 243?

"You lost, kid?"

A huge guy with a tag saying STUDENT GUIDE stopped me. I handed him my card without speaking.

"Down the hall, then go upstairs, but be sure you take the steps marked UP not DOWN."

My feet echoed on the steps.

I found 241, 242, 243 . . .

And I didn't want to go in.

Through the little window in the door I could see kids laughing and joking. No doubt, in *English*. No doubt, they already all knew each other. I went in.

The teacher was just inside, sitting at his desk. He took my white card. "Welcome," he said, and shook my hand. "My name is Schwartz. Let's see what yours is." He looked at the card.

"Nice to have you—" he started to say, when a familiar voice said, "Hey, Rafe! You in my homeroom? Hey, great!"

"Wow, Josh!"

"Well, I guess the two of you already know each other." The teacher grinned. Then he called the class to order. And he sat us next to each other.

It was one of the longest days in my life, but it turned out not to be quite the worst. Not only was Josh in my homeroom, but Miguel was in my social studies class. Twice I saw Karen in the hall. I felt—a little—like I belonged in the new school.

That night after dinner I decided to write a real letter to my parents. Miguel lay on his bed reading while I propped up my notebook (it had the name of the school on it and the school seal) and put a clean sheet of paper on top of it. I wanted my parents to miss me. But I also wanted them to know things were really going all right with me. I wrote:

Dear Mother and Father:
I am well and I hope you are, too. School has started now and I have made some new friends. I hope you are enjoying London and Paris and Zurich. I mean I hope you are enjoying Europe but not too much, because I hope you are homesick—a little—for Mexico. Like I am. I don't like school as much as my school in Mexico. But I guess I can stand it. Miguel wants to know if I can stay all year. I told him I would let him know. Aunt Teresa sends love and kisses. So do Miguel and Francisco.
Love from your son,
Rafael
P.S. I still have the obsidian ring.

Reader's Response ∾ After Rafael returns to Mexico, what do you think he will say about his experience in New York City?

Library Link ∾ *This excerpt is from the book* Rafael and the Raiders *by Hilary Beckett. Read it to find out more about Rafael's adventures in New York.*

# A GLIMPSE OF
# MEXICO CITY

Mexico City is the capital of Mexico. As home to almost ten million people it is also one of the most populated cities in the world. It lies over 7,000 feet above sea level and is surrounded by mountains and two extinct volcanoes.

Seven hundred years ago the Aztecs built their capital at Tenochtitlán, on an island in Lake Texcoco. It was the first capital city in North or South America. The Spanish conquistador Hernán Cortés defeated the Aztecs in 1521 and destroyed much of Tenochtitlán. The Spanish colonists went on to use the Aztec stones to build their own capital on the same site.

La Torre Latinamericano ("Latin American Tower") is a modern skyscraper.

The magnificent Paseo de la Reforma is Mexico City's main thoroughfare.

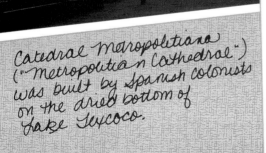

Catedral Metropolitiana ("Metropolitian Cathedral") was built by Spanish colonists on the dried bottom of Lake Texcoco.

Chapultepec Park and Castle. This city park is one of the largest in the world.

31

# THE FOOTBALL PLAYER

from <u>The Two Worlds of Jim Yoshida</u>
by JIM YOSHIDA with BILL HOSOKAWA

My father was a sturdily built man, fairly tall for a Japanese, and he became heavier as he grew older. He sported a bristly Charlie Chaplin mustache and one of his indulgences was cigars. He never learned much English, so he always spoke to us in Japanese. I could understand him, but I couldn't express myself in Japanese so I replied in English. This is the way most Japanese American families communicated, and we got along quite well.

I could never seem to penetrate my father's gruff exterior and I feared him as much as I loved him. I can't ever remember hearing him praise me. Whenever I did anything well, he simply said he expected me to do better next time, and eventually I came to understand that this was his way. When I was sixteen years old I picked a hundred-pound sack of rice off the floor and held it up over my head, the way a weight lifter lifts barbells. This was a feat of strength recognized among Japanese families as a sign that a lad had reached manhood. If Dad was proud, he didn't show any sign. But later Mother told me how really happy he was. About the same time I defeated my father for the first time at arm wrestling. We sat at the kitchen table facing each other. With elbows down on the table, we locked right hands and each tried to force the other's arm down. I was surprised at how easily I defeated him, for Dad had a reputation for physical strength. He was proud that I was growing strong and I felt sad that he was getting old, but neither of us said anything. Our relationship was such that we seldom voiced our thoughts to each other, and I suppose that's the way he was brought up.

With my mother, the relationship was altogether different. She was a tiny woman, no more than five feet two inches tall, but she was blessed with enormous vitality. She had a beautiful heart-shaped face. She was gentle; not once did she ever strike me, although I deserved punishment frequently, and I don't recall that she ever raised her voice to me. But she had a way of talking to me when I did wrong; these talks usually left me weeping in remorse.

Mother had an understanding of young people that was extremely unusual in the Japanese immigrant generation. Dad was strict and stern. He wanted to rear his children the way he had been brought up. Mother was wise enough to know that American children could not be reared like Japanese children, that we were products of the new world and we required freedom. Eventually I came to realize she was a mellowing, liberalizing influence on my father. This does not mean she was entirely permissive. In her own way she kept a tight rein on her children. When I became old enough to go out at night she insisted that I let her know when I came home. I would walk by her bedroom door and knock—*tum-ta-ta-tum-tum*. And she would knock back—*tum-tum*. If she slept while I was out, it was only lightly.

Most of our friends were other Japanese American families, with all of us in similarly humble circumstances. My closest friend was Pete Fujino, one of five kids whose family ran a small apartment house in the lower Yesler Way area. Pete was a natural athlete and wore a judo black belt. He was a little taller than I, and could run a lot faster, so that he played end on the Broadway High School varsity. Because we were both of Japanese extraction, and both team mainstays, the newspapers would refer to us as the Bengal Twins, Broadway being the Tigers. Pete's older sister worked as a waitress at the Paramount Cafe on Jackson Street, the heart of Seattle's international settlement, and he and I would go there often after judo practice to have a piece of pie and a glass of milk, and if we had a few nickels, play the pinball machines.

Usually on Friday nights Joe Nakatsu would join us to make plans for the weekend. Joe was about as big as Pete, and we met through judo. Joe's dad owned a fairly good-sized truck farm in Sunnyvale, on the southern outskirts of Seattle. Joe didn't say much, but we got along famously. He and I were usually the top boys in judo tournaments, which meant that often we faced each other. In one match we were both fooling around, each not wanting to throw the other, and the referee was about to call it a draw when Joe's dad jumped up and shouted: "Yoshida, if you're good enough to throw my son, I want you to throw him and win." Well, we both went at it, and I threw Joe. As soon as he hit the mat Joe jumped up and embraced me, and I cried because I had defeated my friend. We were that kind of buddies.

Another one of my closest friends was Kay Nakamura, who had more brothers and sisters than I can remember. Mr. Nakamura had a little dry-cleaning shop, also on Yesler Way, and I don't see how he supported his family. But they were all close; it was a warm family and the Nakamuras were good to be with. All the Nakamura kids were good at singing or tap-dancing or playing musical instruments, and on Fridays they'd put on a very informal "Amateur Night" at their home just to entertain friends. Sometimes Joe and Pete and another friend, Mud Tsuchikawa, and I and some others would go to the Nakamura home to listen to the singing and watch the dancing, and then we'd play penny ante poker. The winner left his money to buy pies and cakes and soft drinks for the next time we got together. It was a warm, happy time.

Kay and I were graduated from grade school together and started Broadway High School, but he found he liked playing pool better than studying. So he dropped out. Kay was good at anything he tried—football, basketball, track, baseball. He had deadly aim when he threw the newspapers on his route. And he was good at pool. He could start with only a dime in his pocket and play all day, winning consistently. He could cup his hand and imitate Louis Armstrong playing the "Sugar Blues," and he could do a great imitation of Fred Astaire tap-dancing on the sidewalk. At the end of my junior year Kay said he was going to Los Angeles to join his brother in a produce market. He'd write once in a while—with pencil on toilet paper. I really missed him.

Mud Tsuchikawa's name needs explaining. His given name was Masakatsu, which is as bad as Katsumi. Well, he had to have a nickname, but what can you make from Masakatsu? His family name, Tsuchikawa, means "Earth" (*tsuchi*) "River" (*kawa*). It was easy to get the nickname "Mud" out of "earth river," so that's what we called him. Mud was the best bowler in our group, and also the smoothest dancer. Dancing made me sweat, and I disliked it. Even when I was going with Pete's sister, Aki, I wouldn't dance, so she and Mud would be out on the floor together while I watched from the table. Mud turned out for the football team, too, but he couldn't quite make it.

After Kay left for Los Angeles, Mud, Pete, Joe and I spent a lot of time together, fooling around, talking about girls, eating, getting into mischief but never really creating trouble or winding up in a jam. Sometimes we'd go up to Madrona Park to play tennis or dance with the car radio going full blast. Some evenings we'd drive out to Magnolia Bluffs for a weiner roast and to dig for butter clams. Some of my other friends were George Tatsumi, who we called Dimples because he had them, Eugene Amabe, known as Beefo because he was heavy-set. Tak Shibuya, who was the best baseball pitcher in our group as well as the best student, and Junelow (Junks) Kurose, who stood six feet tall and weighed 235 pounds. Junks was a senior when I was a sophomore and we played on the same team at Broadway.

We did all the things white kids our age did for fun, but we never forgot we were Japanese Americans.

We lived an oddly mixed but pleasant life. We celebrated the Fourth of July, Thanksgiving and Christmas as well as the Japanese festivals like Boys' Day and Girls' Day and the Festival of the Dead in late summer. As children we went to public schools and learned about George Washington at Valley Forge and the grand heritage of a people who were willing to revolt for liberty and freedom. And after school was dismissed at 3 P.M., we trudged on to the Japanese Language School to learn a little about that very difficult language of our parents. Although some resented the double dose of schooling, we did not think it strange, because many of our Jewish friends in Seattle attended Hebrew school.

Somehow this life must have agreed with me, for by the time I was fifteen years old and a freshman at Broadway High School—in September of 1936—I stood five feet seven inches tall and weighed 168 pounds. Many of the other fellows signed up to try out for the freshman football team. I couldn't, because I had to go to Japanese school.

Still, it wouldn't hurt to watch for a little while. I sat on the sidelines, glancing at my Ingersoll watch frequently to make sure I would leave in time to get to Japanese school before the bell rang. About the third day the freshmen engaged in a scrimmage, and I couldn't tear myself away. I had played some sandlot football, and I figured I could do just as well as the boys in uniform. Before I knew it, it was too late to get to Japanese school on time. It didn't take me long to rationalize—being absent was only a little worse than being tardy. I was going to get a scolding if I showed up late without a good excuse, so I might just as well play hooky for the day. Before long, nothing seemed to be more important than playing football with the Broadway High School freshman team. I found myself walking over to the coach—his name was Bob Heaman—and telling him I wanted to turn out.

Heaman looked up and down my stocky frame. "What's your name?" he asked.

"Katsumi Yoshida," I replied.

"That's no name for a kid who wants to play football," he said. "I'm going to call you Jim." He reached into a pocket and pulled out a mimeographed form. "You have to get your parents' permission," he said. "Take this home and get your father to sign it. Come down to the locker room after school tomorrow and check out a uniform."

My heart sank. Here I was being invited to try out for the team and parental permission—an impossible obstacle—blocked the way.

Full of apprehension, I went home at the normal time. Apparently my mother was unaware of my absence from Japanese school, and if my sister Betty had noticed, she hadn't said anything. I knew that my mother could sense when I had something on my mind. Besides, I wanted to talk to her before Dad came home, so I came straight to the point.

"Mom," I said, "I want to turn out for the football team at school."

She scarcely looked up from her cooking, "Isn't it a very rough game?"

"Not really," I said.

After a moment she replied: "You are our only son, Katsumi, and I don't know what we would do if you were injured permanently playing football. Besides, what would you do about Japanese school? I think we had better forget about football."

I knew it was useless to try to change her mind, and even more useless to talk to Dad.

Next day, during a study period, I gave myself permission to play football. I carefully forged my father's signature on the slip. My hands were clammy when I gave the slip to Coach Heaman. I was sure he could hear the pounding of my heart and see the look of guilt that I knew was written

on my face. But he failed to notice and routinely filed the permission form and issued me an ancient, hand-me-down uniform and a pair of ill-fitting shoes.

I made the team as a running guard. This meant I pulled out of the line and ran interference for the ball-carrier. If I did what I was supposed to do and threw a good block, the ball-carrier had a chance of making a good gain. The position required speed, agility, size, and the willingness to play the part of a human battering ram. I loved the body contact. At the end of the freshman season I was one of several boys invited to suit up with the varsity. In the season finale the varsity coach, Jerry Robinson, let me play half the game.

Meanwhile, for some reason I have never understood, my absence from Japanese school went unnoticed. Perhaps I had dropped out before anyone became aware that I should have been attending classes. At any rate three months had slipped by without my ever setting foot in Japanese school, and I all but forgot that I was really supposed to be studying the intricacies of the ancestral language rather than learning to block and tackle.

I was finally tripped up when Betty brought home her report card from Japanese school right after the football season ended. As usual she had done very well in her studies, and Dad nodded his approval as he examined her record. I knew what was coming next. He turned to me and asked to see my report card.

"Sir," I said, "I don't have one."

His eyebrows shot up. "Why not? Did you lose it?"

"No sir, I haven't been attending Japanese school."

He fixed me with a stare that bored right through me. We were at the dinner table and Mother had served all of us with hot boiled rice to eat with the cooked meat and vegetables. Steam rose from the bowl in front of my father and I could see his temper rising, too. Ordinarily, I was famished by mealtime and made quick work of my dinner, but now I had lost all interest in food.

"Explain yourself," Dad ordered.

So I told him the whole story, including the way I had forged his signature, and his frown grew darker and darker.

*"Bakatare!"* he finally shouted in fury. There is no precise English equivalent for that word. It means fool, or imbecile, but there is much more scorn, vitriol and invective in the word than is indicated by direct translation.

Good old Mom. She averted a very explosive situation by suggesting that the dinner table was not the place for a scolding. She suggested we finish our dinner and then talk about the problem. I picked at my food while all the others seemed to eat with the usual relish. I wasn't too worried about what had happened—that was over the dam. My real concern was whether Dad would let me play football next season.

Sometime during the meal Dad must have seen the humor of my transgression. Perhaps he remembered pranks he had pulled as a boy. I was relieved to see his anger had given way to simply a serious mood when finally the dishes were cleared away.

First, he lectured me about how wrong it was to deceive one's parents, and I had to agree with him. Eventually he got around to football. "I can understand why you would want to play the game," he said. "It is a rough game and it is natural for boys to want to engage in rough sports. But you must remember you are the son of Japanese parents, and therefore you should take an interest in Japanese sports like *kendo* and judo."

*Kendo* is a form of fencing. The participants wear masks, helmets and armor, and whale away at each other with split bamboo staves which simulate the long, curved steel swords used by the samurai warriors of old. Judo is like wrestling, hand-to-hand combat, in which a smaller and weaker man learns to use his opponent's strength to defeat him. I wanted nothing to do with *kendo;* the prospect of fighting with sticks was too much. And I didn't have much enthusiasm for judo either, for I had heard that clever little fellows could whip big ones, and I was one of the "big" guys.

"Either sport is good," Dad was saying. "Either one will give you the discipline you need because they are Japanese sports. American life is too soft. You must learn to grow tougher, physically, mentally and morally."

Football isn't tough? He had never played football. He didn't know what it was to get your brains jarred loose in a hard tackle and then come back for more.

Just then I saw an out. I apologized for what I had done. I was truly sorry. I agreed to go back to Japanese school and try my best to make up for what I had missed. And I said I would go to judo class—and here was the hooker—if I could play football again next year.

The smile that had started to take shape on Dad's face vanished. He raised his arm as though to strike me and just as suddenly he dropped it.

"All right," he said with resignation. "Play football if you must, if it's that important to you. But remember there are things that are important to me, too. So go to Japanese school and try to learn a little about the language. And go to judo classes and learn a little about discipline." We shook hands and I think I gained a deeper understanding of Dad that night than ever before.

Several nights later when I came home from Japanese school Dad introduced me to a handsome, curly-haired fellow who was about eight or ten years older than I. His name was Kenny Kuniyuki; he was an instructor at the Tentokukwan Judo School and the son of one of Dad's best friends. Dad told me Kenny would be my judo teacher. Kenny was a little taller than I, powerfully built with broad, square shoulders that tapered down to slim hips and the muscular legs of an athlete. I liked him immediately. We had dinner together and then he drove me to the judo school.

There were perhaps two dozen boys, many of whom I knew, fooling around on the judo mats. All were wearing padded jackets and short trousers. When Kenny entered, their yelling and laughing stopped abruptly and they snapped to attention. Apparently he was a very important person at the school. Kenny led me to the framed portrait of a little, half-bald old man which hung on one wall and told me to bow before it each time I entered the hall. Later I learned he was Jigoro Kano, father of modern judo and regarded as a near-deity by devotees of the art.

For the next three weeks, every Monday, Wednesday and Friday, I went to the school and learned to sit Japanese-style with my legs folded under me, and to fall. Falling without hurting yourself is an art in itself. Gradually I learned to roll to absorb the impact as I hit the mat, to break the

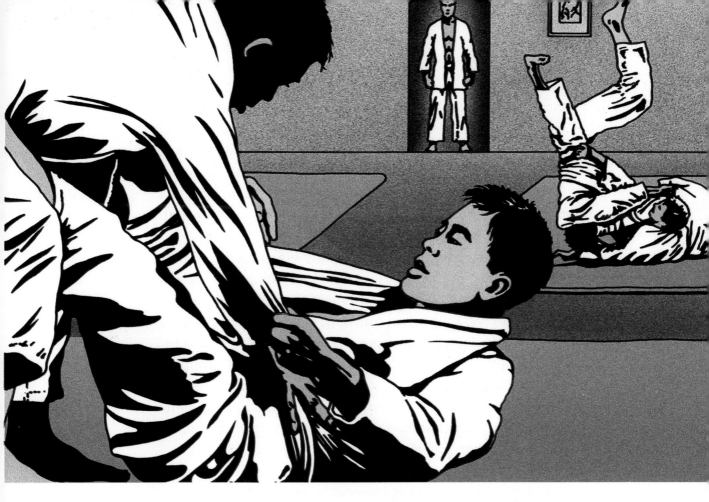

momentum with my arms and legs and shoulders before I crashed to the floor. Then Kenny—I was supposed to call him Kuniyuki Sensei (Instructor Kuniyuki)—began on the holds and throws. He seemed to think the best way to teach was to demonstrate. From seven to nine thirty I would practice with the other boys, throwing and being thrown almost without a break. Then the others were told to shower and change, but my evening was just starting.

"Come on, Yoshida," Kenny would say. He would let me throw him a few times, then *wham,* I would find myself thrown flat on the mat. "Get up," he would say. "We don't have time to sit around." *Wham,* I would go down again. Or he would say something like, "How would you like to see Tokyo?" I would drop my guard for the barest instant to reply, and *wham,* I would crash into the wall. He would pick me up, sweep my legs from under me and slam me to the mat, scolding me all the time for not taking the offensive. Once he put the choke hold on me and I was too exhausted to struggle. The bright lights overhead faded and I blacked out. Next thing I remember, I was sitting up with someone's knee in my back and arms across my chest. He jerked back on my shoulders while jabbing his knee into my spine and miraculously everything was in focus again.

Some of my friends felt that Kenny was picking on me unfairly. "Jim," one of them asked, "how come you take all that punishment? I'd quit if I were in your place." I must admit that I thought about quitting, especially on mornings after a particularly strenuous workout when I was so sore I could hardly crawl out of bed. But I knew that if I dropped judo I could forget about playing football. I also suspected that Dad had given Kenny orders to make it as rough as he could for me, and that only firmed up my determination to stick it out. Then one day it occurred to me that Kenny wouldn't be spending all that time with me if he didn't think a lot of me. And after that I vowed to take all the punishment he dealt out and come back for more. When Mom asked how I was getting along, I assured her that Kuniyuki Sensei was being extra nice to me.

About six months after I began judo lessons, everything began to fall in place. I was tough physically. I had learned, finally, to take the hardest falls without hurting myself, and now I was able to coordinate my skill together with my strength and dish it out as well as take it. I found a new exhilaration in the combat of judo, and excitement in the smell of the judo mats. Judo was as much fun as football.

Once a month we would have an intra-club tournament. The boys at the Tentokukwan School would be divided into two teams; then we would engage in elimination matches starting with the youngest and newest students. If you threw an opponent, or won a decision over him, you took on the next man and remained in the ring until you were defeated. Although I was bigger than most of the fellows, I still wore the white belt of the novice and was about in the middle of our lineup. In my first tournament I threw seven boys in a row, including two wearing the black belt of experts. I was having the time of my life. A black-belter must throw a white-belter or lose face. I had nothing to lose and could go all out. Kuniyuki Sensei gave me an approving look. Not long afterward I was jumped over all the intermediate steps—yellow, green, brown and purple—and given a black belt. It usually takes a student three or four years of hard work to win black-belt rating. I had done it in a fraction of that time. Dad beamed approval.

He raised no objection when I turned out for football in the fall of 1937, my sophomore year. I had kept my end of the bargain and he kept his. I made the team as running guard and was lucky enough to be an all-city selection even though we didn't win a single game. This was a busy time for I continued with judo after the daily football workouts. Still, I managed to keep my grades up. After football season I returned to Japanese school and made a valiant but futile effort to catch up with the other students trying to master an almost incomprehensible language.

In the summer of 1938 Kenny took me with him to Taku Harbor, Alaska, where he was foreman in a salmon cannery. It was common practice for Nisei teenagers in Seattle to work as cannery laborers during the two to three months of the summer season. We were paid about seventy-five dollars a month, plus transportation and room and board in a bunkhouse. Some of the boys gave their earnings to their parents to help support the family. Others saved the money for a college education. We ate rice and salmon at every meal and put in heavy physical labor ten hours a day, six days a week. Anything over sixty hours paid overtime—at thirty cents an hour if I remember correctly. I thrived on the

hard work. I returned to Broadway High for my junior year
with 190 muscular pounds on my five-foot nine-and-a-half-
inch frame. We had a new coach and although I was a
letterman, I had to start from scratch to earn my position.
But I was bigger and stronger than most of the boys, and
more experienced, and had no trouble keeping my job. Again
we went through the season without a victory, and once
more I was named all-city.

These were happy times. As a football star, I was a "big
man" in school. My teammates were of many ethnic origins—
Italians, Germans, Jews, Irish—but it never occurred to us
that we were different. We were all Americans held together
by a common love for football and loyalty to our school. I can
remember only one fight, and that was with some college
fellows. After judo practice one Friday night, Pete, Joe, Mud
and I drove to a drive-in for some root beer. There was some
difficulty getting out of the parking lot and four big fellows
in another car made some loud remarks. One of them made
the mistake of calling us "Japs," a fighting word like "Dago"
or "Kike." We piled out in a hurry. Pete grabbed one of the
fellows and threw him to the pavement. Joe had his man

helpless in an armlock. The biggest fellow swung at me. I
ducked, came up under him and flipped him to the ground. It
was all over in about thirty seconds.

That evening I learned strength is power. When we
demonstrated to those college guys that with judo we were
their physical masters, they quickly lost their belligerence.
They wanted to be friends. They invited us to have a drink
with them. We turned them down, feeling like cocks of the
walk. But we paid for it at Tentokukwan where, somehow,
the officials had heard of the fight. It had been drilled into us
time and again that judo skills were not to be demeaned by
street brawls. Each night for the next two weeks we had to
sit Japanese-style on our knees and meditate about our
"sin." Our American knees weren't made for kneeling. We
quickly got the point.

By the time my senior year rolled around, both my parents had become ardent football fans. Since someone had to
stay at the barbershop, they alternated in coming out to
watch me play. We had still another new coach, Al Lindquist.
He figured that since I was fast enough to run in front of the
ball-carrier, why couldn't I play in the backfield where my

size would be useful? He shifted me to fullback and I guess
the experiment was a success because, even though we still
didn't win a game, we scored a touchdown—the first in
three years. I took it over against Garfield High, and this is
what I kept dreaming about when everything else in my life
had turned to ashes. We eventually lost the game 27 to 7.
The crowd had overflowed from the stands onto the field
and as I picked myself up after scoring I saw Dad standing
just outside the end zone in his big brown overcoat, a cigar
in his mouth and a big grin on his face. I think the sight of
that grin made me happier than scoring the touchdown.

Reader's Response ～ Why do you think pleasing his
father meant so much to Jim?

Library Link ～ *To find out more about Jim Yoshida,
look for* The Two Worlds of Jim Yoshida *by Jim Yoshida
with Bill Hosokawa.*

# THE WORLD'S GREATEST ATHLETE

In Stockholm, Sweden, in the summer of 1912, King Gustav V of Sweden presented trophies to a young American man. He shook the young man's hand and said, "You, sir, are the greatest athlete in the world."

The young man was Jim Thorpe and he had just performed an amazing feat at the Olympic Games. He had competed in fifteen separate track and field events, winning both the pentathlon and the decathlon. A Sac and Fox Indian, Jim Thorpe had already been called the greatest football player ever—as the star performer on the nationally known Carlisle Indian School team. He also excelled in lacrosse, wrestling, swimming, baseball, and track.

But soon after winning at the Olympics, Jim Thorpe had to give back his medals and trophies. For two summers, it was revealed, he had played baseball for fifteen dollars a week. His sports earnings meant that he had not been an amateur when he competed at the Olympics. According to Olympic rules at the time, only amateur athletes were eligible to participate in the games. Thorpe defended himself by saying he had not known he was violating any rules.

After Thorpe's death in 1953, his children began a long fight for their father's honor. At last, in 1982, the International Olympic Committee restored Thorpe's name to the official record books and returned his medals to his family. Despite the controversy surrounding his Olympic achievements, Jim Thorpe is still considered by many to be the greatest athlete of all time.

# 🍂 THE ROAD 🍂
# NOT TAKEN

Two roads diverged in a yellow wood,
And sorry I could not travel both
And be one traveler, long I stood
And looked down one as far as I could
To where it bent in the undergrowth;

Then took the other, as just as fair,
And having perhaps the better claim,
Because it was grassy and wanted wear;
Though as for that the passing there
Had worn them really about the same,

And both that morning equally lay
In leaves no step had trodden black.
Oh, I kept the first for another day!
Yet knowing how way leads on to way,
I doubted if I should ever come back.

I shall be telling this with a sigh
Somewhere ages and ages hence:
Two roads diverged in a wood, and I—
I took the one less traveled by,
And that has made all the difference.

ROBERT FROST

THE PRELUDE, *oil on canvas by William L. Metcalf, American, 1909.*

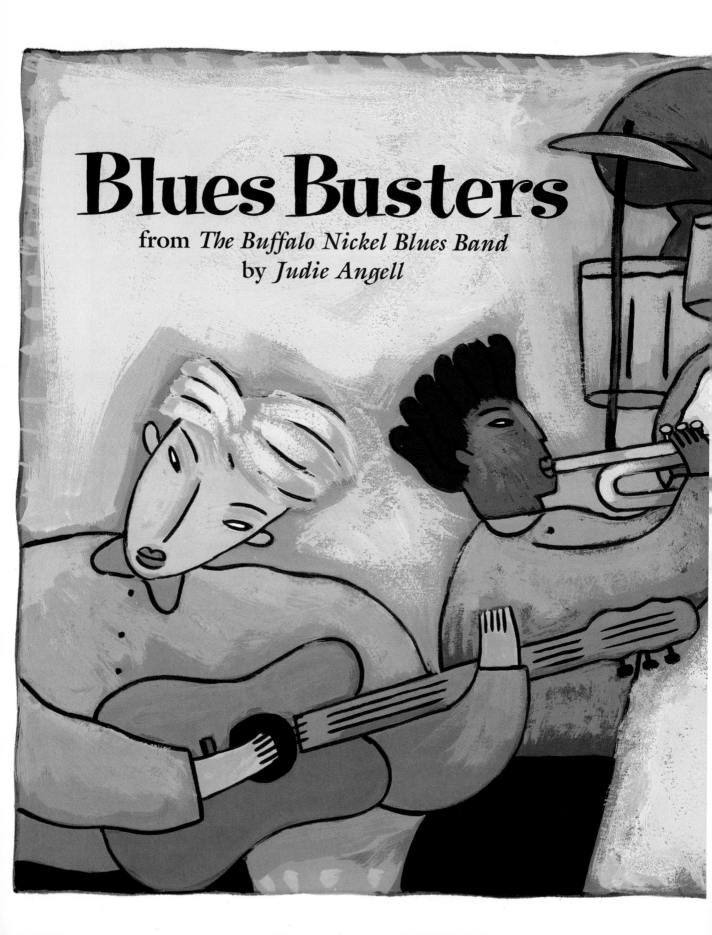

# Blues Busters

from *The Buffalo Nickel Blues Band*
by *Judie Angell*

With Ivy on drums, Georgie on guitar, and Eddie on keyboards, the Centerin City Blues Trio was a big hit at the neighborhood picnic. On the advice of an experienced musician, they decided to develop their own "blues" sound. They added Shelby—a brilliant trumpet player—to the group. Now they need a good bass player. They've tacked up notices all over town: "Wanted: Bass guitar player for blues band. Must be fourteen or under. Call Eddie: 555-4234."

"Eddie."

"Yes, Pop?"

"Your music is going well? You've added a horn now?"

"A trumpet. Shelby Powell. You'll meet him soon, Pop, he's really good, but he can never stay past about quarter-to-five."

"Your mother says it sounds loud in there. In the garage."

"She doesn't like it?"

"No, no, you know your mother, she loves that you're making music. I was thinking about Dr. Broigen."

"No problem! Shelby's been with us a couple of weeks now and we haven't heard a word from Broigen. Him and his chestnut trees. What is he, anyway?"

"He's a plant pathologist."

"Oh."

"Haven't you been wondering why you haven't heard him complain lately?"

"No . . ."

"Well, I'll tell you the reason. It's because he's not home. Your sister's been watering his plants and feeding his cats."

"She has?"

"You've been very busy, Eddie, you haven't noticed. Dr. Broigen is in Michigan."

"What's he doing there?"

"There are eight groves of trees in Michigan that have survived the blight. He's out there studying them."

"Oh. Great!"

"Not great. He's coming back soon and now that you're adding musicians to your group you might be in for some trouble. From him. You'd better think about that."

"But Pop, we only practice in the afternoons after school. It's not as if we play loud at night or anything . . ."

"I'm just telling you."

"Yeah, okay, Pop, thanks."

I couldn't worry about Mr. Broigen and his chestnut trees. I had much more important things to think about like where

we were going to get our bass. Every night I sat by the phone, but nothing happened.

As it turned out, our bass player didn't phone. He kind of hunched up to me on my way out of school one afternoon in late October. Just as we had begun to think there were no bass players anywhere near Centerin City!

"You Eddie?"

"Yeah . . ."

"I wanna talk to you."

"I'm in a hurry," I said. I was. We had to get to practice before Shelby the Mystery Man had to go home.

"You want a bass player or not?"

I stopped and looked him over. He was kind of mangy-looking and he had his hair all slicked back except for one curl that hung down over his forehead.

"You mean you?" I asked stupidly.

"Yeah, me, what's wrong with that?"

"Nothing. Nothing. You have to audition, though."

"Yeah, okay. When, now?"

"Now is fine. We're rehearsing at my house. Out in back in the garage. Where's your axe?"

"I'll get it. Where do you live?"

"24 Coral."

"I'll be there."

"You have to be there soon. We quit at four-forty-five."

"You punch a clock?"

"It's a long story. What's your name?"

"Reese."

"First or last?"

"Both."

I barely had enough time to explain about Reese to the others before he showed up. He was carrying a burlap bag and the smallest amp I'd ever seen.

I introduced him to Ivy and Shelby and Georgie, whose eyebrows went through his hairline as Reese pulled his guitar out of the bag.

"Where do I plug in?" Reese asked, holding the power cord from his amp and looking around.

"You're not going to get any power out of that thing," Georgie wailed. "When was it made, 1909? That's no bass amp, that toy'll never give you any bottom!"

"Oh, yeah?" Reese snarled.

Things were getting off to a flying start. I elbowed Georgie who decided that amends were in order.

"Hey. I'm sorry. Look, the outlet's over there, but why don't you plug into my amp, okay?" And then he added, "I didn't mean anything . . ."

Reese accepted the apology by plugging into Georgie's amp.

"What'll you have?" I asked Reese.

"Crossroads," he answered, and then it was my turn for raised eyebrows.

"Really?" I asked.

"You're a blues band, aren't you? That's what the sign said."

"Yeah, we sure are!" I cried. "Crossroads is a great number! Shelby does a terrific wah-wah trumpet in that, don't you, Shel? Hey, you like Eric Clapton?"

"My brother says Eric Clapton is the best guitarist in the world."

"What's your brother play?" Ivy asked.

"Bass. Same as me. He taught me."

"How come he didn't come around to audition?"

Reese laughed.

"What's so funny?"

"Nothin', man. He's twenty-eight years old, anyway, he got no time for band-playin'."

"All right," I said, sitting down at my keyboard, "let's do it, one . . . two . . . one, two, three, four—"

When the song was over, we chewed our lips and nodded our heads at each other.

"He sure was right on top of the beat," Ivy said.

"Whatever changes I played, he heard," I added.

"Good beat," Georgie said. "Very nice."

Shelby smiled. "He seems real good," he said.

"You got a job with us if you want it, Reese," I said.

"You guys make any money?" he asked.

"Not yet. We just completed our band. Now we have to go to work, build up a repertoire, learn to work together. Then we can advertise and stuff."

Ivy said, "If we try real hard, maybe we can be ready by Christmas and pick up on all the holiday parties!"

"Yeah! Well, let's start right now! How about it?" I cried. "Let's do *Crossroads* again, let's see what we can do this time."

We were halfway through it when the garage door burst open.

We stopped instantly. Ivy muttered, "Uh oh."

"Welcome home, Mr. Broigen," I sighed.

"*Doctor* Broigen. And this is not what I consider a welcome. I thought you said this wasn't going to continue, Eddie."

I wanted to say "It's Edward," but I didn't. I said, "Well, I promised there wouldn't be any more firecrackers, Dr. Broigen, and there won't be."

"I can't work with this, Eddie. You're going to have to find another place to practice. Besides, it's getting cold now. Aren't you cold working in here?"

"No . . . we're not cold . . ."

"Who's *that*, man?" Reese asked, jerking his head toward Broigen.

"Our neighbor. Dr. Broigen. He works at his house right next door."

"What's your problem, man?" Reese asked, looking directly at him. "What is it, music bother you or something?"

Dr. Broigen opened his mouth but nothing came out. His face was purple.

"Listen, stay cool," Reese said, as Ivy covered her mouth to stifle a giggle. "We're not here to interfere with anyone's work, right?" Reese looked at the four of us but didn't wait for our answer. "Right," he

said, "so don't worry about it, man. I'll take care of it."

Mr.—*Dr.* Broigen looked at me. I looked at Reese and shrugged. "He'll take care of it," I said and prayed silently.

"What're you starin' at *me* for?" Reese asked after Dr. Broigen left.

"This is our only practice place," I said. "How are you going to take care of the sound? What can you do?"

Reese put up both his palms and closed his eyes. "I said I'd take care of it and I'll take care of it. You got the word of Reese."

I decided to take the word of Reese. I still didn't want to worry about Broigen. Now, just when our band was complete I only wanted to think about that. I told Reese when we rehearsed and he said it was okay with him. He wouldn't tell us what grade he was in or even how old he was. He seemed mysterious, too, although not in the way Shelby was.

"It doesn't matter," Ivy said, as I walked her home that afternoon. "If he shows up and works hard and we have a good group with a new sound, that's what matters."

"But don't you wonder, though? Don't you wonder why shy ol' Shelby gets hyper if a tune runs over four-forty-five? Don't you wonder about Reese and why he won't even say what grade he's in?"

"Yeah, I wonder," she said, "but I don't lose sleep over it. Neither should you."

"Oh, I don't, I don't. But . . . remember when we were talking about special friends and being up front and all that?"

"Uh huh . . ."

"Well, you're like that with me . . . and so is Ham, I guess, but Ham's pretty laid back most of the time . . ."

"But Shelby's not that kind of special friend? Is that what you mean? Because he doesn't talk about himself much, or Reese either?"

"Maybe," I answered. "But not exactly. I mean, Georgie's pretty straight and I like him, it's just more than that. I tried to tell you before . . . You know, before we started working together last year—before all our free time was taken up practicing and stuff—I had a couple of friends, guys I used to hang out with—used to play D and D with them all the time . . ."

"Me, too," she said. "I mean, I had some girlfriends I just don't see any more."

"Yeah, same with me. But you know, I don't really mind it so much because I always have somebody to talk to about anything. You. I guess you're my best friend, Ivy." I wasn't sure if she knew, so I thought I'd better tell her.

"Does that bother you?" she asked after a minute. It wasn't the response I had expected.

"Bother me? No! What do you mean, *bother* me?"

"Well, for one thing, I'm a girl."

"No kidding."

"Usually twelve-year-old boys don't have best friends who are girls. Not to mention that I'm black and Presbyterian and you're white and Jewish, and—"

"Hey, Ivy, does it bother *you?*" I interrupted.

"Not at all," she said firmly. "You're my best friend now, too. Only sometimes I think about what other people think."

"What difference does that—"

"Not that what other people think is going to change me, no way," she said. "What I want is to play drums and be in a blues band and have you for my best friend and I want all that to go on forever and ever. The thing is, though, I know that makes me different from other girls my age and sometimes I wonder about that and when you said just now that I was your best friend I knew you were wondering about it too. That's all."

"Oh. Well, yeah, I know what you mean. But our music for example— We want that to be different . . . to stand out from other groups, right?"

"Oh, sure, but there's 'different' and 'different'," she said. "You can stand out by wearing freaky clothes, too, y'know . . ." She laughed.

"Listen," I said, "even if stupid people think we're all freaks right now, I don't even care. We'll show them when we start working. I've never seen such talented people as us, have you?"

"No, you're right," she said. "There never have been such talented people as we are."

The next afternoon when Ivy, Georgie, Shelby, and I arrived at the garage after school, Reese was standing in front of it, leaning against the door. My mother was standing next to him, smiling. Now what was this?

"Ma?"

"We have a surprise for you," she said.

"We?"

"Your friend Reese and I." She winked conspiratorially at Reese who winked back. Talk about your odd couple!

"Well, . . . let's not keep them in suspense," my mother said and flung open the garage door.

The four of us stood there gawking. The walls of the garage were covered with—mattresses.

"Ma?" I said. Ivy's jaw was hanging down.

"Instant soundproofing!" my mother cried.

"And insulation!" Reese added. "Energy-saving, like the government wants." He folded his arms across his chest.

"Wha— Where did they come from?"

My mother spread her hands. "Listen," she said, "this morning, right after you left for school, there I was, scouring out the bathroom sink, when my eye catches something crawling down the driveway toward the garage. I put down the Brillo and go over to the window and I see what it is crawling. A mattress."

"Huh?"

"It's a mattress, only it isn't crawling by itself. Reese is under it. I go out there and stand in front of him as he's about to drop it on the ground here. 'Why are you dropping a mattress in front of my garage?' I say. 'And why aren't you in school, you're just a kid.'"

Reese opened his mouth then, but my mother said, "Sh! So the second question he doesn't answer but the first he says, 'It isn't just one mattress I'm delivering, it's twelve.' I say, 'Twelve mattresses? I didn't even order one!'"

Reese and I both opened our mouths then, but my mother said, "Sh! So he explains how he got this idea to soundproof the garage so Dr. Broigen can cure his chestnut tree blight in peace and you musicians can go on with your work uninterrupted. And he said how it would keep out the draft and wind. He said if he worked all day he could probably get five mattresses over here before you got home from school."

"Hey, Reese," I said, beginning to recover a little. "That was a great idea!"

"Yeah, but you got more than five here," Georgie said.

Reese turned to me. "Your mother," he said, "she got her car and helped. We piled the mattresses on the roof and both of us put 'em up on the walls."

I looked around and shook my head. The mattresses sure didn't look like the kind you'd find on the beds at the Ritz Hotel. They were dirty and stained and had stuffing popping out of them all over the place. Not that I cared about that

because they sure would solve our problems, but I was curious.

"Where'd you get them, Reese?" I asked. "Twelve mattresses."

"From buildings," Reese answered with a shrug.

"He had them piled up on the street when I met him with the car," my mother said. "We made two trips."

"Buildings?" Ivy repeated. Shelby and Georgie went inside to inspect the nailing-up job.

"Yeah, you know, abandoned buildings. There's plenty of junk in those places—you'd be surprised. You could live for a long time in one of those. People do, y'know."

"Is that where you live?" I asked. "In one of those?"

Reese stiffened. "No! A-course not. But I know 'em. I used to play there when I was a kid. There's lots of things I know."

"*Nobody* has said 'thank you'," my mother said harshly.

I grinned. "Thank you," I said. "Thanks, Ma! Thanks, Reese! That's really terrific, really."

"It's great, Reese," Ivy said. "Thanks."

Shelby said, "Thanks, both of you," and Georgie cried, "Now we're really all set!"

Look, I'm not bragging. I don't brag. But we really *were* good. Somehow we lucked out in getting together and in all of us digging the same music. And even if two of us were a little mysterious, it didn't affect the way we played or got along . . . most of the time.

GEORGIE: Let's do this in E.

ME: E's too brittle, do it in E*b*.

GEORGIE: Yeah, but my voice squeaks on that top F.

IVY: Sing it in falsetto, then!

ME: Ivy, that's too loud. How about using brushes there instead of sticks? I can't even hear my own solo.

IVY: Loud: I'm never loud! Whaddya mean *loud?*

GEORGIE: Hey, Reese, I know you want to kick us along, but are you trying to set a record for the number of notes you can get into every measure?

REESE: In your ear, Carrothead!

REESE: Shelby, that sounds like 'elevator music'! Can't you get a little *bite* in that horn?

SHELBY: Bite? Reese, did you ever hear the word 'subtle'?

Okay, nobody's perfect. Sure, we argued, but it was always about the music and all five of us really cared about how each song came across. We were five people all working toward making the Centerin City Blues Band something that people would enjoy and remember. And just keeping that in mind was what made us argue and what made us happy.

Reader's Response ∿ What was your opinion of Reese at the beginning of the story? Did it change by the end?

Library Link ∿ *To find out more about Eddie and the band, read* The Buffalo Nickel Blues Band *by Judie Angell, from which this excerpt was taken.*

# Fathers of the Blues

Tracing its origins to the traditional music of west Africa, the blues first appeared about 100 years ago in the Mississippi delta region. Music that sounds both sorrowful and uplifting, the blues is a response to suffering as well as a reaffirmation of the strength of the human spirit. You can hear the blues influence in virtually every form of contemporary American music—from country music to rap. And of the many great blues performers, Robert Johnson and Muddy Waters remain the most influential.

Two years before his suspicious death in 1938, 25-year-old Robert Johnson rambled from his Mississippi home to Texas. There, in two primitive recording sessions, Johnson laid down the 41 classic tracks upon which his reputation rests. Accompanying himself on acoustic guitar, Johnson's live performances were so powerful that, as one listener said, he "caused many a woman to weep, and many a man, too." In the early 1960s, soon-to-be guitar legends Eric Clapton and Keith Richards both patterned their playing on Johnson's unique and innovative style.

Muddy Waters, born McKinley Morganfield in Rolling Fork, Mississippi in 1915, learned traditional blues from listening to Johnson's records and watching other local blues musicians. In the 1940s Waters moved to Chicago and formed a band. Muddy's new sound, with electric guitars, piano, harmonica, bass, and drums, defined the "Chicago blues" style, a style that would profoundly influence a new form of music called rock 'n roll.

Despite its historical influences, the blues remains a vital musical form. Such musicians as Robert Cray and the late Stevie Ray Vaughan introduced the music to a new generation. Blues giants like Buddy Guy, Otis Rush, and Albert Collins keep the fiery spirit of the blues alive. And in 1991, a reissue of recordings made in a hot San Antonio hotel room in 1936 climbed to the top of the album charts.

Robert Johnson–Studio Portrait, circa 1935, © Stephen C. LaVere 1989

Robert Johnson

Muddy Waters

# Anne Frank

## THE DIARY OF A YOUNG GIRL

n 1933 Adolf Hitler and the Nazis, his political party took power in Germany. Hitler soon established a ruthless dictatorship, singling out Jews for the harshest treatment. That same year Anne Frank and her family, who were Jewish, moved from Germany to the Netherlands to escape the oppressive and hostile atmosphere Hitler had created. But in 1939 the German army invaded Poland to start World War II, and one year later Hitler's forces conquered the Netherlands and surrounding countries. Hitler then ordered units of the Nazi armies to destroy all European Jews. As they swept across Europe, the Nazis seized millions of Jews and deported them to Auschwitz and other death camps in Eastern Europe. During the war the Nazis murdered millions of Jews in these camps. Many were worked to death as slave laborers, and many more died horribly of disease and starvation. By the early 1940s Jews throughout Europe had learned of the Nazi atrocities. In 1942 Anne Frank and her family went into hiding in a secret apartment in Amsterdam to avoid being sent to the camps. During her two years in the apartment, young Anne kept a diary describing her life in hiding under the constant threat

*Sunday morning, 5 July, 1942*

... When we walked across our little square together a few days ago, Daddy began to talk of us going into hiding. I asked him why on earth he was beginning to talk of that already. "Yes, Anne," he said, "you know that we have been taking food, clothes, furniture to other people for more than a year now. We don't want our belongings to be seized by the Germans, but we certainly don't want to fall into their clutches ourselves. So we shall disappear of our own accord and not wait until they come and fetch us."

"But, Daddy, when would it be?" He spoke so seriously that I grew very anxious.

"Don't you worry about it, we shall arrange everything. Make the most of your carefree young life while you can." That was all. Oh, may the fulfillment of these somber words remain far distant yet!

Yours, Anne

Anne (THIRD FROM RIGHT), Mr. Frank (CENTER), and friends on their way to a 1941 wedding.

*Wednesday, 8 July, 1942*

Dear Kitty,

Years seem to have passed between Sunday and now. So much has happened, it is just as if the whole world had turned upside down. But I am still alive, Kitty, and that is the main thing, Daddy says.

Yes, I'm still alive, indeed, but don't ask where or how. You wouldn't understand a word, so I will begin by telling you what happened on Sunday afternoon.

At three o'clock (Harry had just gone, but was coming back later) someone rang the front doorbell. I was lying lazily reading a book on the veranda in the sunshine, so I didn't hear it. A bit later Margot appeared at the kitchen door looking very excited. "The S.S. have sent a call-up notice for Daddy," she whispered. "Mummy has gone to see Mr. Van Daan already." (Van Daan is a friend who works with Daddy in the business.) It was a great shock to me, a call-up; everyone knows what that means. I picture concentration camps and lonely cells—should we allow him to be doomed to this? "Of course he won't go," declared Margot, while we waited together. "Mummy has gone to the Van Daans to discuss whether we should move into our hiding place tomorrow. The Van Daans are going with us, so we shall be seven in all." Silence. We couldn't talk any more, thinking about Daddy, who, little knowing what was going on, was visiting some old people in the Joodse Invalide; waiting for Mummy, the heat and suspense, all made us very overawed and silent.

Suddenly the bell rang again. "That is Harry," I said. "Don't open the door." Margot held me back, but it was not necessary as we heard Mummy and Mr. Van Daan downstairs, talking to Harry, then they came in and closed the door behind them. Each time the bell went, Margot or I had to creep softly down to see if it was Daddy, not opening the door to anyone else.

Margot and I were sent out of the room. Van Daan wanted to talk to Mummy alone. When we were alone together in our bedroom, Margot told me that the call-up was not for Daddy, but for her. I was more frightened than ever and began to cry. Margot is sixteen; would they really take girls of that age away alone? But thank goodness she

ABOVE: **Mrs. Frank.** TOP RIGHT: **Mr. Frank and Miep.** BOTTOM RIGHT: **Margot Frank**

won't go, Mummy said so herself; that must be what Daddy meant when he talked about us going into hiding.

Into hiding—where would we go, in a town or the country, in a house or a cottage, when, how, where. . . ?

These were questions I was not allowed to ask, but I couldn't get them out of my mind. Margot and I began to pack some of our most vital belongings into a school satchel. The first thing I put in was this diary, then hair curlers, handkerchiefs, schoolbooks, a comb, old letters; I put in the craziest things with the idea that we were going into hiding. But I'm not sorry, memories mean more to me than dresses.

At five o'clock Daddy finally arrived, and we phoned Mr. Koophuis to ask if he could come around in the evening. Van Daan went and fetched Miep. Miep has been in the business with Daddy since

1933 and has become a close friend, likewise her brand-new husband, Henk. Miep came and took some shoes, dresses, coats, underwear, and stockings away in her bag, promising to return in the evening. Then silence fell on the house; not one of us felt like eating anything, it was still hot and everything was very strange. We let our large upstairs room to a certain Mr. Goudsmit, a divorced man in his thirties, who appeared to have nothing to do on this particular evening; we simply could not get rid of him without being rude; he hung about until ten o'clock. At eleven o'clock Miep and Henk Van Santen arrived. Once again, shoes, stockings, books, and underclothes disappeared into Miep's bag and Henk's deep pockets, and at eleven-thirty they too disappeared. I was dog-tired and although I knew that it would be my last night in my own bed, I fell asleep immediately and didn't wake up until Mummy called me at five-thirty the next morning. Luckily it was not so hot as Sunday; warm rain fell steadily all day. We put on heaps of clothes as if we were going to the North Pole, the sole reason being to take clothes with us. No Jew in our situation would have dreamed of going out with a suitcase full of clothing. I had on two vests, three pairs of pants, a dress, on top of that a skirt, jacket, summer coat, two pairs of stockings, lace-up shoes, woolly cap, scarf, and still more; I was nearly stifled before we started, but no one inquired about that.

Margot filled her satchel with schoolbooks, fetched her bicycle, and rode off behind Miep into the unknown, as far as I was concerned. You see I still didn't know where our secret hiding place was to be. At seven-thirty the door closed behind us. Moortje, my little cat, was the only creature to whom I said farewell. She would have a good home with the neighbors. This was all written in a letter addressed to Mr. Goudsmit.

There was one pound of meat in the kitchen for the cat, breakfast things lying on the table, stripped beds, all giving the impression that we had left helter-skelter. But we didn't care about impressions, we only wanted to get away, only escape and arrive safely, nothing else. Continued tomorrow.

Yours, Anne

*Thursday, 9 July, 1942*

Dear Kitty,

So we walked in the pouring rain, Daddy, Mummy, and I, each with a school satchel and shopping bag filled to the brim with all kinds of things thrown together anyhow.

We got sympathetic looks from people on their way to work. You could see by their faces how sorry they were they couldn't offer us a lift; the gaudy yellow star spoke for itself.

Only when we were on the road did Mummy and Daddy begin to tell me bits and pieces about the plan. For months as many of our goods and chattels and necessities of life as possible had been sent away and they were sufficiently ready for us to have gone into hiding of our own accord on July 16. The plan had had to be speeded up ten days because of the call-up, so our quarters would not be so well organized, but we had to make the best of it. The hiding place itself would be in the building where Daddy has his office. It will be hard for outsiders to understand, but I shall explain that later on. Daddy didn't have many people working for him: Mr. Kraler, Koophuis, Miep, and Elli Vossen, a twenty-three-year-old typist, who all knew of our arrival. Mr. Vossen, Elli's father, and two boys worked in the warehouse; they had not been told.

I will describe the building: there is a large warehouse on the ground floor which is used as a store. The front door to the house is next to the warehouse door, and inside the front door is a second doorway which leads to a staircase (A). There is another door at the top of the stairs, with a frosted glass window in it, which has "Office" written in black letters across it. That is the large main office, very big, very light, and very full. Elli, Miep, and Mr. Koophuis work there in the daytime. A small dark room containing the safe, a wardrobe, and a large cupboard leads to a small somewhat dark second office. Mr. Kraler and Mr. Van Daan used to sit here, now it is only Mr. Kraler. One can reach Kraler's office from the passage, but only via a glass door which can be opened from the inside, but not easily from the outside.

From Kraler's office a long passage goes past the coal store, up four steps and leads to the showroom of the whole building: the private office. Dark dignified furniture, linoleum and carpets on the floor, radio, smart lamp, everything first-class. Next door there is a roomy kitchen with a hot-water faucet and a gas stove. Next door the W.C. That is the first floor.

A wooden staircase leads from the downstairs passage to the next floor (B). There is a small landing at the top. There is a door at each end of the landing, the left one leading to a storeroom at the front of the house and to the attics. One of those really steep Dutch staircases runs from the side to the other door opening on to the street (C).

The right-hand door leads to our "Secret Annexe." No one would ever guess that there would be so many rooms hidden behind that plain gray door. There's a little step in front of the door and then you are inside.

There is a steep staircase immediately opposite the entrance (D). On the left a tiny passage brings you into a room which was to become the Frank family's bed-sitting-room, next door a smaller

ABOVE: **The yellow star that Dutch Jews were ordered to wear.**
RIGHT: **Floor plan of the building.**

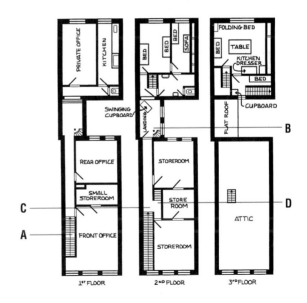

room, study and bedroom for the two young ladies of the family. On the right a little room without windows containing the washbasin and a small W.C. compartment, with another door leading to Margot's and my room. If you go up the next flight of stairs and open the door, you are simply amazed that there could be such a big light room in such an old house by the canal. There is a gas stove in this room (thanks to the fact that it was used as a laboratory) and a sink. This is now the kitchen for the Van Daan couple, besides being general living room, dining room, and scullery.

A tiny little corridor room will become Peter Van Daan's apartment. Then, just as on the lower landing, there is a large attic. So there you are, I've introduced you to the whole of our beautiful "Secret Annexe."

Yours, Anne

LEFT: **Front view of the Annex, or hiding place.** RIGHT: **Back view of the Annex.**

*Friday, 10 July, 1942*

Dear Kitty,

I expect I have thoroughly bored you with my long-winded descriptions of our dwelling. But still I think you should know where we've landed.

But to continue my story—you see, I've not finished yet—when we arrived at the Prinsengracht, Miep took us quickly upstairs and into the "Secret Annexe." She closed the door behind us and we were alone. Margot was already waiting for us, having come much faster on her bicycle. Our living room and all the other rooms were chock-full of rubbish, indescribably so. All the cardboard boxes which had been sent to the office in the previous months lay piled on the floor and the beds. The little room was filled to the ceiling with bedclothes. We had to start clearing up immediately, if we wished to sleep in decent beds that night. Mummy and Margot were not in a fit state to take part; they were tired and lay down on their beds, they were miserable, and lots more besides. But the two "clearers-up" of the family—Daddy and myself—wanted to start at once.

The whole day long we unpacked boxes, filled cupboards, hammered and tidied, until we were dead beat. We sank into clean beds that night. We hadn't had a bit of anything warm the whole day, but we didn't care; Mummy and Margot were too tired and keyed up to eat, and Daddy and I were too busy.

On Tuesday morning we went on where we left off the day before. Elli and Miep collected our rations for us, Daddy improved the poor blackout, we scrubbed the kitchen floor, and were on the go the whole day long again. I hardly had time to think about the great change in my life until Wednesday. Then I had a chance, for the first time since our arrival, to tell you all about it, and at the same time to realize myself what had actually happened to me and what was still going to happen.

Yours, Anne

*Saturday, 11 July, 1942*

Dear Kitty,

Daddy, Mummy, and Margot can't get used to the sound of the Westertoren clock yet, which tells us the time every quarter of an hour. I can. I loved it from the start, and especially in the night it's like a faithful friend. I expect you will be interested to hear what it feels like to "disappear"; well, all I can say is that I don't know myself yet. I don't think I shall ever feel really at home in this house, but that does not mean that I loathe it here, it is more like being on vacation in a very peculiar boardinghouse. Rather a mad idea, perhaps, but that is how it strikes me. The "Secret Annexe" is an ideal hiding place. Although it leans to one side and is damp, you'd never find such a comfortable hiding place anywhere in Amsterdam, no, perhaps not even in the whole of Holland. Our little room looked very bare at first with nothing on the walls; but thanks to Daddy who had brought my film-star collection and picture postcards on beforehand, and with the aid of paste pot and brush, I have transformed the walls into one gigantic picture. This makes it look much more cheerful, and, when the Van Daans come, we'll get some wood from the attic, and make a few little cupboards for the walls and other odds and ends to make it look more lively.

Margot and Mummy are a little bit better now. Mummy felt well enough to cook some soup for the first time yesterday, but then forgot all about it, while she was downstairs talking, so the peas were burned to a cinder and utterly refused to leave the pan. Mr. Koophuis has brought me a book called *Young People's Annual*. The four of us went to the private office yesterday evening and turned on the radio. I was so terribly frightened that someone might hear it that I simply begged Daddy to come upstairs with me. Mummy understood how I felt and came too. We are very nervous in other ways, too, that the neighbors might hear us or see something going on. We made curtains straight away on the first day. Really one can hardly call them curtains, they are just light, loose strips of material, all different shapes, quality, and pattern, which Daddy and I sewed together in a most unprofessional way. These works of art are fixed in position with drawing pins, not to come down until we emerge from here.

There are some large business premises on the right of us, and on the left a furniture workshop; there is no one there after working hours but even so, sounds could travel through the walls. We have forbidden Margot to cough at night, although she has a bad cold, and make her swallow large doses of codeine. I am looking for Tuesday when the Van Daans arrive; it will be much more fun and not so quiet. It is the silence that frightens me so in the evenings and at night. I wish like anything that one of our protectors could sleep here at night. I can't tell you how oppressive it is *never* to be able to go out-doors, also I'm very afraid that we shall be discovered and be shot. That is not exactly a pleasant prospect. We have to whisper and tread lightly during the day, otherwise the people in the warehouse might hear us.

Someone is calling me.

Yours, Anne

**A wall in Anne's room**

*Friday, 14 August, 1942*

Dear Kitty,

I have deserted you for a whole month, but honestly, there is so little news here that I can't find amusing things to tell you every day. The Van Daans arrived on July 13. We thought they were coming on the fourteenth, but between the thirteenth and the sixteenth of July the Germans called up people right and left which created more and more unrest, so they played for safety, better a day too early than a day too late. At nine-thirty in the morning (we were still having breakfast) Peter arrived, the Van Daans' son, not sixteen yet, a rather soft, shy, gawky youth; can't expect much from his company. He brought his cat (Mouschi) with him. Mr. and Mrs. Van Daan arrived half an hour later, and to our great amusement she had a large pottie in her hat box. "I don't feel at home anywhere without my chamber," she declared, so it was the first thing to find its permanent resting

**Mr. and Mrs. Van Daan, and Victor Kraler**

74

place under her divan. Mr. Van Daan did not bring his, but carried a folding tea table under his arm.

From the day they arrived we all had meals cozily together and after three days it was just as if we were one large family. Naturally the Van Daans were able to tell us a lot about the extra week they had spent in the inhabited world. Among other things we were very interested to hear what had happened to our house and to Mr. Goudsmit. Mr. Van Daan told us:

"Mr. Goudsmit phoned at nine o'clock on Monday morning and asked if I could come around. I went immediately and found G. in a state of great agitation. He let me read a letter that the Franks had left behind and wanted to take the cat to the neighbors as indicated in the letter, which pleased me. Mr. G. was afraid that the house would be searched so we went through all the rooms, tidied up a bit, and cleared away the breakfast things. Suddenly I discovered a writing pad on Mrs. Frank's desk with an address in Maastricht written on it. Although I knew that this was done on purpose, I pretended to be very surprised and shocked and urged Mr. G. to tear up this unfortunate little piece of paper without delay.

"I went on pretending that I knew nothing of your disappearance all the time, but after seeing the paper, I got a brain wave. 'Mr. Goudsmit'—I said—'it suddenly dawns on me what this address may refer to. Now it all comes back to me, a high-ranking officer was in

**Peter Van Daan**

75

the office about six months ago, he appeared to be very friendly with Mr. Frank and offered to help him, should the need arise. He was stationed in Maastricht. I think he must have kept his word and somehow or other managed to get them into Belgium and then on to Switzerland. I should tell this to any friends who may inquire. Don't of course, mention Maastricht.'

"With these words I left the house. Most of your friends know already, because I've been told myself several times by different people."

We were highly amused at the story and, when Mr. Van Daan gave us further details, laughed still more at the way people can let their imagination run away with them. One family had seen the pair of us pass on bicycles very early in the morning and another lady knew quite definitely that we were fetched by a military car in the middle of the night.

Yours, Anne

**The church tower seen from the window of the attic in the hiding place.**

*Friday, 21 August, 1942*

Dear Kitty,

The entrance to our hiding place has now been properly concealed. Mr. Kraler thought it would be better to put a cupboard in front of our door (because a lot of houses are being searched for hidden bicycles), but of course it had to be a movable cupboard that can open like a door.

Mr. Vossen made the whole thing. We had already let him into the secret and he can't do enough to help. If we want to go downstairs, we have to first bend down and then jump, because the step has gone. The first three days we were all going about with masses of lumps on our foreheads, because we all knocked ourselves against the low doorway. Now we have nailed a cloth filled with wood wool against the top of the door. Let's see if that helps!

I'm not working much at present; I'm giving myself holidays until September. Then Daddy is going to give me lessons; it's shocking how much I've forgotten already.

There is little change in our life here. Mr. Van Daan and I usually manage to upset each other, it's just the opposite with Margot

LEFT: **The entrance to the hiding place, with the bookcase in front of the doorway.**

RIGHT: **The bookcase moved aside to show the doorway.**

whom he likes very much. Mummy sometimes treats me just like a baby, which I can't bear. Otherwise things are going better. I still don't like Peter any more, he is so boring; he flops lazily on his bed half the time, does a bit of carpentry, and then goes back for another snooze. What a fool!

It is lovely weather and in spite of everything we make the most we can of it by lying on a camp bed in the attic, where the sun shines through an open window.

Yours, Anne

## EPILOGUE

On August 4, 1944, Nazi police, operating on a tip from a Dutch informer, raided the secret annex. They arrested Anne and the others and deported them to German and Dutch concentration camps. Though the Gestapo plundered the annex, they ignored Anne's diary, which lay on the floor among old books and newspapers. Anne Frank died in the concentration camp at Bergen-Belsen in March 1945, just two months before the liberation of the Netherlands.

Reader's Response ∼ How do you think you might react if you were forced to go into hiding?

Library Link ∼ *If you enjoyed this selection you might be interested in* Anne Frank Remembered *by Miep Gies. This fascinating and informative book presents an equally compelling account of the Franks' time in hiding.*

# A REMARKABLE

# Legacy

**"In spite of everything I still believe that people are really good at heart."**

Anne Frank wrote those words in her diary, not knowing whether she and her family would survive the hate and horror of her times. As it turned out, she did not survive. But she left behind one of the most important works ever written during the Holocaust and the Second World War, published in English as *The Diary of a Young Girl*. Her story of the two years she and her family spent hiding from the Nazis, told with wit and insight, provides a compelling message about hope in the face of terror and brutality.

Since its publication, *The Diary of a Young Girl* has been translated into more than fifty-five languages and read by millions of people all over the world. It was turned into a Pulitzer Prize-winning play by Frances Goodrich and Albert Hackett in 1956. The play has since been made into a movie and staged for television.

Miep Gies, the Dutch woman who helped hide Anne and the other Annex residents, held on to the diary after the hideout was discovered and her friends sent to concentration camps. She could not bring herself to read it so she returned it to Otto Frank, Anne's father and the sole survivor of the family, who had it published. Two printings of the book had already been sold out before Miep Gies decided to read it. "The emptiness in my heart was eased," she wrote years later about her reaction to the diary. "So much had been lost, but now Anne's voice would never be lost. My young friend had left a remarkable legacy to the world."

The cover of the first edition of Anne's diary, titled *The Secret Annexe*.

# LEROY "SATCHEL" PAIGE

## FROM TAKE A WALK IN THEIR SHOES

### BY GLENNETTE TILLEY TURNER

THE LEGENDARY BASEBALL PITCHER, LEROY "SATCHEL" PAIGE, USED TO SAY, "I STARTED OUT AS A PITCHER." FOR PRACTICE, "I TOSSED STONES AT TIN CANS ALL DAY LONG." PAIGE'S AFTER-SCHOOL JOBS GAVE HIM EVEN MORE OF A CHANCE TO DEVELOP HIS ARM. ONE JOB WAS DELIVERING LARGE BLOCKS OF ICE. THE OTHER WAS CARRYING BAGGAGE AT UNION STATION IN HIS HOMETOWN OF MOBILE, ALABAMA. SOME SAY HE GOT THE NICKNAME "SATCHEL" BECAUSE THE BAGS WERE CALLED "SATCHELS." OTHERS SAY THAT THE NAME REFERRED TO HIS BIG "SATCHEL-SIZED" FEET.

NOBODY EVER KNEW PAIGE'S EXACT AGE. MOST BIOGRAPHERS SAY HE WAS BORN ON JULY 7, 1906. OTHER WRITERS CLAIM HE WAS BORN IN 1904. THE RECORD BOOKS SAY HE RETIRED AT FIFTY-NINE, BUT HE MAY HAVE BEEN SIXTY-ONE OR EVEN SIXTY-NINE. THERE IS AGREEMENT ON THE FACT THAT HIS PARENTS WERE JOHN AND LULA PAIGE AND THAT HE WAS BORN IN MOBILE, ONE OF A LARGE FAMILY OF CHILDREN.

LIKE MANY THINGS ABOUT PAIGE'S LIFE, THE EXACT TIME AND PLACE OF HIS PROFESSIONAL DEBUT ARE NOT KNOWN. WHAT IS KNOWN IS THAT "SATCHEL" PAIGE WAS ONE OF THE MOST BRILLIANT PITCHERS THAT EVER LIVED. HE PROGRESSED FROM SANDLOT, TO SEMI-PRO, TO PROFESSIONAL BASEBALL. IN THE MID-1920S, HE PLAYED FOR TEAMS IN THE ALL-NEGRO SOUTHERN ASSOCIATION—THE MOBILE TIGERS, THE BLACK LOOKOUTS OF CHATTANOOGA, THE BIRMINGHAM BLACK BARONS, THE NASHVILLE ELITE GIANTS, AND THE NEW ORLEANS BLACK PELICANS. IN THE 1930S, HE PLAYED IN SOUTH AMERICA AND THE CARIBBEAN DURING THE WINTER. IN THE SUMMER HE PLAYED IN WESTERN UNITED STATES—IN DENVER, COLORADO, AND BISMARCK, NORTH DAKOTA. HE BECAME THE FIRST BLACK PLAYER IN THE AMERICAN LEAGUE AS THE CLEVELAND INDIANS MADE THEIR RUN FOR THE PENNANT IN 1948.

Paige commanded one of the highest salaries in baseball in his day. Yet he started out very humbly. His first "paying" job was in 1924. The Mobile Tigers—the first semi-pro team he played for—used to pass the hat among the spectators. If the collection was good, Paige was paid $1.00 per game. Otherwise he was given a keg of lemonade as payment for pitching a game. His first real paying job was with the Black Lookouts of Chattanooga for $50 a month. After that, he was with various black baseball teams, always as pitcher and oftentimes as the star attraction for the team. He joined the Kansas City Monarchs in 1942. With his pitching, the team won the Negro American League pennant that year and again in 1946 when Paige allowed only two runs in 93 innings.

Paige was a real showman, and appreciative black fans came out in large numbers. Sportswriters for the black press kept

PAIGE WITH ENTERTAINER AND DANCER
BILL "BO JANGLES" ROBINSON

their readers well informed, but many other Americans had little knowledge about the teams and players in the Negro leagues. There was little coverage in the big city daily papers, and television was just coming into existence.

American society and major league baseball were not yet integrated. Black organized baseball and white organized baseball operated in two separate worlds. Black teams had to ride segregated buses and trains or crowd nine men into a car and drive to out-of-town games. The players kept their spirits up by singing as they rode. Paige provided accompaniment with his guitar. Frequently after traveling long distances, the teams had a hard time finding lodging. In small towns the players had to stay in private homes or local

boarding houses, for white-owned hotels would not accept them. Sometimes they had to sleep on the bus or in dugouts at the ball park. At other times they'd ride all night and arrive in town just in time for the game. It was equally hard to find eating places. Paige used to refuse to pitch in any town where he could not find a place to stay or eat. In the larger cities, players could find lodging and food at some of the better black hotels and restaurants. In spite of the inconveniences caused by racial segregation, the Negro leagues produced some very fine players—such as eventual Hall of Fame members Josh Gibson, "Cool Papa" Bell, Oscar Charleston, Judy Johnson, and "Satchel" Paige, of course.

Even though they operated separately, the Negro leagues and major leagues met each other in exhibition games. Both black and white sportswriters publicized pitching duels between such greats as "Satchel" Paige and Dizzy Dean or Bob Feller. Paige's pitching earned the respect of outstanding athletes. Dizzy Dean said he'd seen the finest pitchers, and "Paige is the best." Joe DiMaggio called Paige "the fastest pitcher I've ever faced."

Paige's remarkable career spanned portions of five decades. He played from the mid-1920s to the late 1960s. He is credited with having played about 2,500 games and winning 2,000 of them. He pitched 300 shutouts and 55 no-hitters. In 1933 he pitched 31 games and lost only 4. In 1934,

GOING INTO THE WIND-UP FOR THE KANSAS CITY MONARCHS.

when he was in North Dakota, he pitched 29 consecutive games and won 28. He pitched in every game that season. His record was 105 games played, 104 won. Other records include a winning streak of 21 consecutive wins, 64 scoreless innings, and 22 strikeouts in one game.

Paige was often booked as a solo star. He'd pitch for any team that would meet his price, reportedly $500 to $2,000 a game, and would guarantee "9 strikeouts in 3 innings." The Baltimore Black Sox, the Pittsburgh Crawfords, the Newark Eagles, the Homestead (Pennsylvania) Grays, and the Chicago American Giants are some of the teams he pitched for or appeared with at various times.

In 1948, Bill Veeck was president of the Cleveland Indians. Cleveland was fighting to win the American League pennant. It was the year after the Brooklyn Dodgers had hired Jackie Robinson and removed the color bar in the National League. Veeck had seen Paige pitch and thought he was what Cleveland needed, so he signed him. Paige won six games and lost only one. Cleveland cinched the pennant and went on to win the World Series.

Although Paige was past his prime by the time he had an opportunity to play in the major leagues, he could still attract large crowds. He brought in 200,000 fans in three games at Cleveland. In 1951 he moved to the St. Louis Browns and was their most valuable pitcher through the 1953 season. A high point of his stint there was when Casey Stengel chose Paige as a pitcher on the 1952 American League All-Star team. Paige was greatly disappointed when the game was halted by rain prior to his appearance on the mound.

Paige officially retired from the Browns at the end of the 1953 season. Having entered the major leagues late in his career, he held the distinction of being the oldest "rookie." When he retired, he was the oldest player ever to play in a major league game. Although retired from league play, Paige continued to pitch exhibition games and delight the fans. He spent off-seasons at home in Kansas City with his wife, Lahoma, and their children. He became active in politics. In 1968 he made an unsuccessful run for the Missouri legislature. That same year the Atlanta Braves signed him as a coach to make him eligible for a major league pension.

Paige was one of the first players to be enshrined when the National Baseball Hall of Fame was opened to stars in the Negro leagues. At his induction, he said, "I'm the proudest man on the face of the earth today."

"Satchel" Paige died in June of 1982, suffering from emphysema and heart disease. Just three days before, he was the star attraction in a ball park when a stadium in the heart of Kansas City's black community was renamed the "Satchel" Paige Stadium. It was a fitting tribute to the ageless man who was one of the greatest pitchers of all time.

# SATCHEL PAIGE
## FROM BASEBALL ANECDOTES

### BY DANIEL OKRENT AND STEVE WULF

Late in Jackie Robinson's rookie season, Bill Veeck integrated the American League when he signed outfielder Larry Doby. And the next year he brought to the majors black baseball's greatest star, Satchel Paige.

According to both Dizzy Dean and Charlie Gehringer, Paige was the greatest pitcher who ever lived. He was as confident of this fact as anyone, as evidenced by an incident that took place in Pittsburgh on July 21, 1942. Pitching against the Homestead Grays, Paige found himself leading 4-0, with two out in the seventh inning.

Then the Grays' next batter, Jerry Benjamin, tripled.

Paige called his first baseman, Buck O'Neil, over to the mound and informed him he was going to walk the next two hitters, load the bases, and pitch to Josh Gibson—the Babe Ruth of the black leagues. As he threw four straight balls to Jack Leonard, who batted just before Gibson, he called out to the Homestead star in the on-deck circle, "I'm gonna put Buck in and pitch to you."

Before his first pitch, Paige told Gibson he was going to throw a fastball. Gibson watched it pass, for strike one. He told Gibson another fastball was coming, and again Gibson let it by, for strike two. And on the third pitch, Paige whipped another fastball, right past Gibson's knees. The inning was over.

In Oakland, the season before Joe DiMaggio came up, the Yankees sent a scout to see him play against a Paige-led barnstorming team. Richard Donovan said the Yankee scout wired the home office, "DIMAGGIO ALL WE HOPED HE'D BE. HIT SATCH ONE FOR FOUR."

When Veeck signed him in '48, Paige was already past forty. In *The Sporting*

*News,* editor Taylor Spink wrote, "To bring in a pitching 'rookie' of Paige's age casts a reflection on the entire scheme of operation in the major leagues. To sign a hurler at Paige's age is to demean the standards of baseball in the big circuits. Further complicating the situation is the suspicion that if Satchel were white, he would not have drawn a second thought from Veeck."

As Veeck would later write, "If Satch were white, of course, he would have been in the majors twenty-five years earlier, and the question would not have been before the House." As it turned out, Paige won six games and lost only one for the pennant-bound Indians that season—and after each victory, Veeck would send a telegram to Spink, adjusted to the circumstances: "NINE INNINGS. FOUR HITS, FIVE STRIKEOUTS. WINNING PITCHER: PAIGE. DEFINITELY IN LINE FOR THE SPORTING NEWS AWARD AS ROOKIE OF THE YEAR."

There is no end to Satchel Paige stories, just as there was in his lifetime no end to writers who tried to pry them out of him. Though generally obliging, Paige could at times get resistant. According to Richard Donovan, when Paige was finishing up his second career, the one in the major leagues, he said about all the questioning, "Who's gonna straighten out 2,500 ball games in my head? How many cow pastures you played on, Satchel? they wanta know. How many bus rides you took? Who put the spike scars on your shinbone? Why is your feet flat? Who was it offered you $50 to pitch a triple-header that time?

"Man," he concluded, "the past is a long and twisty road."

## TO SATCH/SAMUEL ALLEN

Sometimes I feel like I will *never* stop
Just go on forever
Till one fine mornin'
I'm gonna reach up and grab me a
    handfulla stars
Swing out my long lean leg
And whip three hot strikes burnin' down
    the heavens
And look over at God and say
*How about that!*

**Reader's Response** ∼ What do you find to be the most inspirational aspect of Satchel Paige's life?

**Library Link** ∼ *To find out more about Satchel Paige and other greats of the Negro Leagues, read* Invisible Men, Life in Baseball's Negro Leagues *by Donn Rogosin.*

# HALL OF FAMERS

Satchel Paige once described a fellow ballplayer this way: "That man was so fast he could turn out the light and jump into bed before it was dark." That man was James "Cool Papa" Bell, a talented switch-hitter with phenomenal speed. In one season Bell stole 175 bases. He played in the Negro leagues in the years of segregated baseball, and was later inducted into the Baseball Hall of Fame.

Another Hall of Famer from the Negro leagues is Martin Dihigo, originally from Cuba. He could play both the infield and the outfield, and he could pitch, too. A fellow player once said of Dihigo, "He was the best ballplayer of all time, black or white."

Andrew "Rube" Foster is in the Hall of Fame too. A 6-foot 4-inch, 200-pound pitcher with a notorious fastball, Foster helped organize the Negro leagues in the 1920s. William "Judy" Johnson, a Hall of Famer who came up through the leagues Foster helped organize, once said that an all-star team made up only of Negro league players could beat any major league team.

But black players were not allowed to join the all-white teams of orga-

JAMES "COOL PAPA" BELL

nized baseball until 1947, when Jackie Robinson left the Negro leagues for the Dodgers and broke the so-called "color barrier." By that time, many of the great Negro league players were too old to join the major league teams. Some, such as Satchel Paige, became "rookies" in their thirties and forties. Others, such as the legendary Willie Mays, were luckier because they still had their best years ahead of them. Had the color barrier been broken earlier it is certain that many more stars from the Negro leagues would have gone on to become Hall of Famers.

Mixed Singles.

She tosses the tennis ball    high

                                  into    the    air.

Her

racket comes down harder    than I    e v e r

                                      k n e w

a

racket could hit.

It

is a serve into the inside corner,

that I barely see: kicking    chalk

as

it flies away, untouched    by    me.

I know this will be love.

ARNOLD ADOFF

89

# LEAVING HOME

## from *Sing to the Dawn* by Minfong Ho

*Dawan and her brother, Kwai, have lived in a small Thai farming village all their lives. They both worked hard to earn a scholarship to attend school in the city; but there could be only one recipient. When Dawan finished first in the competition, a disappointed Kwai helped convince their father that Dawan deserved the chance to continue her education. Now, on the morning Dawan is to leave for school, both she and Kwai must face the consequences of their decisions.*

She could not believe that she was leaving in an hour, and yet she sensed that everything, the river, the fields, the bridge, even her brother, were all bidding her goodbye.

She walked over to the bridge, her feet knowing their own way. Kwai took no notice of her approach, but was completely absorbed in throwing pebbles into the river, sullenly watching each one as it hit the water and sank from sight.

When she reached the foot of the bridge, she called up to him, but he gave no sign of acknowledgment. "Kwai," she called again, "can I come up too?" Still he ignored her, and continued to throw his pebbles in, each one with more force and anger.

Finally he muttered to himself, "Stupid stones! All they can do is sink, sink, sink, to the bottom. No matter how hard you throw them, no matter how big a splash they make, all they do is sink." He threw another one in and watched in disgust as it sank from sight. "And even their ripples fade away, and the water flows on, as if nothing ever happened. Stupid, stupid, stupid." He stopped abruptly and glared down at his sister, "I didn't get in your way after all, did I? Now are you satisfied?"

Dawan felt a sharp pain and pity shoot through her, and she wanted to run up to him and hold him, rock him clumsily like she did when they were both very little. Instead, she climbed up the bridge and sat down next to him, with the little pile of pebbles between them.

They maintained an uneasy silence, each staring directly ahead into the tendrils of the rising sun. Finally Dawan said gently, "Kwai, thank you. Thank you very much."

For answer, Kwai threw another pebble into the water. "Why do you have to go anyway?" he challenged. And although his voice was hostile, Dawan knew that, in his way, this was a plea too. Quietly, without looking up, she said to the ripples in the water, "You know why. We've just begun studying, and there's still so much more I need to learn, Kwai."

"Why go and study more when all you're going to end up doing sooner or later is cook and raise babies anyway, like Mama?" he demanded, punctuating every few words by hurling a pebble onto the smooth river surface.

"Well, why do _you_ want to go study then?" she retorted angrily. She reached over for a pebble and flung one into the water herself. "All father's ever done with _his_ life is plant some rice and raise chickens, and a buffalo or two. He's never gone to school, so why should you, when all you're going to be is just another peasant anyway?"

She grabbed another pebble from the pile, but her fingers touched something warm and bony: it was Kwai's hand reaching for his own pebble. They glared at each other for a split second, and then Dawan snatched her hand away.

"Kwai," Dawan continued in a softer tone, "I'm not even sure I really want to go to the City to study. You know how scared I am of crowded places. You're not helping me any with your angry questions, Kwai. Can't you see that I'm confused and scared too?"

She could feel the tears welling up from her lower eyelids as she spoke. All the things that had been pent up inside her for the past few days streamed forth as she continued, "Why can't you be happy for me, Kwai? I know it's hard, but if you had won the scholarship and were going instead of me, I would have been so happy for you, really, really I would have! Remember all the ideas you used to talk about? You dreamed of learning enough to help Father improve his crops, or to take the land away from the landlord and divide it among all the villagers, or to . . ."

"Well, I can't do any of that now, can I?" Kwai broke in bitterly, and although he still sounded angry, his voice was choked.

"But Kwai, don't you see? I can do all those things," Dawan continued eagerly. "All those mornings that we watched the sun rising, I listened to you talk of building a new world. I never said anything much because I never thought I'd have a chance to do anything. But I did listen and I believed in what you dreamed. And now that I've been given this chance to fulfill our ideals, you should be glad for me. Oh Kwai, everything will be better, I promise! I'll make things better!"

Kwai stared at his sister, whose face was shining with a new hope and strength. Then he lowered his gaze to his small pile of pebbles, and felt all the more lonely and deserted.

"Sure, things will be better," he blurted out. "Better for you! What am I supposed to do while you tromp off to a big fancy school in the City? Go sit with the dirty old buffalo all day and be glad for you? And in the early mornings, am I supposed to come out to this stupid old bridge and watch the stupid old sunrise and talk to myself?"

His voice broke, but he took a deep breath and went on more calmly, and yet with more urgency. "Nothing will ever be the same, Sister. I don't care if things will be better or worse, it's just that when . . . if you come back, we couldn't ever sit on the bridge and just watch the dawn like we used to anymore. You've changed that, you've gone and changed all that already." Almost automatically,

Kwai's hand stretched out for a pebble, then stopped half-way in midair. "Oh, what's the use?" he said softly to himself.

In the silence that followed, he picked up a lotus bud lying on the other side of him, and began restlessly plucking off its petals.

Dawan noticed this, and because she hated to see fresh flowers destroyed, said sharply, "Stop that! Why are you tearing that lotus apart?" She was about to snatch it away from him when he shrugged, and tossed the bud aside.

"I liked watching the dawn with you too," she continued in a gentler, sad tone. "Can't you imagine how much I will miss that when I'm alone in the City? I won't have a chance to watch a quiet sunrise over river water anymore. Kwai, you know I'll keep wishing I could be back here on the bridge with you. I'll miss everything so much."

There was a pause, and then she said softly, "Hey, Kwai, when you're out here in the early mornings, will you watch the dawn for me too? And maybe you can sing my morning song for me, because it belongs here, and I'll never sing it anywhere else. Please, Kwai? Do you understand? Watch the dawn for me, and sing."

Her brother's face was now streaked with tears, cool, lonely tears which he didn't want his sister to see. Abruptly, without looking at her, he ran down the bridge and across to the fields, until he disappeared between the tall ricestalks. Dawan watched him run away, but this time made no move to follow him.

She picked up a pebble and dropped it into the water, and as the ripples slowly quivered their way outwards, she started singing her morning song one last time:

"Misty morning,
  mist is rising,
  melody of trees,
  slowly sifting . . ."

and as she sang, she let the hope of the morning light filter through her pores, until the delicate wonder of being home and leaving home blended together like sunlight through rainclouds in her heart. "How can I leave this?" she thought to herself, her song left unfinished. "How can I bear the loneliness in the big City, without friends, without Kwai, without the quiet dawns? I don't want to go off all alone and yet I have to. I don't, don't, want to but I have to, have to leave." It was as if these confused thoughts swirling inside her blurred over the morning scene itself with a misted film. Funny, she thought to herself, how the world looks like after-rain when I'm crying inside.

Then she noticed the half-torn lotus bud lying forlornly by her side, where Kwai had tossed it just now. Out of some feeling of kinship for it, Dawan reached over and picked it up, holding it with both hands, much the way she used to hold onto her grandmother's thumb when she was just learning to walk. Then she knelt up and carefully gathered the petals Kwai had stripped off and sprinkled them gently over the surface of the klong-water.

Like a fleet of tiny pink boats, the petals floated lazily down the water, rising and falling with each ripple of the river. Dawan watched them silently, then whispered, "See, see, Kwai, these don't sink. See, don't be sad, don't be sad, these don't sink." Then wiping away a stray tear, she got up and walked slowly down the bridge.

She knew that at home the bus would soon be arriving, and people would be waiting for her to leave.


Peering out from the leafy shelter of the path, Dawan watched the crowd of villagers gathered around her home. Naked babies scurried between people's legs chasing chickens; a cluster of solemn young monks talked in low whispers among themselves; little girls peeped out from behind the curtain of their mothers' sarongs.

Dawan caught glimpses of a few people who were special to her. Her teacher was standing rather awkwardly by himself, Bao was carelessly holding onto her baby brother while arguing with her older one. Noi was chattering and giggling with a knot of young wives while Ghan stood behind her sullenly.

Dawan stared at all this bustle for a moment, then hastily retreated into the shadows of the tree. But her mother, tying the last rope around her daughter's luggage, caught sight of the movement. She straightened up and hurried over to her daughter, shouting, "There you are! I was getting worried, child. Your father has already gone out to look for you. We thought you had suddenly decided not

to go. It's a good thing you didn't run off for the day, child. Why, look at all the people here to see you off. . . ."

By this time the villagers were swarming around, fussing and cooing over her. Dawan cringed back, muttered something about having to change her clothes, and wiggled her way through them. She clambered up the ladder to the hut, which she knew would be empty except for her old grandmother.

In the dim light of the house, Dawan saw a pair of steady eyes gleaming in the corner. "Don't be afraid child. Calm down," her grandmother said gently. "I have put your new clothes and shoes on the matting there. Are they all waiting for you outside?" She clucked softly, "Never *mind,* child, take your time."

Dawan smiled gratefully at her grandmother, and walked over to the piece of matting where her new things lay waiting. As she bent down to put her shoes on, she realized that she was still clutching Kwai's discarded lotus bud in her hand. Tossing the bud aside, she dressed hurriedly, her nervousness increasing as she heard the sound of the heavy old bus rumbling in. Outside, the noise of the crowd grew, like palm fronds rustling in the wind before a monsoon storm.

"Child, you come here."

Dawan obediently crawled to the corner where her grandmother sat, and knelt down in front of the old woman, hands neatly folded and head bowed. This was the leavetaking that pained her most.

In a voice slow and heavy with age, the old woman said, "You have a long life ahead of you yet, child, and this is just the first step. If you're this timid now how on earth are you going to face all the struggle still before you? Gather yourself together and face the world out there with clear bold eyes. You hear me?"

Dawan nodded, but did not budge. It was the rhythm more than the meaning of the aged voice that calmed the young girl.

Her grandmother gave her a gentle shove, "Well, child, you must go now. You've packed everything you want to take with you, haven't you?"

Dawan stared at her blankly, then shook her head. "No, no, I can't go yet!" she blurted out. Swallowing hard, she continued desperately, "Please Grandmama, I'm not ready. I haven't packed everything yet. There's the sunrise I want to take, and the bridge over the river-bend. And, oh Grandma, how can I pack Kwai, and home here, and the chickens, even the bullfrogs in the forest, and . . ." She could feel a sob rising from her throat, but could not stop it.

Already it seemed as if these precious drops of childhood were slipping through her fingers, like sun-sparkles when she washed her hands in the river. Dawan glanced down at her one outstretched hand, and it looked so small, so helplessly empty. She wept then, shoulders hunched over as sob after sob was wrenched from her thin frame.

The old woman reached out and cupped her granddaughter's ears with feeble hands, but Dawan only shook them off.

"Let me cry, Grandmama," she sobbed brokenly. "Let me cry now and I promise, I won't ever cry anymore. Oh, let me cry now!"

So the grandmother withdrew her hands, and waited patiently until Dawan's sobs began to subside.

After a while the gentle old woman got up and hobbled, back-bent, to the rain barrel. There, she picked up a small glass jar and scooped some fresh rainwater into it. Walking back to where the lotus bud lay on the matting, she bent over and put it carefully in the jar.

Dawan wiped away her tears with the back of her hand, and watched curiously. There was a solemnity about her grandmother's movements that suggested a sacred ritual, like the sprinkling of holy water over a newly-wed couple.

It was not until the old woman had unhurriedly reseated herself beside Dawan, that she handed the glass jar to her granddaughter.

"Hold on to this lotus carefully, child," the grandmother said. "Watch it unfold during your long bus-ride to the City. It's like your-self, this lotus bud, all shut up tight, small and afraid of the outside. But with good water and strong sunlight, it'll unfold, petal by petal by petal. And you will too, Dawan, you will unfold too."

"But, but I don't want to," the schoolgirl mumbled. "I don't want to change."

"I'm sure that bud you have there is pretty contented the way it is," the old woman smiled, nodding towards the lotus. "But if it refuses to change, it'll never become a lotus in full bloom, will it?"

Dawan shook her head reluctantly.

"And remember, the lotus shrinks back into a bud when night falls, only to unfold again in the dawn. Just because you're leaving now doesn't mean you'll never come back. And when you come back, of course some things will change. Anybody can see there's always change. What people seem to forget is that there is a beautiful pattern to all this change."

"But I'm not afraid I won't ever come back, Grandma," Dawan protested weakly. "Right now I don't know if I even want to leave in the first place."

"Don't think of this as leaving, then," the old woman answered firmly. "Think of it as just another of your petals unfolding. For me, child, life has always been an endless unfolding: night unfolding into day, girls unfolding into women, women unfolding babies from themselves. Why, life itself unfolds to death, and death unfolds to life again. There is no cause for sorrow or for fear in this."

Then, as Dawan still hesitated, her grandmother gave her another light push and said, "Go now, child."

Dawan looked at the lotus bud uncertainly. The glass jar was smooth and cool in her hands; somehow it seemed able to absorb the anxiety within her. She swept her eyes over the familiar walls of her home. Sunlight and laughter stole in through the windows and hopped about on the wooden floorboards. Dawan took a deep breath, and nodded. She was ready now.

Setting the jar aside, Dawan pressed her palms together and bent her head over them to her grandmother in the traditional gesture of leave-taking. Then she stood up and, lotus-jar in hand, went outside to the veranda. Her mother and some other women were busy loading her luggage onto the already crowded bus, trying to wedge the bags between a big basket full of bananas and a coop full of squawking chickens. Everybody was fluttering about excitedly trying to help.

As she climbed down the stairs, her father rushed out from the jungle path, panting and scowling fiercely. He caught sight of Dawan at once, and strode up to her.

"Why did you disappear like that just before you're supposed to leave?" he yelled at her angrily. "Do you know that I've been chasing

around the countryside the whole morning looking for you and
Kwai? I thought the two of you had taken off together, until I saw
Kwai alone. Where the hell have you been anyway?"

Ignoring his last question, Dawan asked eagerly, "Where is
Kwai, Father? Where did you see him? Is he coming?"

Her father snorted loudly. "Huh! That brother of yours! And I
thought the two of you were such good friends!"

"But where is he, Father? Is he coming?" Dawan craned her
neck to peer behind her father, but no-one was in sight.

"Where is he? He's sitting out on the old bridge, calm as a
water-buffalo, that's where he is. I asked him where you were, and
he said he didn't know and didn't care. Then I asked if he was coming back to see you off. He . . ." The strong peasant paused and
eyed his daughter shrewdly, "You two had a fight, didn't you?"

Dawan did not seem to have heard the question. "Is he coming
or not, Father? What did he say?" she asked tersely.

"You really want to know what he said? He looked down at me
from his bridge and said, 'She's got the whole village seeing her off.
Isn't that enough? What does she need me there for?' And I thought
you two were . . ."

Dawan turned away so that her father could not see her face.
She felt more lonely on the fringe of that chattering crowd than she
had ever felt before. Looking at all the faces around her, she realized
that there was not a single one she really cared to say goodbye to.

So her brother was still bitter and angry at her. She wondered
again if fighting with him to go to the City had been worth it after
all. She was leaving, but there was nothing left to say goodbye to.

The bus honked sharply, and Dawan saw the bus driver wave
impatiently for her to board. Immediately the crowd surged over to
her, and she was shoved, patted, hugged and somehow pushed to
the steps of the bus. She caught a glimpse of her mother crying, but
she herself felt no more sadness, only a throbbing disappointment.

As soon as she got on, the big bus ground to a start and roared
off. She groped her way clumsily to a seat and leaned out the window to watch the crowd. Her grandmother was standing on the
veranda above them all, smiling slightly. Then the faces all receded
into the distance. When they had disappeared from view, green

stretches of paddy-fields slid past her window, going by as quickly as slippery fish. Ahead of them now was the river, and Dawan stuck her head way out of the window to catch a last glimpse of the bridge on which she had so often greeted the sun.

Suddenly, carried by the breeze, she heard a very familiar voice singing a very familiar song—

"Misty morning,
mist is lifting,
melody of trees
slowly sifting . . ."

He was there. Etched sharply against the cloudless sky, Kwai was standing on the old arched bridge, both arms thrown back in a gesture meant both to embrace her and send her off.

Dawan burst out laughing and the laughter was so strong and round that it seemed to jam in her throat. Flinging her arms out too, to hug him and the land, she joined him in song.

"Dappled morning,
sun is flying
breaths of breezes
rising, dying,
brushing over the earth's brown skin . . ."

The bus was fast approaching the slim figure now. A grin, a streak of wetness gleaming on one cheek, an out-stretched palm, and Kwai had already flashed past her.

Leaning out as far as she could, Dawan watched her brother wave until he was only a speck on the bridge, until the bridge was only a speck on the river, and until finally even the ribbon of water faded into the distance.

Dawan watched for a moment longer, and then, gently picking up the glass jar from her seat, she leaned back. The morning song was still in her. So, brushing the lotus bud with her fingertips, she sang the last verse.

"Happy morning
my heart is singing
arms spread wide,
the dawn is bringing
its sunglow to this land, my home."

And as she sang, a shaft of sunlight pierced through the grimy bus windows and cradled the lotus. Dawan noticed that the first few petals of the flower had already begun to unfold.

Reader's Response ∼ If you were Dawan, what choice would you have made?

# Making Connections

**W**e are beginning
to understand how
animals communicate.
What do they have
to say to each other
and to us?

ROUSSEAU, Henri: THE SLEEPING GYPSY, *1987. Oil, 51" x 6'7". Gift of Mrs. Simon Guggenheim. 646.39. Collection, The Museum of Modern Art, New York*

# Theme Books for
# Making Connections

A nimals, like people, have unique and varied languages. When we pay close attention, we can better understand how they communicate and what their signals mean.

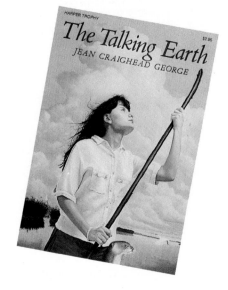

A two-day retreat into the Everglades to learn the language of the animals turns into a twelve-week ordeal for a Seminole girl. Author Jean Craighead George leads her heroine through a series of frightening experiences as Billie Wind learns to listen to *The Talking Earth*

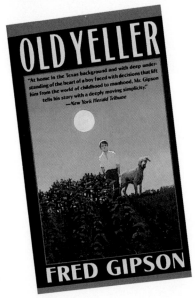

He was just an old yellow hound, but he won the hearts of a Texas farm family in Fred Gipson's classic tale of the special relationship between a boy and his dog. At first, fourteen-year-old Travis wanted nothing to do with the thieving dog. Could *Old Yeller* change his mind?

In Robert Siegel's **Whalesong**, Hruna sings his story—the saga of a young humpback whale's rite of passage. His is a life of sacrifice, terror, and joy— and puzzlement over the human need to kill, trap, and pollute.

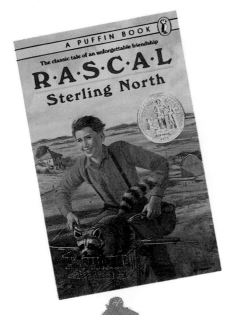

Author Sterling North takes a nostalgic look back at one special year of his boyhood—1918, the year of *Rascal*. This heartwarming portrait of a boy's special friendship with a raccoon is both entertaining and uplifting.

*More Books to Enjoy*

*Irish Red* by Jim Kjelgaard
*The Wolfling* by Sterling North
*Animal Partners: Training Animals to Help People*
    by Patricia Curtis
*National Velvet* by Enid Bagnold

# RIVER RESCUE

by Sheila Burnford
from The Incredible Journey:
A Tale of Three Animals

*Three animals—a Labrador retriever, a bull terrier, and a Siamese cat—have embarked on a daring 250-mile trek across the Canadian wilderness to return to their home. Together they have battled hunger, cold, bobcat, and bear—until the moment when the Siamese is unable to cross a large river, and the powerful waters carry the cat downstream, away from his companions.*

Many miles downstream on the side to which the dogs had crossed, a small cabin stood near the bank of the river, surrounded by three or four acres of cleared land, its solid, uncompromising appearance lightened only by the scarlet geraniums at the window sills and a bright blue door. A log barn stood back from it, and a steam-bath house at the side nearer the river. The patch of vegetable garden, the young orchard and the neatly fenced fields, each with their piles of cleared boulders and stumps, were small orderly miracles of victory won from the dark encroaching forest that surrounded them.

Reino Nurmi and his wife lived here, as sturdy and uncompromising as the cabin they had built with their own hand-hewn logs, their lives as frugal and orderly as the fields they had wrested from the wilderness. They had tamed the bush, and in return it yielded them their food and their scant living from trap lines and a wood lot, but the struggle to keep it in subjection was endless. They had retained their Finnish identity complete when they left their homeland, exchanging only one country's set of solitudes and vast lonely forests for another's, and as yet their only real contact with the new world that lay beyond their property line was through their ten-year-old daughter Helvi, who knew no other homeland. Helvi walked the lonely miles to the waiting school bus each day, and through her they strengthened their roots in the security of the New World, and were content meanwhile with horizons limited by their labor.

On the Sunday afternoon that the beaver dam broke, a day of some relaxation, Helvi was down by the river, skipping flat stones across the water, and wishing that she had a companion; for she found it difficult to be entirely fair in a competition always held against herself. The riverbank was steep and high here, so she was quite safe when a rushing torrent of water, heralded by a great curling wave, swept past. She stood watching it, fascinated by the spectacle, thinking that she must go and tell her father, when her eye was caught by a piece of debris that had been whirling around in a back eddy and was now caught on some boulders at the edge of the bank. She could see what looked like a small, limp body on the surface. She ran along by the boiling water to investigate, scrambling down the bank, to stand looking pityingly at the wet, bedraggled body, wondering what it was, for she had never seen anything like it before. She dragged the mass of twigs and branches further up on land, then ran to call her mother.

Mrs. Nurmi was out in the yard by an old wood stove which she still used for boiling the vegetable dyes for her weaving, or peelings and scraps for the hens. She followed Helvi, calling out to her husband to come and see this strange animal washed up by an unfamiliar, swift-surging river.

He came, with his unhurried countryman's walk and quiet thoughtful face, and joined the others to look down in silence at the small limp body, the darkly plastered fur betraying its slight-ness, the frail skull bones and thin crooked tail mercilessly exposed. Suddenly he bent down and laid his hand lightly on it for a moment, then pulled back the skin above and below one eye and looked more closely. He turned and saw Helvi's anxious, question-ing face close to his own, and beyond that her mother's. "Is a drowned *cat* worth trying to save?" he asked them, and when her mother nodded, before Helvi's pleading eyes, he said no more, but scooped the soaking bundle up and walked back to the cabin, tell-ing Helvi to run ahead and bring some dry sacks.

He laid the cat down in a sunny patch by the wood stove and rubbed it vigorously with sacking, turning the body from side to side until the fur stood out in every direction and it looked like some disheveled old scarf. Then, as he wrapped the sacking firmly around and her mother pried the clenched teeth open, Helvi poured a little warm milk and precious brandy down the pale cold throat.

She watched as a spasm ran through the body, followed by a faint cough, then held her breath in sympathy as the cat retched and choked convulsively, a thin dribble of milk appearing at the side of its mouth. Reino laid the straining body over his knee and pressed gently over the ribcage. The cat choked and struggled for breath, until at last a sudden gush of water streamed out, and it lay relaxed. Reino gave a slow smile of satisfaction and handed the bundle of sacking to Helvi, telling her to keep it warm and quiet for a while—if she was sure that she still wanted a cat.

She felt the oven, still warm though the fire had long died out, then placed the cat on a tray inside, leaving the door open. When her mother went into the cabin to prepare supper and Reino left to milk the cow, Helvi sat cross-legged on the ground by the stove, anxiously chewing the end of one fair braid, watching and waiting. Every now and then she would put her hand into the oven to touch the cat, to loosen the sacking or to stroke the soft fur, which was beginning to pulsate with life under her fingers.

After half an hour she was rewarded: the cat opened his eyes. She leaned over and looked closely into them—their blackness now contracted, slowly, to pinpoints, and a pair of astonishingly vivid blue eyes looked up instead. Presently, under her gentle strok-ing, she felt a throaty vibration, then heard a rusty, feeble purring. Wildly excited, she called to her parents.

Within another half-hour the little Finnish girl held in her lap a sleek, purring, Siamese cat, who had already finished two saucers of milk (which normally he detested, drinking only water), and who had groomed himself from head to foot. By the time the Nurmi family were eating their supper around the scrubbed pine table, he had finished a bowl of chopped meat, and was weaving his way around the table legs, begging in his plaintive, odd voice for more food, his eyes crossed intently, his kinked tail held straight in the air like a banner. Helvi was fascinated by him, and by his gentle-ness when she picked him up.

That night the Nurmis were having fresh pickerel, cooked in the old-country way with the head still on and surrounded by potatoes. Helvi ladled the head with some broth and potatoes into a saucer and put it on the floor. Soon the fishhead had disappeared to the accompaniment of pleased rumbling growls. The potatoes followed; then, holding down the plate with his paw, the cat polished it clean. Satisfied at last, he stretched superbly, his front paws extended so that he looked like a heraldic lion, then jumped onto Helvi's lap, curled himself around and purred loudly.

The parents' acceptance was completed by his action, though there had never before been a time or place in the economy of their lives for an animal that did not earn its keep, or lived anywhere else except the barn or kennel. For the first time in her life Helvi had a pet.

Helvi carried the cat up to bed with her, and he draped himself with familiar ease over her shoulder as she climbed the steep ladder stairs leading up to her little room in the eaves. She tucked him tenderly into an old wooden cradle, and he lay in sleepy contentment, his dark face incongruous against a doll's pillow.

Late in the night she woke to a loud purring in her ear, and felt him treading a circle at her back. The wind blew a gust of cold rain across her face and she leaned over to shut the window, hearing far away, so faint that it died in the second of wind-borne sound, the thin, high keening of a wolf. She shivered as she lay down, then drew the new comforting warmth of the cat closely to her.

When Helvi left in the morning for the long walk and ride to the distant school the cat lay curled on the window sill among the geraniums. He had eaten a large plate of oatmeal, and his coat shone in the sun as he licked it sleepily, his eyes following Mrs. Nurmi as she moved about the cabin. But when she went outside with a basket of washing she looked back to see him standing on his hind legs peering after, his soundless mouth opening and shutting behind the window. She hurried back, fearful of her geraniums, and opened the door—at which he was already scratching—half expecting him to run. Instead he followed her to the washing line and sat by the basket, purring. He followed her back and forth between the cabin and the wood stove, the henhouse and the stable. When she shut him out once by mistake he wailed pitifully.

This was the pattern of his behavior all day—he shadowed the Nurmis as they went about their chores, appearing silently on some point of vantage—the seat of the harrow, a sack of potatoes, the manger or the well platform—his eyes on them constantly. Mrs. Nurmi was touched by his apparent need for companionship: that his behavior was unlike that of any other cat she attributed to his foreign appearance. But her husband was not so easily deceived—he had noticed the unusual intensity in the blue eyes. When a passing raven mocked the cat's voice and he did not

look up, then later sat unheeding in the stable to a quick rustle in the straw behind, Reino knew then that the cat was deaf.

Carrying her schoolbooks and lunch pail, Helvi ran most of the way home across the fields and picked up the cat as well when he came to meet her. He clung to her shoulder, balancing easily, while she performed the routine evening chores that awaited her. Undeterred by his weight she fed the hens, gathered eggs, fetched water, then sat at the table stringing dried mushrooms. When she put him down before supper she saw that her father was right— the pointed ears did not respond to any sound, though she noticed that he started and turned his head at the vibration if she clapped her hands or dropped even a small pebble on the bare floor.

She had brought home two books from the traveling library, and after the supper dishes had been cleared away her parents sat by the stove in the short interval before bed while she read aloud to them, translating as she went. They sat, in their moment of rare relaxation, with the cat stretched out on his back at their feet, and the child's soft voice, flowing through the dark austerity of the cabin, carried them beyond the circle of light from the oil lamp to the warmth and brightness of strange lands. . . .

They heard of seafaring Siamese cats who worked their passages the world over, their small hammocks made and slung by their human messmates, who held them second to none as ship's cats; and of the great proud Siamese Ratting Corps who patrolled the dockyards of Le Havre with unceasing vigilance; they saw, with eyes withdrawn and dreaming, the palace watch-cats of long-ago Siam, walking delicately on long simian legs around the fountained courtyards, their softly padding feet polishing the mosaics to a lustred path of centuries. And at last they learned how these nobly born Siamese acquired the kink at the end of their tails and bequeathed it to all their descendants.

And as they listened, they looked down in wonder, for there on the rag rug lay one of these, stretched out flat on his royal back, his illustrious tail twitching idly, and his jeweled eyes on their daughter's hand as she turned the pages that spoke of his ancestors—the guardian cats of the Siamese princesses. Each princess, when she came down to bathe in the palace lake, would slip her rings for safekeeping on the tail of her attendant cat. So zealous in their charge were these proud cats that they bent the last joint sideways for safer custody, and in time the faithful tails became crooked forever, and their childrens' and their childrens' children. . . .

One after another the Nurmis passed their hands admiringly down the tail before them to feel the truth in its bent bony tip; then Helvi gave him a bowl of milk, which he drank with regal condescension before she carried him up the ladder to bed.

That night, and for one more, the cat lay curled peacefully in Helvi's arms, and in the daytime during her absence he followed her parents everywhere. He trailed through the bush after her mother as she searched for late mushrooms, then sat on the cabin steps and patted the dropped corn kernels as she shucked a stack of cobs. He followed Reino and his work horse across the fields to the wood lot and perched on a newly felled pungent stump, his head following their every movement, and he curled by the door of the stable and watched the man mending harness and oiling traps. And in the late afternoons when Helvi returned he was there waiting for her, a rare and beautiful enigma in the certain routine of the day. He was one of them.

But on the fourth night he was restless, shaking his head and pawing his ears, his voice distressed at her back. At last he lay down, purring loudly, and pushed his head into her hand—the fur below his ears was soaking. She saw their sharp black triangles outlined against the little square of window and watched them flicker and quiver in response to every small night sound. Glad for him in his newfound hearing, she fell asleep.

When she woke, later in the night, aware of a lost warmth, she saw him crouched at the open window, looking out over the pale fields and the tall, dark trees below. His long sinuous tail thrashed to and fro as he measured the distance to the ground. Even as her hand moved out impulsively towards him he sprang, landing with a soft thud.

She looked down and saw his head turn for the first time to her voice, his eyes like glowing rubies as they caught the moonlight, then turn away—and with sudden desolate knowledge she knew that he had no further need of her. Through a blur of tears, she watched him go, stealing like a wraith in the night towards the river that had brought him. Soon the low, swiftly running form was lost among the shadows.

# Epilogue

Even though the Siamese found comfort and love with the Nurmi family, he had stronger ties elsewhere. To stay would have been to abandon his ''first'' family. It didn't take him long to pick up the trail of the dogs, but he had another narrow escape from death before he could reach them. When he finally did, their joy was boundless. All three had lighter hearts as they continued their incredible journey.

Reader's Response ∽ Why do you think Helvi was so taken with the Siamese?

Library Link ∽ *If you'd like to find out whether the Siamese cat finds his real family, read the book* The Incredible Journey: A Tale of Three Animals *by Sheila Burnford.*

# A GALLERY OF CATS

The most popular short-haired cat is the *Siamese*.

The *Burmese* is noted for its round eyes and dark brown coat.

With its short, curly fur, the *Rex* first appeared in 1950.

Like the short-haired *Burmese*, the *Birman* originated in Burma, but the two cats are not related.

The coat of the popular *Persian* can vary in color.

The *Maine coon* originated in New England in the nineteenth century.

# THE NAMING OF CATS

L'HIVER: CHAT SUR UN COUSSIN, *color lithograph by Théophile-Alexandre Steinlen, French, 1950.*

## T.S. Eliot

The Naming of Cats is a difficult matter,
    It isn't just one of your holiday games;
You may think at first I'm as mad as a hatter
When I tell you, a cat must have THREE DIFFERENT NAMES.
First of all, there's the name that the family use daily,
    Such as Peter, Augustus, Alonzo or James,
Such as Victor or Jonathan, George or Bill Bailey—
    All of them sensible everyday names.
There are fancier names if you think they sound sweeter,
    Some for the gentlemen, some for the dames:
Such as Plato, Admetus, Electra, Demeter—
    But all of them sensible everyday names.
But I tell you, a cat needs a name that's particular,
    A name that's peculiar, and more dignified,
Else how can he keep up his tail perpendicular,
    Or spread out his whiskers, or cherish his pride?
Of names of this kind, I can give you a quorum,
    Such as Munkustrap, Quaxo, or Coricopat,
Such as Bombalurina, or else Jellylorum—
    Names that never belong to more than one cat.
But above and beyond there's still one name left over,
    And that is the name that you never will guess;
The name that no human research can discover—
    But THE CAT HIMSELF KNOWS, and will never confess.
When you notice a cat in profound meditation,
    The reason, I tell you, is always the same:
His mind is engaged in a rapt contemplation
    Of the thought, of the thought, of the thought of his name:
        His ineffable effable
        Effanineffable
Deep and inscrutable singular Name.

## Gentleman Cat

·from *The Fur Person*·
by M·a·y S·a·r·t·o·n

*The Fur Person is a very independent tomcat who has been on his own for two years. Now he has decided it is time to find a suitable housekeeper and settle down. Will he be able to find a happy home?*

The Fur Person raised his head and took in a terrible series of smells, the smell of a small stuffy apartment, of overheated radiators, of cheap perfume, of talcum powder, of yesterday's bacon; he stood there, his tail standing out straight behind him in amazement, his nose trembling slightly in dismay. Then he cast a quick glance behind him, but the door was shut tight. No escape. The lady meanwhile had not stopped talking since she set him down. He could hear her while she ran water in the kitchen and rattled the dishes, telling him over and over (almost as bad as Hannah she was) how much she loved kitties, how much she loved him, and what he would have for breakfast. The Fur Person could not pay attention right away to this. He had first to explore the apartment and any possible avenues of escape. He had first to sniff at every inch of the dirty pink carpet stretched from wall to wall, with moldy crumbs, as he soon discovered, concealed along the edges. He had never been in a human house with so many objects in it, and he was only about a third of the way through, had in fact just reached a stand with three potted ferns on it, had stood up on his hindlegs to feel the quality of a green velvet armchair (for claw-sharpening purposes), had taken a quick look at the bed, almost entirely covered with small satin pillows and with, of all things, an imitation cat sitting on it, when the lady suddenly pounced on him from the back and hauled him ignominiously into the kitchen, setting him down in front of a plate of scrambled eggs and bacon. Now, no Gentleman Cat likes to be plunked down in front of his food. The law is that he shall approach it slowly from a distance, without haste, however hungry he may be, that he shall smell it from afar and decide at least three feet away what his verdict is going to be: Good, Fair, Passable or Unworthy.

If the verdict is Good, he will approach it very slowly, settle himself down in a crouching position and curl his tail around him before he takes a mouthful. If it is Fair, he will crouch, but leave his tail behind him, stretched out along the floor. If it is merely Passable, he will eat standing up, and if it is Unworthy he will perform the rite of pretending to scratch earth over it and bury it.

The Fur Person backed away, ruffled and indignant, and had to put his clothes in order before he would even look at the food. Then he very carefully extracted the bacon, bit by bit, and ate it with considerable relish. Scrambled eggs were considered "Unworthy" and were left on the plate.

When the lady saw him performing the usual rite demanded by Unworthy food, she clapped her hands with delight and said he was a terribly clever cat (little she knew!), she had never seen anything so sweet in her life, and he should have a can of crabmeat for his lunch.

Then she picked him up and tried to fold him together onto her lap. Foolish woman! Though a little crumbled bacon is not a heavy meal for a Gentleman Cat who has spent the night out, it is enough of a meal to require at least fifteen minutes of solitary meditation after it. The Fur Person jumped down at once and went as far away from her as he could get, as her smell of cheap narcissus or rose (he was not quite sure which) made him feel rather ill. The farthest away he could get was under the bed; there he stayed for some time, licking his chops, for the slightest sensation of oiliness or fat around his whiskers is something a Gentleman Cat cannot endure. Then he sat, crouching, but not in any way "settled" and thought things over. He did not fancy the lady, but she had mentioned crabmeat for lunch. Also there was at present no way of escape that he could see. By now, it should be clear that the Fur Person was of a philosophical nature, capable of considerable reflection. He had waited six months before making up his mind to leave Alexander and two years before deciding to settle down, and after all, he had only been here for half an hour. Sometimes first impressions could be misleading. Also he was very susceptible to flattery, and the lady's admiration was unstinted. Although he was completely concealed from her under the bed, she was still talking about him and to him. Things could be worse.

The trouble was, as he soon found out, that as soon as he came into reach, the lady could not resist hugging and kissing him with utter disregard for the dignity of his person. There are times when a Gentleman Cat likes very much to be scratched gently under his chin, and if this is done with *savoir-faire*[1] he may afterwards enjoy a short siesta on a lap and some very refined stroking, but he does not like to be held upside down like a human baby and he does not like to be cooed over, and to be pressed to a bosom smelling of narcissus or rose. The Fur Person struggled furiously against the ardent ministrations of the lady and took refuge behind the garbage pail in the kitchen when he could. It was crystal clear that he was in jail, and, even at the risk of not having crabmeat for lunch, he must escape. His eyes behind the garbage pail had become slits; he did not tuck his paws in but sat upright, thinking very fast. While he was thinking he nibbled one back foot—he had observed before that there was nothing like thinking to make one itch all over—then he had to bite a place rather difficult to reach on his back, and then his front paw, and soon he was quite absorbed in licking himself all over. It is best to be clean before attempting to escape, and—this thought occurred to him suddenly—it is also best to have sharp claws. From behind the garbage pail he could see the green velvet armchair, and as soon as the lady disappeared for a moment into the bedroom, he emerged from his hiding place and stretched, then walked sedately to the chair, sat up and began to sharpen his claws on the thick plush, a very satisfactory claw-sharpening place indeed.

"Oh," screamed the lady, and swooped down and picked him up, "you naughty cat. Stop it at once!" She even shook him quite violently. This, on top of all he had suffered that morning, was suddenly more than the Fur Person could endure. He turned and bit her arm, not very hard, but just enough so she dropped him unceremoniously and gave a penetrating yell.

[1]savoir-faire: French term indicating the ability to act properly under any conditions

122

"You're not a nice cat at all," she said, and she began to whimper. "You don't like me," she whimpered, "do you?"

But this last remark was addressed to his back. He was sitting in front of the door. It is a known fact that if one sits long enough in front of a door, doing the proper yoga exercises, the door will open. It is not necessary to indulge in childish noises. Commandment Four: "A Gentleman Cat does not mew except in extremity. He makes his wishes known and then waits." So he sat with his back to the lady and wished with the whole force of his fur person; his whiskers even trembled slightly with the degree of concentration. Meanwhile the lady grumbled and mumbled to herself and said "Nobody loves me." But the Fur Person's whiskers only trembled a little more violently, so huge had become his wish to get away. By comparison with this prison, the grocery shop looked like Heaven. He might even bring himself to eat day-old hamburger if only he could get away from this infernal apartment. He noticed also that it was much too hot and his skin was prickling all over, but he schooled himself not to move, not to lick, not to nibble. He became a single ever-more-powerful WISH TO GET OUT.

"Very well," said the lady, blowing her nose. He gave her one last cold look out of his green eyes, and then she opened the door. She even followed him downstairs, his tail held perfectly straight like a flag to show his thanks, and opened the front door. The Fur Person bounded out and ran all the way up the street, sniffing the fresh air with intense pleasure. He ran halfway up an elm tree and down again before you could say "Gentleman Cat," and then he sauntered down the street, his tail at half-mast, and his heart at peace.

On his roves and rambles, on his rounds and travels, he had never found himself exactly where he now found himself, on the border of a dangerous street—very dangerous, he realized after a short exposure to the roar of cars, the squeaking of brakes, the lurching, weaving, rumbling, interspersed with loud bangs and horns of a really incredible amount of traffic. It was quite bewildering, and the Fur Person looked about for a place where he could withdraw and sit awhile. He was rather tired. It was time, he considered, for a short snooze, after which the question of Lunch might be approached in the proper frame of mind. And there, providentially indeed, he noticed that he was standing in front of a house bounded on one side by a porch with a very suitable railing running along it. He took the porch in one leap, sat for a second measuring the distance to the square platform on top of the railing post, then swung up to it rather casually, and there he was, safe and free as you please, in a little patch of sunlight which seemed to have been laid down there just for him. He tucked in his paws and closed his eyes. The sun was delicious on his back, so much so that he began to sing very softly, accompanying himself this time with one of his lighter purrs, just a tremolo to keep things going.

And there he sat for maybe an hour, or maybe even two, enjoying the peace and quiet, and restoring himself after the rather helter-skelter life he had been leading for two days, since his metamorphosis into a Gentlemen Cat in search of a housekeeper. He was so deep down in the peace and the quiet that when a window went up right beside him on the porch, he did not jump into the air as he might have done had it not been such a very fine May morning or had he been a little less tired. As it was, he merely opened his eyes very wide and looked.

"Come here," a voice said inside the house, "there's a pussin on the porch."

The Fur Person waited politely, for he had rather enjoyed the timbre of the voice, quite low and sweet, and he was always prepared to be admired. Pretty soon two faces appeared in the window and looked at him, and he looked back.

"Well," said another voice, "perhaps he would like some lunch."

The Fur Person woke right up then, rose, and stretched on the tips of his toes, his tail making a wide arc to keep his balance.

"He is rather thin," said the first voice. "I wonder where he belongs. We've never seen him before, have we?"

"And what are we having for lunch?" said the second voice.

"There's that haddock left over—I could cream it."

The Fur Person pivoted on the fence post and stamped three times with his back feet, to show how dearly he loved the sound of haddock.

"What is he doing now?" said the first voice and chuckled.

"Saying he likes haddock, I expect."

Then, quite unexpectedly, the window was closed. Dear me, he thought, won't I do? For the first time, he began to be really anxious about his appearance. Was the tip of his tail as white as it could be? How about his shirt front? Dear me, he thought, won't I do? And his heart began to beat rather fast, for he was, after all, tired and empty and in a highly emotional state. This made him unusually impulsive. He jumped down to the porch and then to the ground below and trotted round to the back door, for as he expected, there was a garden at the back, with a pear tree at the end of it, and excellent posts for claw-sharpening in a small laundry yard. He could not resist casting a glance at the flower beds, nicely dug up and raked, in just the right condition for making holes, and in fact the thought of a neat little hole was quite irresistible, so he dug one there and then.

When he had finished, he saw that the crocuses were teeming with bees. His whiskers trembled. He crouched down in an ecstasy of impatience and coiled himself tight as a spring, lashed his tail, and before he knew it himself was in the air and down like lightning on an unsuspecting crocus. The bee escaped, though the crocus did not. Well, thought the Fur Person, a little madness in the spring is all very well, but I must remember that this is serious business and I must get down to it. So he sat and looked the house over. It was already evident that there were innumerable entrances and exits like the window opening to the porch, that there were places of safety in case he was locked out, and that (extraordinary bit of luck) he had found not one old maid with a garden and a house but *two*. Still, his hopes had been dashed rather often in the last twenty-four hours and he reminded himself this time to be circumspect and hummed a bit of the tune about being a free cat, just to give himself courage.

Then he walked very slowly, stopping to stretch out one back leg and lick it, for he remembered the Fifth Commandment: "Never hurry towards an objective, never look as if you had only one thing in mind, it is not polite." Just as he was nibbling the muscle in his back foot with considerable pleasure, for he was always discovering delightful things about himself, he heard the back door open. Cagey, now, he told himself. So he went on nibbling and even spread his toes and licked his foot quite thoroughly, and all this time, a very sweet voice was saying:

"Are you hungry, puss-cat? Come, pussin . . ."

And so at last he came, his tail tentatively raised in a question mark; he came slowly, picking up his paws with care, and gazing all the while in a quite romantic way (for he couldn't help it) at the saucer held in the old maid's hand. At the foot of the back stairs he sat down and waited the necessary interval.

"Well, come on," said the voice, a slightly impatient one, with a little roughness to it, a great relief after the syrupy lady in the hot apartment from which he had escaped.

At this the Fur Person bounded up the stairs, and at the very instant he entered the kitchen, the purrs began to swell inside him and he wound himself round and round two pairs of legs (for he must be impartial), his nose in the air, his tail straight up like a flag, on tiptoe, and roaring with thanks.

"He's awfully thin," said the first voice.

"And not very beautiful, I must say," said the second voice.

But the Fur Person fortunately was not listening. He was delicately and with great deliberation sniffing the plate of haddock; he was settling down; he was even winding his tail around him, because here at last was a meal worthy of a Gentleman Cat.

The most remarkable thing about the two kind ladies was that they left him to eat in peace and did not say one word. They had the tact to withdraw into the next room and to talk about other things, and leave him entirely to himself. It seemed to him that he had been looked up and down, remarked upon, and hugged and squeezed far too much in the last days, and now he was terribly grateful for the chance to savor this delicious meal with no exclaiming this or that, and without the slightest interruption. When he had finished every single scrap and then licked over the plate several times (For if a

meal is Worthy, the Sixth Commandment says, "The plate must be left clean, so clean that a person might think it had been washed."), the Fur Person sat up and licked his chops. He licked them perhaps twenty or twenty-five times, maybe even fifty times, his raspberry-colored tongue devoting itself to each whisker, until his face was quite clean. Then he began on his front paws and rubbed his face gently with a nice wet piece of fur, and rubbed right over his ears, and all this took a considerable time. While he was

127

doing it he could hear a steady gentle murmur of conversation in the next room and pretty soon he stopped with one paw in the air, shook it once, shook his head the way a person does whose hair has just been washed in the bowl, and then took a discreet ramble.

"Just make yourself at home," said the voice he liked best. "Just look around."

His tail went straight up so they would understand that he was out for a rove and did not intend, at the moment, to catch a mouse, that in fact he was looking around, and not committing himself one way or another. The house, he discovered, was quite large enough, quite nice and dark, with a long hall for playing and at least three sleeping places. He preferred a bed, but there was a large comfortable armchair that would do in a pinch. Still, he reminded himself, one must not be hasty. Just then he walked into a rather small room lined with books and with (this was really splendid) a huge flat desk in it. There are times in a Gentleman Cat's life when what he likes best is to stretch out full length (and the Fur Person's length was considerable) on a clean hard place. The floor is apt to be dirty and to smell of old crumbs, but a desk, preferably with papers strewn across it, is quite the thing. The Fur Person felt a light elegant obbligato² of purrs rising in his throat.

Neither of the old maids had, until now, touched him. And this, he felt, was a sign of understanding. They had given him a superior lunch and allowed him to rove and ramble in peace. Now he suddenly felt quite curious to discover what they were like. It is amazing how much a cat learns about life by the way he is stroked. His heart was beating rather fast as he approached the table. One of the two old maids had almost disappeared in a cloud of smoke, the brusque one; he did not like smoke, so he made a beeline toward the other, gazing out of wide-open eyes, preceded by his purrs.

"Well, old thing, do you want a lap?" the gentle voice inquired very politely. She did not reach down and gather him up. She leaned forward and ran one finger down his head and along his spine. Then she scratched him between the ears in a most delightful way. The purrs began to sound like bass drums very lightly drummed, and the Fur Person felt himself swell with pleasure. It was incredibly enjoyable, after all he had been through, to be handled with such *savoir-faire*, and before he knew it himself he had jumped up on this welcoming lap and begun to knead. The Fur Person, you remember, had lost his mother when he was such a small kitten that his ears were still buttoned down and his eyes quite blue, but when he jumped up onto this lady's lap, he seemed dimly to remember kneading his mother like this, with tiny starfish paws that went in and out, in and out.

"I wish he'd settle," the gentle voice said, "his claws are rather sharp."

But the Fur Person did not hear this for he was in a trance of home-coming and while he kneaded he composed a song,

²obbligato: an accompanying part in music

128

and while he composed it, it seemed as if every hair on his body tingled and was burnished, so happy was he at last.

"He actually looks fatter," the brusque voice said, "he must have been awfully hungry."

The Fur Person closed his eyes and sang his song and it went like this:

Thank you, thank you,
You and no other
Dear gentle voice,
Dear human mother,
For your delicate air,
For your *savoir-faire*
For your kind soft touch
Thank you very much.

He was so terribly sleepy that the last line became inextricably confused in a purr and in his suddenly making himself into a round circle of peace, all kneading spent, and one paw over his nose.

There was an indefinite interval of silence; but it must not be forgotten that the Fur Person had led a hectic and disillusioning life, and while he slept his nose twitched and his paws twitched and he imagined that he was caught and being smothered, and before he even quite woke up or had his eyes open he had leapt off the kind lap, in a great state of nerves.

It is all very well, he told himself severely, but this time you have to be careful. Remember Alexander, remember the grocer, remember the lady and her suffocating apartment. It was not easy to do, but without

giving the old maids a parting look, he walked in great dignity down the long dark hall to the front door and sat down before it, wishing it to open. Pretty soon he heard footsteps, but he did not turn his head. I must have time to think this over, he was telling himself. Never be hasty when choosing a housekeeper. The door opened and he was outside. Never be hasty, he was telling himself, as he bounded down the steps and into the sweet May afternoon. But at the same time, quite without intending it, he found that he had composed a short poem, and as he sharpened his claws on the elm by the door and as he ran up it, just to show

what a fine Gentleman Cat he was, he hummed it over. It was very short and sweet:

> East and West
> Home is Best.

And though he spent several days coming and going, it was very queer how, wherever he went, he always found himself somehow coming back to the two old maids, just to be sure they were still there, and also, it must be confessed, to find out what they were having for supper. And on the fourth day it rained and that settled it: he spent the night. The next morning while he was washing his face after eating a nice little dish of stew beef cut up into small pieces, he made his decision. After all, if a Gentleman Cat spends the night, it is a kind of promise. I will be your cat, he said to himself, sitting on the desk with his paws tucked in and his eyes looking gravely at the two old maids standing in the doorway, if you will be my housekeepers. And of course they agreed, because of the white tip to his tail, because he hummed such a variety of purrs and songs, because he really was quite a handsome fellow, and because they had very soft hearts.

Reader's Response ∾ As you read the story, which particular episode did you enjoy the most?

Library Link ∾ *Share more of the Gentleman Cat's adventures by reading* The Fur Person *by May Sarton.*

# A Humorous Look at Cats

Because of their finnicky nature and often disinterested behavior, cats are viewed as humorous creatures by many people. Among those who find cats to be humorous are cartoonists, whose unique perspectives on these interesting animals can produce highly amusing results.

*"We had her declawed, but she's still impossible."*
Drawing by W. Miller; © 1988 The New Yorker Magazine, Inc.

*"Makes you wonder, doesn't it?"*
Drawing by Dedini; © 1988 The New Yorker Magazine, Inc.

Drawing by Mankoff; © 1990 The New Yorker Magazine, Inc.

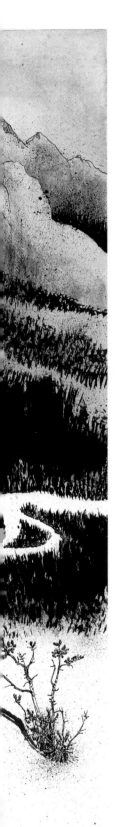

# THE WOUNDED WOLF

## by Jean Craighead George

A wounded wolf climbs Toklat Ridge,
a massive spine of rock and ice.
As he limps, dawn strikes the ridge
and lights it up with sparks and stars.
Roko, the wounded wolf, blinks in the ice fire,
then stops to rest and watch his pack
run the thawing Arctic valley.
They plunge and turn.
They fight the mighty caribou
that struck young Roko with his hoof
and wounded him.
He jumped between the beast and
Kiglo, leader of the Toklat pack.

Young Roko spun and fell.
Hooves, paws and teeth roared over him.
And then his pack and the beast were gone.

Gravely injured, Roko pulls himself
toward the shelter rock.

133

Weakness overcomes him. He stops.
He and his pack are thin and hungry.
This is the season of starvation.
The winter's harvest has been taken.
The produce of spring has not begun.

Young Roko glances down the valley.
He droops his head and stiffens his tail
to signal to his pack
that he is badly hurt.

Winds wail.
A frigid blast picks up long shawls of snow
and drapes them between young Roko
and his pack.
And so his message is not read.

A raven scouting Toklat Ridge
sees Roko's signal.
"Kong, Kong, Kong," he bells—

death is coming to the Ridge;
there will be flesh and bone for all.

His voice rolls out across the valley.
It penetrates the rocky cracks
where the Toklat ravens rest.
One by one they hear and spread their wings.
They beat their way to Toklat Ridge.

They alight upon the snow
and walk behind the wounded wolf.
"Kong," they toll with keen excitement
for the raven clan is hungry, too.
"Kong, Kong"—
there will be flesh and bone for all.

Roko snarls
and hurries toward the shelter rock.

A cloud of snow envelops him.
He limps in blinding whiteness now.
A ghostly presence flits around.

135

"Hahahahahahaha," the white fox states—
death is coming to the Ridge.
Roko smells the fox tagging at his heels.

The cloud whirls off.
Two golden eyes look up at Roko.
The snowy owl has heard the ravens
and joined the deathwatch.

Roko limps along.
The ravens walk.
The white fox leaps.
The snowy owl flies and hops
along the rim of Toklat Ridge.

Roko stops.
Below the ledge out on the flats
the musk-ox herd is circling.
They form a ring and all face out,
a fort of heads and horns
and fur that sweeps down to their hooves.
Their circle means to Roko that
an enemy is present.

He squints and smells the wind.

It carries scents of thawing ice,
broken grass—and earth.
The grizzly bear is up!
He has awakened from his winter's sleep.
A craving need for flesh will drive him.

Roko sees the shelter rock.
He strains to reach it.

He stumbles.
The ravens move in closer.
The white fox boldly walks beside him.
"Hahaha," he yaps.
The snowy owl flies ahead, alights and waits.

The grizzly hears the eager fox
and rises on his flat hind feet.
He twists his powerful neck and head.
His great paws dangle at his chest.

He sees the animal procession
and hears the ravens' knell of death.
Dropping to all fours
he joins the march up Toklat Ridge.

Roko stops, his breath comes hard.
A raven alights upon his back
and picks the open wound.

137

Roko snaps. The raven flies
and circles back.
The white fox nips at Roko's toes.
The snowy owl inches closer.

The grizzly bear, still dulled by sleep,
stumbles onto Toklat Ridge.

Only yards from the shelter rock,
Roko falls.

Instantly the ravens mob him.
They scream and peck and stab his eyes.
The white fox leaps upon his wound.
The snowy owl sits and waits.

Young Roko struggles to his feet.
He bites the ravens.
Snaps the fox.
And lunges at the stoic owl.
He turns and warns the grizzly bear.
Then he bursts into a run
and falls against the shelter rock.

The wounded wolf wedges down
between the rock and barren ground.
Now protected on three sides
he turns and faces all his foes.

The ravens step a few feet closer.
The fox slides toward him on his belly.
The snowy owl blinks and waits,
and on the Ridge rim
roars the hungry grizzly bear.

Roko growls.

The sun comes up.

Far across the Toklat Valley
Roko hears his pack's "hunt's end" song.
The music wails and sobs,
wilder than the bleating wind.

The hunt song ends.
Next comes the roll call.
Each member of the Toklat pack barks
to say that he is home and well.
"Kiglo here," Roko hears his leader bark.
There is a pause. It is young Roko's turn.
He cannot lift his head to answer.

The pack is silent.
The leader starts the count once more.
"Kiglo here."
—A pause.
Roko cannot answer.

The wounded wolf whimpers softly.
A mindful raven hears.
"KONG, KONG, KONG," he tolls
—this is the end.

His booming sounds across the valley.
The wolf pack hears the raven's message
that something is dying.
They know it is Roko
who has not answered roll call.

The hours pass.
The wind slams snow on Toklat Ridge.
Massive clouds blot out the sun.
In their gloom Roko sees
the deathwatch move in closer.

Suddenly he hears the musk-oxen
thundering into their circle.
The ice cracks as the grizzly leaves.
The ravens burst into the air.
The white fox runs.
The snowy owl flaps to the top of the shelter rock

and Kiglo rounds the knoll.

In his mouth he carries meat.
He drops it close to Roko's head
and wags his tail excitedly.
Roko licks Kiglo's chin to honor him.
Then Kiglo puts his mouth around Roko's nose.
This gesture says "I am your leader."
And by mouthing Roko he binds him
and all the wolves together.

The wounded wolf wags his tail.
Kiglo trots away.

Already Roko's wound feels better.
He gulps the food
and feels his strength return.

He shatters bone, flesh, and gristle
and shakes the scraps out on the snow.

The hungry ravens swoop upon them.
The white fox snatches up a bone.
The snowy owl gulps down flesh and fur.
And Roko wags his tail and watches.

For days Kiglo brings young Roko food.
He gnashes, gorges, and shatters bits upon the snow.

A purple sandpiper winging north
sees ravens, owl and fox.
And he drops in upon the feast.

The long-tailed jaeger gull flies down
and joins the crowd on Toklat Ridge.

Roko wags his tail.

One dawn he moves his wounded leg.
He stretches it and pulls himself into the sunlight.
He walks—he romps. He runs in circles.
He leaps and plays with chunks of ice.
Suddenly he stops.
The "hunt's end" song rings out.

Next comes the roll call.
"Kiglo here."
"Roko here," he barks out strongly.
The pack is silent.
"Kiglo here," the leader repeats.
"Roko here."

Across the distance comes the sound
of whoops and yipes and barks and howls.
They fill the dawn with celebration.

And Roko prances down the Ridge.

# OF WOLVES
AND MEN

BY BARRY HOLSTUN LOPEZ

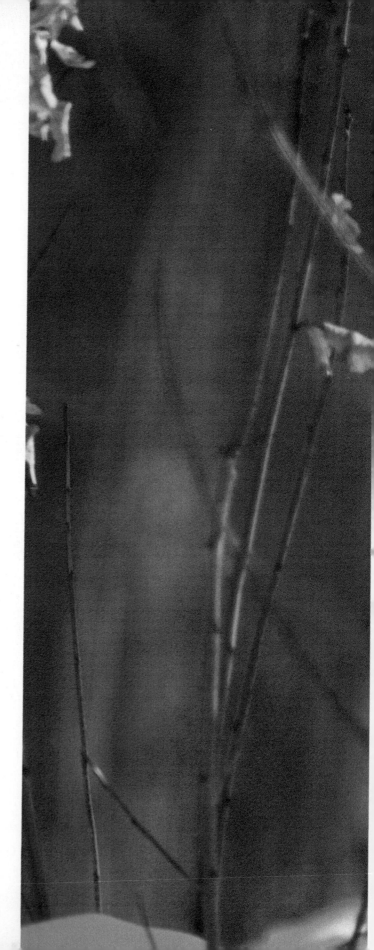

Imagine a wolf moving through the northern woods. The movement, over a trail he has traversed many times before, is distinctive, unlike that of a cougar or a bear, yet he appears, if you are watching, sometimes catlike or bearlike. It is purposeful, deliberate movement. Occasionally the rhythm is broken by the wolf's pause to inspect a scent mark, or a move off the trail to paw among stones where a year before he had cached meat.

The movement down the trail would seem relentless if it did not appear so effortless. The wolf's body, from neck to hips, appears to float over the long, almost spindly legs and the flicker of wrists, a bicycling drift through the trees, reminiscent of the movement of water or of shadows.

The wolf is three years old. A male. He is of the subspecies *occidentalis,* and the trees he is moving among are spruce and subalpine fir on the eastern slope of the Rockies in northern Canada. He is light gray; that is, there are more blond and white hairs mixed with gray in the saddle of fur that covers his shoulders and extends down his spine than there are black and brown. But there are silver and even red hairs mixed in, too.

It is early September, an easy time of year, and he has not seen the other wolves in his pack for three or four days. He has heard no howls, but

he knows the others are about, in ones and twos like himself. It is not a time of year for much howling. It is an easy time. The weather is pleasant. Moose are fat. Suddenly the wolf stops in mid-stride. A moment, then his feet slowly come alongside each other. He is staring into the grass. His ears are rammed forward, stiff. His back arches and he rears up and pounces like a cat. A deer mouse is pinned between his forepaws. Eaten. The wolf drifts on. He approaches a trail crossing, an undistinguished crossroads. His movement is now slower and he sniffs the air as though aware of a possibility

for scents. He sniffs a scent post, a scrawny blueberry bush in use for years, and goes on.

The wolf weighs ninety-four pounds and stands thirty inches at the shoulder. His feet are enormous, leaving prints in the mud along a creek (where he pauses to hunt crayfish but not with much interest) more than five inches long by just over four wide. He has two fractured ribs, broken by a moose a year before. They are healed now, but a sharp eye would notice the irregularity. The skin on his right hip is scarred, from a fight with another wolf in a neighboring

pack when he was a yearling. He has not had anything but a few mice and a piece of arctic char in three days, but he is not hungry. He is traveling. The char was a day old, left on rocks along the river by bears.

The wolf is tied by subtle threads to the woods he moves through. His fur carries seeds that will fall off, effectively dispersed, along the trail some miles from where they first caught in his fur. And miles distant is a raven perched on the ribs of a caribou the wolf helped kill ten days ago, pecking like a chicken at the decaying scraps of meat. A smart snowshoe hare that eluded the wolf and left him exhausted when he was a pup has been dead a year now, food for an owl. The den in which he was born one

April evening was home to porcupines last winter.

It is now late in the afternoon. The wolf has stopped traveling, has lain down to sleep on cool earth beneath a rock outcropping. Mosquitoes rest on his ears. His ears flicker. He begins to waken. He rolls on his back and lies motionless with his front legs pointed toward the sky but folded like wilted flowers, his back legs splayed, and his nose and tail curved toward each other on one side of his body. After a few moments he flops on his side, rises, stretches, and moves a few feet to inspect—minutely, delicately—a crevice in the rock outcropping and finds or doesn't find what draws him there. And then he ascends the rock face, bounding and balancing momentarily before bounding again, appearing slightly unsure of the process—but committed. A few minutes later he bolts suddenly into the woods, achieving full speed, almost forty miles per hour, for forty or fifty yards before he begins to skid, to lunge at a lodgepole pine cone. He trots away with it, his head erect, tail erect, his hips slightly to one side and out of line with his shoulders, as though hindquarters were impatient with forequarters, the cone inert in his mouth. He carries it for a hundred feet before dropping it by the trail. He sniffs it. He goes on.

The underfur next to his skin has begun to thicken with the coming of fall. In the months to follow it will become so dense between his shoulders it will be almost impossible to work a finger down to his skin. In seven months he will weigh less: eighty-nine pounds. He will have tried unsuccessfully to mate with another wolf in the pack. He will have helped kill four moose and thirteen caribou. He will have fallen through ice into a creek at twenty-two below zero but not frozen. He will have fought with other wolves.

He moves along now at the edge of a clearing. The wind coming down-valley surrounds him with a river of odors, as if he were a migrating salmon. He can smell ptarmigan and deer

droppings. He can smell willow and spruce and the fading sweetness of fireweed. Above, he sees a hawk circling, and farther south, lower on the horizon, a flock of sharp-tailed sparrows going east. He senses through his pads with each step the dryness of the moss beneath his feet, and the ridges of old tracks, some his own. He hears the sound his feet make. He hears the occasional movement of deer mice and voles. Summer food.

Toward dusk he is standing by a creek, lapping the cool water, when a wolf howls—a long wail that quickly reaches pitch and then tapers, with several harmonics, long moments to a tremolo. He recognizes his sister. He waits a few moments, then, throwing his head back and closing his eyes, he howls. The howl is shorter and it

changes pitch twice in the beginning, very quickly. There is no answer.

The female is a mile away and she trots off obliquely through the trees. The other wolf stands listening, laps water again, then he too departs, moving quickly, quietly through the trees, away from the trail he had been on. In a few minutes the two wolves meet. They approach each other briskly, almost formally, tails erect and moving somewhat as deer move. When they come together they make high squeaking noises and encircle each other, rubbing and pushing, poking their noses into each other's neck fur, backing away to stretch, chasing each other for a few steps, then standing quietly together, one putting a head over the other's back. And then they are gone, down a vague trail,

the female first. After a few hundred yards they begin, simultaneously, to wag their tails.

In the days to follow, they will meet another wolf from the pack, a second female, younger by a year, and the three of them will kill a caribou. They will travel together ten or twenty miles a day, through the country where they live, eating and sleeping, birthing, playing with sticks, chasing ravens, growing old, barking at bears, scent-marking trails, killing moose, and staring at the way the water in a creek breaks around their legs and flows on.

Reader's Response ∽ Which of the two selections about wolves did you enjoy more? Why?

Library Link ∽ *To find out more about wolves, look for* Wolf Pack: Tracking Wolves in the Wild *by Sylvia A. Johnson and Alice Aamodt.*

# WOLVES
## IN LITERATURE AND LEGEND

■ An ancient legend tells of a she-wolf that saves the lives of abandoned twin babies. One of the babies grows up to found a great city in 753 B.C. Who is the baby, and what is the city?

■ This classic tale reveals Europeans' fear and hatred of the wolf. So wicked is the wolf in this story that it even threatens a little girl. What is the tale?

■ Brer Wolf is a character in tales that originated in the American South. What other character often tricks Brer Wolf?

■ Awarded the Newbery Medal in 1973, this realistic novel tells about an Alaskan Eskimo girl's adventures with her wolf companions. What is the book, and who wrote it?

■ This famous novel, published in 1905, shows how a wolf-dog might see its world. The wolf-dog is taught to hate by brutal human masters until it meets a different kind of human being. What is the novel, and who wrote it?

■ ANSWERS: 1. The baby who grows up to found the city of Rome is named Romulus. 2. The tale is *Little Red Riding Hood*. 3. Brer Wolf is often outwitted by the weak but clever Brer Rabbit. 4. *Julie of the Wolves* by Jean Craighead George. 5. *White Fang* by Jack London.

# ONLY ONE
# WOOF

## by James Herriot

"Is this the thing you've been telling me about?" I asked.

Mr. Wilkin nodded. "Aye, that's it, it's always like that."

I looked down at the helpless convulsions of the big dog lying at my feet; at the staring eyes, the wildly pedalling limbs. The farmer had told me about the periodic attacks which had begun to affect his sheepdog, Gyp, but it was coincidence that one should occur when I was on the farm for another reason.

"And he's all right afterwards, you say?"

"Right as a bobbin. Seems a bit dazed, maybe, for about an hour, then he's back to normal." The farmer shrugged. "I've had lots o' dogs through my hands as you know and I've seen plenty of dogs with fits. I thought I knew all the causes—worms, wrong feeding, distemper—but this has me beat. I've tried everything."

"Well you can stop trying, Mr. Wilkin," I said. "You won't be able to do much for Gyp. He's got epilepsy."

"Epilepsy? But he's a grand, normal dog most of t'time."

"Yes, I know. That's how it goes. There's nothing actually wrong with his brain—it's a mysterious condition. The cause is unknown but it's almost certainly hereditary."

Mr. Wilkin raised his eyebrows. "Well that's a rum 'un. If it's hereditary why hasn't it shown up before now? He's nearly two years old and he didn't start this till a few weeks ago."

"That's typical," I replied. "Eighteen months to two years is about the time it usually appears."

Gyp interrupted us by getting up and staggering towards his master, wagging his tail. He seemed untroubled by his experience. In fact the whole thing had lasted less than two minutes.

Mr. Wilkin bent and stroked the rough head briefly. His craggy features were set in a thoughtful cast. He was a big powerful man in his forties and now as the eyes narrowed in that face which rarely smiled he looked almost menacing. I had heard more than one man say he wouldn't like to get on the wrong side of Sep Wilkin and I could see what they meant. But he had always treated me right and since he farmed nearly a thousand acres I saw quite a lot of him.

His passion was sheepdogs. A lot of farmers like to run dogs at the trials but Mr. Wilkin was one of the top men. He bred and trained dogs which regularly won at the local events and occasionally at the national trials. And what was troubling me was that Gyp was his main hope.

He had picked out the two best pups from a litter—Gyp and Sweep—and had trained them with the dedication that had made him a winner. I don't think I have ever seen two dogs enjoy each other quite as much; whenever I was on the farm I would see them together, sometimes peeping nose by nose over the half-door of the loose box where they slept, occasionally slinking devotedly round the feet of their master but usually just playing together. They must have spent hours rolling about in ecstatic wrestling matches, growling and panting, gnawing gently at each other's limbs.

A few months ago George Crossley, one of Mr. Wilkin's oldest friends and a keen trial man, had lost his best dog with nephritis and Mr. Wilkin had let him have Sweep. I was surprised at the time because Sweep was shaping better than Gyp in his training and looked like he was turning out to be a real champion. But it was Gyp who remained. He must have missed his friend but there were other dogs on the farm and if they didn't quite make up for Sweep he was never really lonely.

As I watched, I could see the dog recovering rapidly. It was extraordinary how soon normality was restored after that frightening convulsion. And I waited with some apprehension to hear what his master would say.

The cold, logical decision for him to make would be to have Gyp put down and, looking at the friendly, tail-wagging animal, I didn't like the idea at all. There was something very attractive about him. The big-boned, well-marked body was handsome but his most distinctive feature

154

was his head, where one ear somehow contrived to stick up while the other lay flat, giving him a lop-sided, comic appeal. Gyp, in fact, looked a bit of a clown. But a clown who radiated good-will and camaraderie.

Mr. Wilkin spoke at last. "Will he get any better as he grows older?"

"Almost certainly not," I replied.

"Then he'll always 'ave these fits?"

"I'm afraid so. You say he has them every two or three weeks—well it will probably carry on more or less like that with occasional variations."

"But he could have one any time?"

"Yes."

"In the middle of a trial, like." The farmer sunk his head on his chest and his voice rumbled deep. "That's it, then."

In the long silence which followed, the fateful words became more and more inevitable. Sep Wilkin wasn't the man to hesitate in a matter which concerned his ruling passion. Ruthless culling of any animal which didn't come up to standard would be his policy. When he finally cleared his throat I had a sinking pre-monition of what he was going to say.

But I was wrong.

"If I kept him, could you do any-thing for him?" he asked.

"Well I could give you some pills for him. They might decrease the fre-quency of the fits." I tried to keep the eagerness out of my voice.

"Right . . . right . . . I'll come into t'surgery and get some," he muttered.

"Fine. But . . . er . . . you won't ever breed from him, will you?" I said.

"Naw, naw, naw," the farmer grunted with a touch of irritability as though he didn't want to pursue the mat-ter further.

And I held my peace because I felt intuitively that he did not want to be detected in a weakness; that he was pre-pared to keep the dog simply as a pet. It was funny how events began to slot into place and suddenly make sense. That was why he had let Sweep, the superior trial dog, go. He just liked Gyp. In fact Sep Wilkin, hard man though he may be, had succumbed to that off-beat charm.

So I shifted to some light chatter about the weather as I walked back to the car, but when I was about to drive off the farmer returned to the main subject.

"There's one thing about Gyp I never mentioned," he said, bending to the window. "I don't know whether it has owt to do with the job or not. He has never barked in his life."

I looked at him in surprise. "You mean never, ever?"

"That's right. Not a single bark. T'other dogs make a noise when stran-gers come on the farm but I've never heard Gyp utter a sound since he was born."

"Well that's very strange," I said. "But I can't see that it is connected with his condition in any way."

And as I switched on the engine I noticed for the first time that while a bitch and two half-grown pups gave tongue to see me on my way, Gyp merely regarded me in his comradely way, mouth open, tongue lolling, but made no noise. A silent dog.

The thing intrigued me. So much so that whenever I was on the farm over the next few months I made a point of watching the big sheepdog at whatever he was doing. But there was never any change. Between the convulsions which had settled down to around three-week intervals he was a normal active happy animal. But soundless.

I saw him, too, in Darrowby when his master came in to market. Gyp was often seated comfortably in the back of the car, but if I happened to speak to Mr. Wilkin on these occasions I kept off the subject because, as I said, I had the feeling that he more than most farmers would hate to be exposed in keeping a dog for other than working purposes.

And yet I have always entertained a suspicion that most farm dogs were more or less pets. The dogs on sheep farms were of course indispensable working animals and on other establishments they no doubt performed a function in helping to bring in the cows. But watching them on my daily rounds I often wondered. I saw them rocking along on carts at hay-time, chasing rats among the stooks at harvest, pottering around the buildings or roaming the fields at the side of the farmer; and I wondered . . . what did they really do?

My suspicions were strengthened at other times—as when I was trying to round up some cattle into a corner and the dog tried to get into the act by nipping at a hock or tail. There was

invariably a hoarse yell of "Siddown, dog!" or "Gerrout, dog!"

So right up to the present day I still stick to my theory: most farm dogs are pets and they are there mainly because the farmer just likes to have them around. You would have to put a farmer on the rack to get him to admit it but I think I am right. And in the process those dogs have a wonderful time. They don't have to beg for walks, they are out all day long, and in the company of their masters. If I want to find a man on a farm I look for his dog, knowing the man won't be far away. I try to give my own dogs a good life but it cannot compare with the life of the average farm dog.

There was a long spell when Sep Wilkin's stock stayed healthy and I didn't see either him or Gyp, then I came across them both by accident at a sheepdog trial. It was a local event run in conjunction with the Mellerton Agricultural Show and since I was in the district I decided to steal an hour off.

I took Helen[1] with me, too, because these trials have always fascinated us. The wonderful control of the owners over their animals, the intense involvement of the dogs themselves, the sheer skill of the whole operation always held us spellbound.

She put her arm through mine as we went in at the entrance gate to where a crescent of cars was drawn up at one end of a long field. The field was on the river's edge and through a fringe of trees the afternoon sunshine glinted on the tumbling water of the shallows and turned the long beach of bleached stones to a dazzling white. Groups of men, mainly competitors, stood around chatting as they watched. They were quiet, easy, bronzed men and as they seemed to be drawn from all social strata from prosperous farmers to working men their garb was varied: cloth caps, trilbies, deerstalkers or no hat at all; tweed jackets, stiff best suits, open-necked shirts, fancy ties, sometimes neither collar nor tie. Nearly all of them leaned on long crooks with the handles fashioned from rams' horns.

Snatches of talk reached us as we walked among them.

"You got 'ere, then, Fred." "That's a good gather." "Nay, 'e's missed one, 'e'll get nowt for that." "Them sheep's a bit flighty." "Aye they're buggers." And above it all the whistles of the man running a dog; every conceivable level and pitch of whistle with now and then a shout. "Sit!" "Get by!" Every man had his own way with his dog.

The dogs waiting their turn were tied up to a fence with a hedge growing over it. There were about seventy of them and it was rather wonderful to see that long row of waving tails and friendly expressions. They were mostly strangers to each other but there wasn't even the semblance of disagreement, never mind a fight. It seemed that the natural obedience of

these little creatures was linked to an amicable disposition.

This appeared to be common to their owners, too. There was no animosity, no resentment at defeat, no unseemly display of triumph in victory. If a man overran his time he ushered his group of sheep quietly in the corner and returned with a philosophical grin to his colleagues. There was a little quiet leg-pulling but that was all.

We came across Sep Wilkin leaning against his car at the best vantage point about thirty yards away from the final pen. Gyp, tied to the bumper, turned and gave me his crooked grin while Mrs. Wilkin on a camp stool by his side rested a hand on his shoulder. Gyp, it seemed, had got under her skin too.

Helen went over to speak to her and I turned to her husband. "Are you running a dog today, Mr. Wilkin?"

"No, not this time, just come to watch. I know a lot o' the dogs."

I stood near him for a while watching the competitors in action, breathing in the clean smell of trampled grass and plug tobacco. In front of us next to the pen the judge stood by his post.

I had been there for about ten minutes when Mr. Wilkin lifted a pointing finger. "Look who's there!"

George Crossley with Sweep trotting at his heels was making his way

unhurriedly to the post. Gyp suddenly
stiffened and sat up very straight, his
cocked ears accentuating the lop-sided
look. It was many months since he had
seen his brother and companion; it
seemed unlikely, I thought, that he would
remember him. But his interest was clearly intense, and as the judge waved his
white handkerchief and the three sheep
were released from the far corner he rose
slowly to his feet.

A gesture from Mr. Crossley sent
Sweep winging round the perimeter of
the field in a wide, joyous gallop and as
he neared the sheep a whistle dropped
him on his belly. From then on it was an
object lesson in the cooperation of man
and dog. Sep Wilkin had always said
Sweep would be a champion and he
looked the part, darting and falling at his
master's commands. Short piercing whistles, shrill plaintive whistles; he was in
tune with them all.

No dog all day had brought his
sheep through the three lots of gates as
effortlessly as Sweep did now and as he
approached the pen near us it was obvious
that he would win the cup unless some
disaster struck. But this was the touchy
bit; more than once with other dogs the
sheep had broken free and gone bounding
away within feet of the wooden rails.

George Crossley held the gate wide
and extended his crook. You could see

now why they all carried those long sticks. His commands to Sweep, huddled flat along the turf, were now almost inaudible but the quiet words brought the dog inching first one way then the other. The sheep were in the entrance to the pen now but they still looked around them irresolutely and the game was not over yet. But as Sweep wriggled towards them almost imperceptibly they turned and entered and Mr. Crossley crashed the gate behind them.

As he did so he turned to Sweep with a happy cry of *"Good lad!"* and the dog responded with a quick jerking wag of his tail.

At that, Gyp, who had been standing very tall, watching every move with the most intense concentration, raised his head and emitted a single resounding bark.

*"Woof!"* went Gyp as we all stared at him in astonishment.

"Did you hear that?" gasped Mrs. Wilkin.

"Well, by gaw!" her husband burst out, looking open-mouthed at his dog.

Gyp didn't seem to be aware that he had done anything unusual. He was too preoccupied by the reunion with his brother and within seconds the two dogs were rolling around, chewing playfully at each other as of old.

I suppose the Wilkins as well as myself had the feeling that this event might start Gyp barking like any other dog, but it was not to be.

Six years later I was on the farm and went to the house to get some hot water. As Mrs. Wilkin handed me the bucket she looked down at Gyp who was basking in the sunshine outside the kitchen window.

"There you are, then, funny fellow," she said to the dog.

I laughed. "Has he ever barked since that day?"

Mrs. Wilkin shook her head. "No he hasn't, not a sound. I waited a long time but I know he's not going to do it now."

"Ah well, it's not important. But still, I'll never forget that afternoon at the trial," I said.

"Nor will I!" She looked at Gyp again and her eyes softened in reminiscence. "Poor old lad, eight years old and only one woof!"

Reader's Response ∽ If you had been Gyp's owner, how would you have handled Gyp's problems?

# A LIFE-SAVING DOG

Over the centuries, dogs have been bred and trained to do many jobs. Some herd sheep and cattle, while others are used to pull sleds across the frozen terrain of the north. Some dogs serve as guides for the blind, while others are trained for police work.

Among the working dogs are some whose stories have become famous. One such dog lived about two hundred years ago. His name was Barry. His breed had long been trained by monks who ran a shelter for travelers in a snowy mountain pass between Italy and Switzerland. The breed was large and strong, with acute hearing and the ability to detect human scent from a great distance. Barry and the other dogs of his breed were trained to rescue travelers trapped or lost in the snow.

During the winter of 1806, snowfall in Switzerland had been quite heavy. In early spring a woman set out with her baby to traverse the trail through the mountain pass. As she made her way along the mountainside, the woman heard the roar of an avalanche. Within minutes she and her baby were trapped as the rushing snow thundered down the cliffs onto the trail.

But Barry had heard the distant avalanche and somehow sensed that people were buried in it. When his trainer called for him to return to the shelter, Barry did not appear. He did not return that night, nor the next day, nor the next night. The monks went out to look for him with other dogs, but they had no luck. Finally, on the third night, Barry returned to the shelter with a bundle on his back. It was a baby—still alive! Barry's instincts had led him to the buried travelers, and the mother, with her last bit of strength, had managed to strap her baby to Barry's back.

This was just one of Barry's legendary rescues. By the time Barry "retired" at the age of twelve, he had saved more than forty lives. About seventy years after Barry's death, his breed was given an official name. These massive dogs were named after the Hospice of Saint Bernard, where the monks had worked with them for hundreds of years. Today the Saint Bernard is the national dog of Switzerland.

# The Peace of Wild Things

WENDELL BERRY

When despair for the world grows in me
and I wake in the night at the least sound
in fear of what my life and my children's lives may be,
I go and lie down where the wood drake
rests in his beauty on the water, and the great heron feeds.
I come into the peace of wild things
who do not tax their lives with forethought
of grief.  I come into the presence of still water.
And I feel above me the day-blind stars
waiting with their light.  For a time
I rest in the grace of the world, and am free.

WIVENHOE PARK, *oil on canvas by John Constable, British, 1816.*

# The Wild Swans at Coole

WILLIAM BUTLER YEATS

The trees are in their autumn beauty,
The woodland paths are dry,
Under the October twilight the water
Mirrors a still sky;
Upon the brimming water among the stones
Are nine-and-fifty swans.

The nineteenth autumn has come upon me
Since I first made my count;
I saw, before I had well finished,
All suddenly mount
And scatter wheeling in great broken rings
Upon their clamorous wings.

I have looked upon those brilliant creatures,
And now my heart is sore.
All's changed since I, hearing at twilight,
The first time on this shore,
The bell-beat of their wings above my head,
Trod with a lighter tread.

Unwearied still, lover by lover,
They paddle in the cold
Companionable streams or climb the air;
Their hearts have not grown old,
Passion or conquest, wander where they will,
Attend upon them still.

But now they drift on the still water,
Mysterious, beautiful;
Among what rushes will they build,
By what lake's edge or pool
Delight men's eyes when I awake some day
To find they have flown away?

# *Helping Hands*

### *from* **People Who Make a Difference**
### *by Brent Ashabranner*

YOU ARE thirsty. A cold drink is in the refrigerator ten feet way, but it might as well be ten miles away. You can't move a muscle to reach it. Your nose itches until your eyes water, but you can't lift a hand to scratch. You want to watch a videotape, but all you can do is look helplessly at your VCR across the room and wait until someone comes to put in the cassette.

Your name is Mitch Coffman, and you are a prisoner in your own body. Your mind is clear and sharp; you can talk and move your head, but you can't move any other part of your body. Like almost a hundred thousand other men and women in the United States, you are a quadriplegic, totally paralyzed from the neck down.

Mitch Coffman's entry into the world of the quadriplegic came on a day that should have been a happy one. He was returning from a party to celebrate his thirtieth birthday when his car skidded on a bridge and went into a spin. Mitch was thrown out with an impact that broke his neck.

When Mitch regained consciousness, he came instantly face-to-face with a terrible reality: he had suffered permanent damage to his spine between the third and fifth cervical vertebrae. He would be paralyzed for the rest of his life.

After months of physical therapy, Mitch regained enough movement in his left hand to operate the control for an electric wheelchair. And he was more fortunate than most quadriplegics because he was able to move into a government-subsidized apartment building especially equipped for people with severe physical disabilities. The building has ramps instead of stairs, roll-in showers, light switches and other electrical and kitchen equipment that are easy to reach and operate. Attendants are also on duty at all times. Still, there were endless hours every day and night when Mitch was alone in his apartment waiting, waiting for the simplest tasks to be performed for him.

And then one day a stranger arrived in Mitch's little apartment. She was only eighteen inches tall, weighed but a furry six pounds, and communicated in excited squeaks and endless trills. But she could open the refrigerator door and bring Mitch a cold drink or a sandwich. She could scratch his nose with a soft cloth when it itched. She could put a videotape in the VCR. She could do dozens of other things for him that he could not do for himself.

The stranger was a black and brown capuchin monkey, and her improbable name was Peepers. Almost as important as what she could do for him was the fact that she was there, a companion, a constant presence in the apartment where, for most of the long hours of long days, there had been only Mitch.

"It took us months to learn to live together," Mitch explains as Peepers sits quietly in his lap. "Now I can't imagine living without her."

The modest quarters of Helping Hands: Simian Aides for the Disabled are on the fourth floor of an office building on Commonwealth Avenue in Boston. On my first visit there I could hear monkeys chattering in the training room. I was eager to watch the training, but before that I wanted to talk to Mary Joan Willard, the educational psychologist who started and is director of Helping Hands.

Quantum leaps of the imagination have always fascinated me, and I opened our conversation on that point. "How did you get the idea that monkeys might be trained to do things for paralyzed human beings?" I asked. "What made you think it was possible?"

Mary Joan explained that after receiving her doctorate in educational psychology from Boston University, she began a postdoctoral fellowship in 1977 at Tufts New England Medical Center in Boston. The fellowship was for rehabilitative study and work with persons who had suffered severe physical injury. In her daily rounds she soon came to know Joe, a patient at the center. One minute, he had been a happy, healthy twenty-three-year old. The next minute, because of a diving accident, he was a quadriplegic, paralyzed from the neck down. His story was an all-too-familiar one, but he was the first quadriplegic Mary Joan had ever known.

"I was shocked," she said. "I found it inconceivable that someone so young, so full of life was going to spend the rest of his days completely dependent on other people, dependent for a drink of water, for a bite of food, dependent on someone to bring him a book or turn out a light. I am a psychologist, and I kept thinking, There has to be some way to make him more independent.

"I couldn't get him out of my mind. I would sit in my room and think about him lying there in his room, helpless. And then one night it hit me out of the blue. Chimps! Why couldn't chimpanzees be trained to do things for quadriplegics like Joe? I kept thinking about it, and I didn't get much sleep that night."

The next day Mary Joan went to see B. F. Skinner, the famous Harvard psychologist who has done extensive pioneering research with animals, using reward and punishment techniques to alter their behavior. Mary Joan had worked three years for Skinner as a part-time assistant. He might not think her idea was workable, but she knew he would not scoff at it.

Skinner was amused at his assistant's excitement over her new idea; he pointed out that chimpanzees grow to be almost as big as humans, are stronger than humans, and often are bad-tempered. Chimpanzees would be too risky. But Mary Joan was right; Skinner did not laugh. The idea intrigued him.

Why not, he asked, think about using capuchins, the little creatures traditionally known as organ-grinder monkeys? They are small, usually no more than six or seven pounds and seldom more than eighteen inches tall. They are intelligent, easy to train, and form strong bonds of loyalty to their human masters. Furthermore, they have a long life expectancy, an average of about thirty years.

That was all the encouragement Mary Joan needed. She did some reading about capuchins, found out where they could be purchased, then went to the director of postdoctoral programs at Tufts and asked for money to start an experimental capuchin training program.

"He nearly fell off his chair laughing," Mary Joan said, remembering the director's first reaction to her proposal.

But Mary Joan was persistent and persuasive. When the director stopped laughing, he came through with a grant and some training space. The grant was just two thousand dollars, but it was enough for Mary Joan to buy four monkeys, some cages, and hire student trainers at one dollar an hour.

"I thought we could train them in eight weeks," Mary Joan recalled. "I had never touched a monkey! It took us eight weeks just to coax them out of their cages. The monkeys I was able to buy had had some pretty hard treatment. They weren't in a mood to trust any human being."

But a beginning had been made, and patience and dedication paid off in training the monkeys in an astonishing variety of tasks; taking food from a refrigerator and putting it in a microwave oven, turning lights on and off; doing the same with a television set, stereo, heater, air conditioner; opening and closing curtains; setting up books, magazines, and computer printouts on a reading stand.

One piece of equipment essential to most quadriplegics is a mouthstick which is used for turning pages, dialing a phone, typing, working a computer, and many other actions which improve the quality of a quadriplegic's life. One problem is that the mouthstick often falls to the floor or onto the wheelchair tray. The monkey helper is quickly taught to pick up the stick and replace it correctly in its master's mouth.

"The capuchins have great manual dexterity, greater than a human adult's,"

Mary Joan said "and they're very bright. But we don't try to train them to do tasks where they have to think."

Judi Zazula, an occupational therapist, has been with Helping Hands almost from the beginning. Her title is program director, but Mary Joan describes her as a partner. Judi makes the same point about not putting a monkey in a situation where it has to think about the right way to do something. "Everything," she says, "is planned so that the monkey has just one way to respond if it does the task right."

The basic motivation for a monkey to perform a task correctly is a simple reward system. When it carries out a command as it is supposed to—turning on a VCR or bringing a drink—the trainer, and later the quadriplegic owner, praises the monkey for doing a good job and at the same time gives it a treat, usually a few drops of strawberry-flavored syrup. The quadriplegic releases the syrup by means of a wheelchair control.

There is also a system of punishment because capuchins are endlessly curious and occasionally mischievous. One monkey, for example, began dimming the lights when its owner was reading so that it would get a reward when it was told to turn them up again. More often, however, misbehavior is likely to be opening a drawer without being asked to or throwing paper out of a wastebasket in the hope of finding something interesting.

The monkeys are taught that anything with a white circular sticker pasted on it—

*Dr. Willard with a new trainee.*

such as a medicine cabinet—is off-limits. If a monkey violates the off-limits rule, it is warned with a buzz from a small battery-operated device that it wears on a belt around its waist. If it doesn't obey the warning, the quadriplegic master can use remote controls to give the monkey a tiny electrical shock. The warning buzz is usually sufficient, and most owners report that they almost never have to use the shock treatment. Judi Zazula points out that buzz-shock collars are also used in dog training.

Late in 1979 Robert Foster, a twenty-five-year-old quadriplegic living near Boston, became the first person to take part in a pilot project to test the feasibility of using a capuchin monkey aide. Robert, paralyzed from the shoulders down as the result of an automobile accident at the age of eighteen, had been living by himself for several years with the help of a personal care attendant. The attendant lived in the apartment with

Robert but worked full time in a nearby hospital. That meant that Robert was alone in the apartment for nine hours or more at least five days a week.

Robert's new helper, a six-pound capuchin female named Hellion, helped to fill the long hours and continues to do so eight years after the experiment began. Robert communicates with Hellion—who deserves a nicer name—by aiming a small laser pointer at what he wants the monkey to bring or do. The laser is mounted on the chin control mechanism of his wheelchair. He also gives her a voice command such as "Bring" or "Open."

*An aide practices turning the pages of a magazine.*

Hellion feeds Robert, brushes his hair, tidies up his wheelchair tray, brings him books, and carries out a whole range of other helpful tasks. For his part Robert dispenses strawberry-syrup rewards and tells Hellion how nice she is. Hellion is close by Robert's wheelchair all day, but when he tells her it is time for bed, she will go into her cage and lock the door.

As publicity about simian aides has spread across the country, Helping Hands has been swamped with requests for monkeys. Mary Joan and Judi are proceeding slowly with placements, however, still treating each case as an experiment. A number of additional capuchins have been placed with quadriplegics, and there have been no failures.

Mary Joan has had to spend an increasing amount of her time in fund raising and in administrative details of making Helping Hands a smoothly functioning nonprofit organization. "For the first two years we had to get along on three thousand dollars a year," Mary Joan said. "Fortunately, we don't have to pay student trainers much, and they love the experience."

Several major organizations and agencies concerned with severely disabled persons were interested, but all were skeptical. In the early stages Mary Joan wrote thirty-nine grant proposals and sent them to philanthropic foundations and government agencies, but not one was approved. But she persisted and, as evidence mounted that the capuchins could do the job, a trickle of financial support began. Now the Veterans Administration, National Medical Enterprises, the Educational Foundation of America, and the Paralyzed Veterans of America give some financial help to Helping Hands. Money is also received though private contributions, but fund raising still requires time that Mary Joan would rather be giving to other parts of the program.

Lack of money was not the only problem in the early days of the program. Some critics said that the idea of monkeys serving as helpers was demeaning to the quadriplegics as human beings. Some medical authorities said that mechanical equipment—robotics is the technical term—could be developed to do a better job than monkeys.

To the first criticism, Mary Joan points out that no one thinks it is beneath the dignity of a blind person to have a dog serve as a guide. As to robotic equipment, she agrees that for some quadriplegics mechanical tools may be best. But she points out that no piece of equipment can provide the companionship and sheer pleasure that an affectionate capuchin can.

"A robot won't sit in your lap and put its arms around you," Mary Joan said.

Developing a reliable supply of trainable monkeys was a problem that Helping Hands solved through the cooperation of Walt Disney World in Florida. A capuchin breeding colony has been established on Discovery Island in this world-famous recreational-educational center, and it will produce most of the monkeys needed in the quadriplegic program. Other monkeys are received through private donation, and Helping Hands has become a safe haven for monkeys that have been confiscated by government agencies because of mistreatment or having been brought into the country illegally.

Trial-and-error testing proved to the Helping Hands crew that early socialization was necessary to train a monkey that would be affectionate and happy when it became part of a human household. The answer has been the creation of a foster home program. When the monkeys from Walt Disney World are young babies, six to eight weeks old, they are placed with foster families. These volunteer families agree to raise the monkeys in their homes for about three years and then turn them over to Helping Hands to be trained as aides to quadriplegics.

The carefully selected volunteer families agree to spend ten hours a day with their primate babies for the first six months—ten hours with the monkey outside its cage. This means that the foster mother and father and other children are actually carrying the baby monkey as they go about their household routines. Older monkeys require less time, but members of the household still must spend at least four hours daily with the young capuchin if it is to become a truly "humanized" primate.

Being a foster parent to a young monkey may sound like fun, and in many ways it can be a delightful experience. But it is time-consuming and demanding, and the time inevitably comes when the monkey must be given over to Helping Hands. "Everyone knows this moment of parting is coming, and most people handle it well," Mary Joan said, "but for some it is very hard. We have been offered as much as five thousand dollars to let a family keep a monkey. But, of course, we can't do that."

If for any reason a monkey does not successfully complete its training at Helping Hands, it is offered to its foster care family as a pet. Should the foster care family be unable to take it, Helping Hands maintains a carefully screened list of other families who have applied for a monkey pet. The "unsuccessful" monkey will be placed in the kind of human home environment to which it is accustomed.

Over sixty-five monkeys are now living with foster families. More than a hundred additional families have passed the screening test and are waiting to receive their foster "children."

Judi Zazula is a rehabilitation engineer. Together with Doug Ely, a solar research specialist for Arthur D. Little, Inc., she has designed most of the special equipment needed in the Helping Hands program: the laser pointer, chin and other wheelchair controls, and equipment that the capuchin's tiny hands can hold and manipulate.

"One of the first things I was asked to design was the nose scratcher," Judi told me and added, "The monkeys helped design a lot of the equipment."

She explained that by watching the monkeys as they carried out their tasks, she and Doug Ely could tell when a piece of equipment needed changing or when some new device was necessary.

Almost all of the monkeys selected for training are females because they tend to be gentler and more affectionate than males. Even so, to preclude the possibility of a capuchin aide hurting anyone, the teeth are extracted from the trainee monkey when they reach maturity at about three-and-a-half to four years.

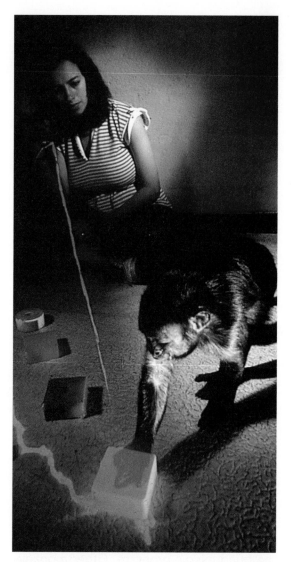

*The laser pointer is used to show the aide which block to pick up.*

This operation has no harmful effects on the monkey or on her ability to eat and digest her food. All Helping Hands monkeys, from soon after they go into foster care, have a diet which is 85 percent commercial monkey food (Purina Monkey Chow). After teeth extraction the food pellets are softened a bit with water, and the monkey can eat them with no difficulty. The rest of the diet usually is fruit—bananas, apple slices, peaches—which the monkey, even without teeth, can eat easily, especially as her gums harden.

The training of a monkey usually takes about eight months. A session with the student trainer may last from half an hour to an hour, but it might be as short as ten minutes depending upon the monkey's personality. There may be several training sessions a day.

"Every monkey is different," Judi said. "Every one has her own personality and her own strengths and weaknesses."

Judi's biggest job within Helping Hands is to match the right monkey with the right quadriplegic who is being considered to receive one. A training log is kept on each monkey, and Judi pores over every page until she knows everything that can be known about a particular capuchin's personality and about her strengths and weaknesses.

Then Judi visits the quadriplegic. She stays at least two days and gets to know as much about the person as she can and about the environment where the monkey is going to live and work for the rest of her life. Judi even makes a video of the quadriplegic's living quarters so that they can be duplicated in the final training of the monkey the quadriplegic will receive.

"I am totally consumed with getting the right monkey in the right place," Judi said to me. "By the time they leave this training room, they are my children. I always think, what kind of life will they have out there? I want to make sure it will be the best and most useful life possible."

Judi has come to know dozens of quadriplegics very well, and she has thought a great deal about the total loss of hope that they suffer. "A spinal cord injury is an especially terrible thing," Judi said, "because it usually happens to young people, and it usually occurs at a happy moment in life—a car accident after a junior-senior prom or having fun diving into a swimming pool or playing football. Then everything is lost in a split second. The person comes to and his or her world has collapsed and a nightmare begins.

"Most people thinking about something like that happening to them say, 'I wouldn't want to live; I'd rather be dead.' But these people aren't dead. Slowly, if they begin to believe that they can do things and affect things, they begin to think that it is worth hanging around."

Both Mary Joan and Judi know very well that the success of Helping Hands depends upon how effective simian aides are in performing tasks that help quadriplegics lead better and more productive lives. But they also believe passionately that having a capuchin helper adds an interest and spice to quadriplegics' lives that can make a huge psychological difference. The companionship is important, but beyond that their ability to control the monkey makes them special. They can do something few other people can do.

As part of her master's degree work, Judi made a study of how people react to a quadriplegic with and without a monkey helper. When one quadriplegic she was using in her study was at a shopping center without his monkey, only two strangers stopped to talk with him in the course of an hour. When the monkey was sitting beside him on the wheelchair, seventy-one people took time from their shopping to speak to the quadriplegic during about the same amount of time.

"The quadriplegic who can control a monkey is an expert in a very unusual way," Judi said, "and that makes him interesting to other people."

One quadriplegic had this to say: "When I go outdoors in my wheelchair, all that people see is the wheelchair. But when I go out with my monkey, the only thing they see is the monkey. Nobody notices the chair at all."

Mary Joan Willard has a sense of history and a vision of the future. In terms of need and demand, Helping Hands may seem slow in getting trained monkeys to the thousands of quadriplegics who want them. But she points out that the possibility of training dogs to guide the blind had been debated and advocated for a century before the Seeing Eye program began early in this century.

"Compared to that, we are doing all right," Mary Joan said to me.

Mary Joan's immediate goal for Helping Hands is to place forty simian aides a year and to move beyond that as fast as the job can be done properly. Costs for training, equipment, and placement are approximately nine thousand dollars for each Helping Hands monkey. If a recipient is able to meet these costs from insurance payments or other personal resources, he or she is expected to do so; however, no one selected to receive a monkey is refused for inability to pay. For most quadriplegics, costs are met from U.S. Veterans Administration and state rehabilitation program funds or from private research or charitable organizations.

Of one thing Mary Joan Willard is sure. "I see this as a life's work," she told me.

Judi Zazula feels the same way. "I can't imagine getting the satisfaction out of anything else that I get from this work," she said.

Judi was recently married to Doug Ely, her long-time partner in equipment development. Instead of a flower girl, Judi decided to have a flower primate. Hellion, the first monkey to become a simian aide in the Helping Hands program, carried a little bouquet of flowers.

Reader's Response ～ In what ways do you think owning a capuchin might be preferable to having a full-time nurse?

Library Link ～ *If you'd like to learn more about people who work to help others, read* People Who Make a Difference, *from which this excerpt was taken.*

# Capuchins In the Wild

Capuchins, considered by many zoologists to be the most intelligent New World monkeys (those that live in Central and South America), get their name from a dark patch of hair on the top of their heads that resembles a capuche, a monk's hood.

Found in tropical rain forests, capuchins spend most of their time in trees, though they are known to leave the trees for the ground during the day. Like other monkeys, capuchins eat most anything they can find, including fruit, insects, lizards, roots, and occasionally young squirrels. Capuchins can live up to forty years on such a diet, although their life expectancy in the wild is less than it is in captivity because of disease and natural predators.

Capuchins live in multimale groups, so called because in each group there is more than one adult male in addition to a large number of adult females. These groups range from five to thirty or more capuchins, with an equal number of young and adult in each group. The young of the group, similar to other young animals, establish social ties with one another as they play. They maintain their social ties into adulthood through continued physical contact, especially through grooming each other's fur.

Because of their keen intelligence, friendly nature, and obvious agility, capuchins are well suited to work with disabled people.

In what other ways do you think capuchins might assist humans?

*A wild capuchin in its natural environment.*

173

# A DREAM SO WILD

~~~~~~~~~~~~~~~~~

### from <u>The Black Pearl</u>
### by Scott O'Dell

Ramón Salazar[1] is a sixteen-year-old boy living in the small town of La Paz, Mexico, where his family makes their living pearling the waters of Baja California. He has grown up hearing the legends of the area—about the great Black Pearl waiting to be found and the monster called the Manta Diablo[2] lurking in the deep. Ramón's father has made him a full partner in the family pearl business, but Ramón's ambition is to sail with the fleet and to learn to dive for pearls. One day he overcomes his father's objections by agreeing to stay on deck and hold the ropes while others dive. The best diver in the fleet is Gaspar Ruiz,[3] known as the Sevillano.[4] He's a braggart who always seems to be taunting Ramón, but Ramón is determined that nothing will diminish this experience.

[1]Ramón Salazar (rä mōn′ sal ä sar′)
[2]Manta Diablo (män′ tä  dē ä′ blō)
[3]Gaspar Ruiz (gas par′ rōō ēs′)
[4]Sevillano (se vē yä′no)

We reached the pearling beds at dawn and anchored the five boats in a cluster over a reef where the shells grew.

Everything was new to me. I had heard many stories of the pearling beds since the time I was old enough to listen, from my father and grandfather and from my friends who were the sons of pearlers. But to be really there on the sea with the sun coming up in a coppery haze and watch the men slip out of the boats into water clear as air, was to me a part of a long dream come true.

My father showed me how to pull up the basket when it was full and how to stack the shells in the boat. Then he took the sink stone in one hand, carefully coiled the rope that was attached to it and tied to the boat, picked up the basket and its rope, and went over the side. Down he went with the heavy stone until he reached the bottom.

Through the clear water I watched him drop the stone, take the big knife from his belt, and start to pry the oyster shells from the rocks. When the basket was full he gave a tug at the rope and I pulled it up. A moment later he rose, trailing a stream of bubbles from his mouth, and I stacked the shells as I had been told and drew up the sink stone for the next dive.

The Sevillano had gone down before my father and was still down as he dived again. When the Sevillano came to the surface he held onto the side of the boat and glanced up at me.

"How does the work go?" he said.

"I learn."

"There is not much to learn, mate. You pull the shells up and then the sink stone and you stack the shells and then you wait a while and do it all over again. It is work for children."

He spoke softly and smiled, but I knew what he meant. "It would be fun to dive," I answered him.

"More fun, mate, but more danger too."

He pointed to the arm he was resting on the gunwale. From his elbow to wrist ran a long, jagged scar, as if the arm had been pulled through the jaws of a steel trap.

"This one," he said, "I got from a burro clam. I put my hand down deep into a crevice and snap, it was not a crevice but the mouth of a burro, the father of all burros. Señor Clam had me tight, but I did not leave my arm with him, as you can see. That was in the Gulf, yet there are many burros here in the Vermilion." He looked up at me again and smiled. "It is better, mate, that you stay in the boat."

The Indian who was working with the Sevillano handed him the sink stone and the Sevillano went down, saying nothing more to me. Nor did he speak to me again that morning. At midday the *Santa Teresa* was loaded with shells and low in the water, because the Sevillano did the work of three divers, so my father sent him out to help in the other boats.

From time to time during the afternoon, when he came up for air, he would call over to me, "Be careful, mate, and do not get your foot caught in the rope," or "There are sharks around, Señor Salazar, mind that you do not fall in the water."

Such things as that I heard during the whole of the afternoon. My father also heard them, though the Sevillano usually spoke to me when he thought my father was not listening.

"He is a troublemaker," my father said, "but let him talk. What do you care what he says? Remember that he is the best gatherer of pearls we have. And it is for pearls that we are here on the sea, not for other reasons."

By dark the boats were piled high with cargo and we set sail for La Paz. The moon came up and a brisk wind that filled the sails. The Sevillano was in good spirits, as if he had not made dozens of deep dives that day. He perched himself on the mound of shells and once more told how he had found the great pearl in the Gulf of Persia, the same tale he had told before but longer. Again I had the feeling that his story was meant for me more than the others.

And as I listened to him a dream began to take shape in my mind. It was a fanciful dream that made me forget the insults that I had suffered silently. I saw myself in a boat anchored in a secret lagoon somewhere on the Vermilion Sea. I put a knife in my belt and grasped the basket and the heavy sink stone and plunged to the bottom. There were sharks swimming around me in slow circles, but I gave no heed to them. I pried clump after clump of shells from the rocks, filling my basket. After I had been down for three or four minutes, I floated to the surface through the circling sharks, and climbed into the boat and pulled up the basket. Then I pried open the shells, one after the other. Nothing. At last there was only one shell left. Discouraged, I opened it and was about to toss it away when I saw before me a pearl larger than my fist that shone as if a fire burned inside . . .

Right at that moment, just as I was about to clutch the pearl in my hand, the Sevillano stopped talking. Suddenly he stood up on the mound and pointed astern, along the path the moon was making on the sea.

"Manta," he shouted, "Manta Diablo."

I jumped to my feet. I could see nothing at first. Then the boat rose on a wave and I made out a silvery shape swimming half out of the water not more than a furlong away.

Truthfully, I must say that for all its beauty the manta is a fearsome sight to those who sail our Vermilion Sea. There are small mantas, no larger when they are full grown than ten feet from one wing tip to the other. But there are some that measure twice that length and weigh most of three tons.

Both kinds are shaped very much like a giant bat and they swim through the water with a regular upward and downward beat of their flippers. And both have a mouth so enormous that a man may easily put his head into it and on either side of this maw are large lobes like arms, which the manta pushes out and then draws in to capture its prey.

Their prey surprisingly is not the shoals of fish that abound in our sea, but shrimp and crabs and such small things. Most of the mantas have a pilot fish that swims along beneath them. These fish swim in and out of their mouths, it is said, to clean up the pieces of food that catch in their plate-like teeth.

And yet for all of his friendly ways, the manta is a fearsome beast. When aroused by some careless insult, it can break a man's neck with a flick of its long tail or lift one flipper and wreck the strongest boat.

"Manta," the Sevillano shouted again. "El Manta Diablo!" His Indian helper quickly scrambled away and crouched down in the bow of the boat and began to mutter to himself.

"No," said my father, "It is not the Diablo. Him I have seen and he is bigger by twice than this one."

"Come where you can see better," said the Sevillano. "It is the Manta Diablo. I know him well."

I was certain that he was trying to scare the Indian and my father was certain of it, too, for he lashed the tiller and climbed to where the Sevillano stood. He glanced astern for a moment and then went back to the tiller.

"No," he said, loud enough for the Indian to hear, "It is not even the small sister of the Diablo."

The Indian fell silent, but he was still frightened. And as I watched the manta swimming along behind us, its outstretched fins like vast silvery wings, I remembered that once I had also been frightened at the very sound of the name.

At last the manta disappeared and near dawn we rounded El Magote, the lizard tongue of land that guards the harbor, and anchored our boats. As my father and I walked home in the moonlight, he said,

"About the Sevillano, let me repeat to you. Treat him with courtesy. Listen to his boasts as if you believed them. For he is a very dangerous young man. Only last week I learned from a friend who lives over in Culiacán that the Sevillano was born there. And that he has never been in Seville nor any part of Spain nor in the Gulf of Persia nor anywhere except here on the Vermilion. Also, he has had many fights in Culiacán, one of them fatal."

I promised my father that I would obey him, but as we walked toward home I again thought of my dream and the big pearl I had found and how surprised the Sevillano would be when he saw it.

Four days passed and I was standing at the desk, with a pen over my ear and the leather-bound ledger open in front of me. I was watching a canoe that moved around the tip of the lizard tongue. It was a red canoe and came swiftly, so I knew it belonged to the Indian Soto Luzon.

I was glad to see old Luzon. He had sold pearls to my father for many years. He came about every three months and never brought more than one, but it always was a pearl of good quality. Soon after I began to work with my father he had brought in a beautiful pearl of more than two carats.

As I watched Luzon beach the canoe and come up the path, I hoped he was bringing another like it, for the yield from our last trip had been poor. Five boatloads of shells had yielded no round or pear-shaped pearls and only a handful of buttons and baroques,[5] all of them dull.

I opened the door at his timid knock and invited him to come in and sit down.

"I have traveled all night," Luzon said. "If it pleases you, I would like to stand."

Luzon never sat. He had an Indian's thin legs but a powerful chest and thick arms that could wield a paddle for hours and not grow tired.

"I passed your boats this morning," he said. "They were near Maldonado."

"They are going to Isla Cerralvo."[6]

The old man gave me a shrewd look. "The fishing is not good around here?"

"Good," I said. It was not wise to say that it was poor, when he had come to sell a pearl. "Very good."

"Then why, señor, do the boats go to Cerralvo?"

"Because my father wants to search there for the black ones."

The old man fumbled in his shirt and pulled out a knotted rag and untied it. "Here is a black one," he said.

I could see at a glance that it was round and of a good quality, like the pearl I had bought from him three months before.

[5]baroques (bä rō′kes): irregularly shaped pearls
[6]Isla Cerralvo (ēs′ lä se räl′ vō)

181

I placed it on the scales and balanced it against the small copper weights.

"Two and a half carats," I said.

My father never haggled with Luzon and always gave him a fair price and had told me to do the same. For that reason old Luzon always brought his pearls to Salazar and Son, although there were four other dealers in our town.

"Two hundred pesos," I said.

This sum was about fifty pesos more than my father would have offered, but a plan was taking shape in my mind and I needed the old man's help. I counted out the money and he put it in his shirt, probably thinking to himself that I was not so smart as my father.

"You always bring in good pearls. Black ones," I said. "There must be many in your lagoon. If you permit me I will come and dive there. All the pearls I find I will pay you for."

The old man looked puzzled. "But you are not a diver," he said.

"You can teach me, señor."

"I have heard your father say many times, since the time you were a child, that he did not raise you to drown in the sea or to give an arm or a leg to a burro shell."

"My father," I said, "has gone to Cerralvo and he will not return for a week or more."

"And your mother and your sister, what will they say?"

"They will say nothing because today they go to Loreto." I paused. "You will teach me to dive and I will look for the big one and when I find it I will pay you what it is worth."

"The big one I have searched for many years," Luzon said. "How is it found in a week?"

"You can find the big one in a single dive."

The old man pulled at his stubbly chin. He was thinking, I knew, about his wife and his two unmarried daughters and his three young sons, and all these mouths he had to feed every day.

"When do you wish to go?" he said.

"I wish to go now."

Luzon hitched up his frayed trousers. "After I buy a sack of frijoles and a sack of flour, then we go."

The old man left and I put the pearls away and locked the safe. I took the bundle from under the desk, my pants, a shirt, and the knife. I closed the door and locked it. As I walked down to the beach, I thought about the great pearl I had dreamed of while the Sevillano was bragging. I thought of how surprised he would be when he came back from Cerralvo and found the whole town of La Paz talking about the monster pearl Ramón Salazar had found.

It was a dream so wild that only a very young man and a stupid one could dream it. And yet, as happens sometimes, the dream came true.

The lagoon where the old man lived was about seven leagues from La Paz and we should have reached it by midnight. But the currents and the wind were against us, so it was near dawn before we sighted the two headlands that marked the lagoon's hidden entrance.

You could pass this entrance many times and think that it was only an opening in the rocks that led nowhere. As soon as you passed the rocks, however, you came to a narrow channel that wound like a snake between the two headlands for a half mile or farther.

The sun was just rising when the channel opened out and suddenly we were in a quiet oval-shaped lagoon. On both sides of the lagoon steep hills came down to the water and at the far end lay a shallow beach of black sand. Beyond were two scraggly trees and beneath them a cluster of huts where breakfast fires were burning.

It was a peaceful scene that lay before me, much like many other lagoons that dot our coast. But there was something about the place that made me feel uneasy. At first I thought it must be the barren hills that closed in upon the lagoon and the coppery haze that lay over it, and the beach of black sand and the quiet. I

was soon to hear that it was something else, something far different from what I thought.

The old man paddled slowly across the lagoon, carefully raising and lowering the paddle, as if he did not want to disturb the water. And though he had talked most of the time before we reached the lagoon he now fell silent. A gray shark circled the canoe and disappeared. He pointed to it, but said nothing.

Nor did he speak again until we beached the canoe and were walking up the path to the huts. Then he said, "It is well to hold the tongue and not to talk needlessly when you are on the lagoon. Remember this when we go out to dive, for there is one who listens and is quickly angered."

Indians are superstitious about the moon and the sun and some animals and birds, especially the coyote and the owl. For this reason I was not surprised that he wished to warn me.

"Who is it that listens and grows angry?" I asked him.

184

Twice he glanced over his shoulder before he answered. "The Manta Diablo," he said.

"El Diablo?" I asked, holding back a smile. "He lives here in your lagoon?"

"In a cave," he answered, "a big one which you can see just as you leave the channel."

"The channel is very narrow," I said, "barely wide enough for a canoe. How does a giant like El Diablo swim through it? But perhaps he does not need to. Perhaps he stays here in your lagoon."

"No," the old man said. "He travels widely and is gone for many weeks at a time."

"Then he must swim through the channel somehow."

"Oh, no, that would be impossible, even for him. There is another opening, a secret one, near the place where you enter the channel. When he swims out to sea, it is this one he uses."

We were nearing the huts clustered beneath the two scraggly trees. A band of children came running out to meet us and the old man said nothing more about El Diablo until we had eaten breakfast, slept the morning away, eaten again, and gone back to the lagoon.

As we floated the canoe and set off for the pearling reefs, the old man said, "When the mist goes, that means El Diablo has gone, too."

It was true that the red mist was gone and the water now shone green and clear. I still smiled to myself at the old man's belief in El Diablo, yet I felt a little of the excitement that I had felt long ago when my mother threatened me with the monster.

"Now that he is gone," I said, "we can talk."

"A little and with much care," Luzon replied, "for he has many friends in the lagoon."

"Friends?"

"Yes, the shark you saw this morning and many small fish. They are all friends and they listen and when he comes back they tell him everything, everything."

"When he leaves the lagoon, where does he go?"

"That I do not know. Some say that he takes the shape of an octopus and seeks out those pearlers who have done him a wrong or spoken ill of him. It is also said that he takes the shape of a human and goes into La Paz and seeks his enemies there in the streets and sometimes even in the church."

"I should think that you would fear for your life and leave the lagoon."

"No, I do not fear El Diablo. Nor did my father before me. Nor his father before him. For many years they had a pact with the Manta Diablo and now I keep this pact. I show him proper respect and tip my hat when I come into the lagoon and when I leave it. For this he allows me to dive for the black pearls which belong to him and which we now go to search for."

Silently the old man guided the canoe toward the south shore of the lagoon, and I asked no more questions for I felt that he had said all he wished to say about the Manta Diablo. In two fathoms of water, over a reef of black rocks, he dropped anchor and told me to do the same.

"Now I teach you to dive," he said. "First we start with the breathing."

The old man lifted his shoulders and began to take in great gulps of air, gulp after gulp, until his chest seemed twice its size. Then he let out the air with a long whoosh.

"This is called 'taking the wind'," he said. "And because it is very important you must try it."

I obeyed his command, but filled my lungs in one breath.

"More," the old man said.

I took in another gulp of air.

"More," the old man said.

I tried again and then began to cough.

"For the first time it is good," the old man said. "But you must practice this much so you stretch the lungs. Now we go down together."

We both filled our lungs with air and slipped over the side of the canoe feet first, each of us holding a sink stone. The water was as warm as milk but clear so that I could see the wrinkled sand and the black rocks and fish swimming about.

When we reached the bottom the old man put a foot in the loop of the rope that held his sink stone and I did likewise with my stone. He placed his hand on my shoulder and took two steps to a crevice in a rock that was covered with trailing weeds. Then he took the knife from his belt and thrust it into the crevice. Instantly the crevice closed, not slowly but with a snap. The old man wrenched the knife free and took his foot out of the loop and motioned for me to do the same and we floated up to the canoe.

The old man held out the knife. "Note the scratches which the burro shell leaves," he said. "With a hand or a foot it is different. Once the burro has you he does not let go and thus you drown. Take care, therefore, where you step and where you place the hand."

We dived until night came, and the old man showed me how to walk carefully on the bottom, so as not to muddy the water,

and how to use the knife to pry loose the oysters that grew in clumps and how to get the shells open and how to search them for pearls.

We gathered many baskets that afternoon but found nothing except a few baroques of little worth. And it was the same the next day and the next, and then on the fourth day, because the old man had cut his hand on a shell, I went out on the lagoon alone.

It was on this day that I found the great Pearl of Heaven.

# EPILOGUE

*Ramón does find the great black pearl of his dream, but Luzon insists that it belongs to Manta Diablo. He warns Ramón that he'd better give it back, but Ramón refuses. Then something happens that makes him wonder if he made the right decision.*

**Reader's Response** ～ Do you think the old man was foolish to fear the Manta Diablo?

**Library Link** ～ *Read about Ramon's exciting encounters with the Manta Diablo in the book from which this excerpt was taken,* The Black Pearl *by Scott O'Dell.*

# On Dreamers' Wings

One of humanity's great dreams
is to soar above it all.
What kinds of adventures have been
inspired by this age-old dream?

BATTERSEA BOX, *enamel, England*

*Theme Books for*

# On Dreamers' Wings

*D*reams of flying have inspired all kinds of adventures. Some dreams you can touch: a better flying machine. Others you can feel: the desire to soar free and strong above old ways of seeing and thinking.

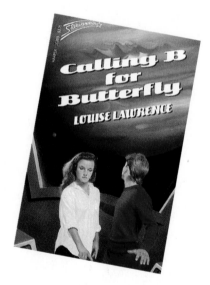

❖ The collision of an asteroid with a galactic spaceliner leaves four teenagers and two small children alone aboard *Life Ferry B* in Louise Lawrence's *Calling B for Butterfly*. The survivors are at odds with each other—and in great danger. Can they pull together in time to save their lives?

❖ Moon Shadow, the young Chinese immigrant in Laurence Yep's *Dragonwings*, learns about flying from his father, Windrider. Life is harsh in turn-of-the-century San Francisco, but Windrider's dream of flying sustains them.

❖ In *The Edge of the Cloud* by K. M. Peyton, seventeen-year-old Christina wants to marry Will and settle into a nice, quiet life. But she has no idea of what looms before her as she faces Will's dream of designing and flying planes—a dangerous business in 1913 England.

❖ Professor Sherman has a pioneering spirit when it comes to hot-air balloons. But his spirit of adventure is sorely tested by a balloon ride that he couldn't have imagined in his wildest dreams. Soar to humorous adventure in *The Twenty-One Balloons* by William Pène du Bois.

*More Books to Enjoy*

*The Wright Brothers: How They Invented the Airplane* by Russell Freedman

*Dragonflight* by Anne McCaffrey

*Hot-Air Ballooning* by Charles Coombs

*Enchantress from the Stars* by Sylvia Engdahl

# DAEDALUS
## and
# ICARUS
### by
### Penelope Farmer

In ancient Greece, the great inventor Daedalus has been banished from Athens, his home, for committing a serious crime. With his beloved son, Icarus, Daedalus has taken refuge on the island of Crete, where the great King Minos rules. Minos asked Daedalus to construct an inescapable stronghold for his son, the Minotaur, a monstrous creature with the head of a huge black bull and a cavernous mouth. To contain the deadly creature, Daedalus created a maze of tunnels and passages so intricate that a hundred people might wander in it for years without ever meeting one another.

In the labyrinth then lived the Minotaur, its roar confined in rock still heard dimly through the palace. People trembled hearing it. Minos, they knew, sent those who had angered him to feed his son, and to the Minotaur all alike were men of tender flesh to tear and devour—Cretan, Spartan, Athenian, none could withstand its furious charge from some dark winding of the labyrinth.

Daedalus, meanwhile, exiled from the city of his birth, lived on at Cnossus in the service of the king. He seemed to grow more clever, more ingenious than ever. He copied in iron a fish's backbone with its row of little teeth; this made the first saw ever seen. He fitted together two pointed rods of iron to make compasses with which a perfect circle could be drawn. His fame grew, all over Greece, all round the Aegean Sea. His pride also burned and puffed itself up till he thought his skill equal to a god's. The sun of Minos' favour[1] shone on him more brilliantly each day, and nothing seemed likely to move him from the favour of the king.

But then one day guards came to seize Daedalus and Icarus and drag them before Minos the king. And he was wrathful, furious, bellowing like a bull himself, like his son the Minotaur.

"So you boasted, Daedalus, that no one could escape your labyrinth. But the Minotaur is dead. A man has killed our son and understood the maze and sailed away unharmed from Crete. Now you and your son shall be cast into the maze, and if you too escape from there, you'll get no further, we swear to it. We, Minos, do not swear in vain. We rule not merely Crete but all the sea about. Without ships no man can escape from Crete, and you, O subtle architect, clever as you are, you command no ships upon our Aegean Sea."

[1]Some words in this selection are spelled in the British style.

So Daedalus, with Icarus his son, was cast into the prison he had made. He took with him there a ball of golden thread, which looked in such darkness like an image of the golden sun. This was the device he'd made secretly to guide himself to the far end of the labyrinth. He tied one end to the entrance place, and slowly the ball began to unroll ahead of them, through all the turns and windings, the confusions of entrances and alleyways. After a while Daedalus smelt a familiar, farmyard reek, but it had a fouler, sicklier note to it, and the stench went on growing all the time till they reached the cave at the heart of the labyrinth where the corpse of the Minotaur lay rotting on dirty straw.

It seemed feeble now, and foolish and puny. Its red eyes were closed, its limbs flaccid and limp. Only the yellow horns still looked dangerous.

Daedalus gazed beyond it, shuddering, holding up his little lamp till its light reached the farthest corners of the cave where human bones and skulls lay scattered everywhere. There were feathers also from birds devoured by the Minotaur. He picked up one and examined minutely its shaft and quill.

"Minos rules the land of Crete," he said. "He may rule the sea that surrounds it too. But remember, Icarus my son, remember that great King Minos does not rule the sky."

Icarus did not know what his father meant by this. He watched Daedalus lay feathers overlapping in four separate rows, each diminishing in size from one end to the other. Then Daedalus brought from his tunic a cake of wax, a needle, and some fine strong thread. He joined the larger feathers with the needle and thread. He softened the wax in the warmth of the lamp and used it to unite the smaller feathers.

Icarus watched his father's patient hands, watched small feathers waver in the heat above the lamp and the wax drip down in slow, dull drops. Sometimes Daedalus made him hold feathers or pull on an end of thread, and he was eager to help, too eager perhaps, jogging his father's arm or letting his shadow fall across the light.

At last Daedalus took the completed rows, bent them and curved them into shape, and then his son could see what they were meant to be; how from the wings of birds, his father Daedalus had made wings for men, one pair each for himself and Icarus.

The oil of the lamp was all burned now. As they left the cave the wick flickered and went out so that the only light was in the guiding thread in the diminishing golden ball, which unrolled ahead of them towards the secret entrance of the labyrinth where no guard would stand in wait. The sound of their breathing magnified itself. On and on they went. Even when they neared the end, there was still no light, not the narrowest rim or chink. The thread doubled round and back again, and they twisted confusedly to follow it.

The light broke suddenly, burst upon them. They had to bury their eyes against the blinding, burning sun. The air rushed at them too, strong air full of honey and wild thyme, for this entrance to the labyrinth lay on the hillside by Cnossus, within sight of the glittering sea.

When Daedalus's eyes accepted the light at last, he took some leather thongs and fixed the smaller pair of wings to the arms of Icarus. He fixed the larger to his own, explaining all the while what they had to do. They would have to use their arms just as the wing bones of a bird, making the feathers gently rise and fall.

"But mind, mind, Icarus my son, don't fly too low, too near the sea, for the feathers once wet will not carry you. But then do not fly too high, too near the sun, for the sun's heat like the lamps, will melt the wax, make the feathers fall away."

Icarus heard his father out. But he was already impatient to begin, moving his arms experimentally, so that the air caught the feathers on the wings.

Daedalus started to run along the hillside. When he had gained some speed he jumped into the air, shouting at Icarus to follow him. Both moved their arms with awkward, chopping strokes; they did not soar as they had expected to, but struggled jerkily, not far above the rock. Daedalus kept close to Icarus, instructing him, but made no more elegant a bird himself. If an even stroke did make him soar, he would lose the knack at once and slip down again. Once Icarus, shooting up, met Daedalus struggling down, their wings entangled and both fell hard onto the bruising stone.

Icarus caught it first, the rhythm, the pattern of flight. He swept into the air and away, filled with joyfulness, shouting with delight, and almost at once Daedalus followed his

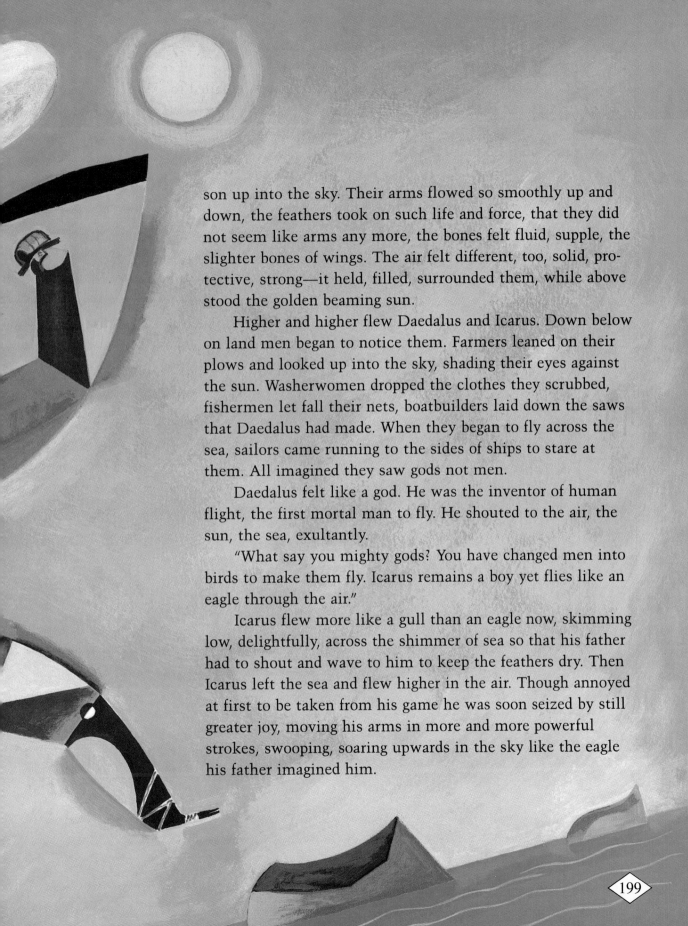

son up into the sky. Their arms flowed so smoothly up and down, the feathers took on such life and force, that they did not seem like arms any more, the bones felt fluid, supple, the slighter bones of wings. The air felt different, too, solid, protective, strong—it held, filled, surrounded them, while above stood the golden beaming sun.

Higher and higher flew Daedalus and Icarus. Down below on land men began to notice them. Farmers leaned on their plows and looked up into the sky, shading their eyes against the sun. Washerwomen dropped the clothes they scrubbed, fishermen let fall their nets, boatbuilders laid down the saws that Daedalus had made. When they began to fly across the sea, sailors came running to the sides of ships to stare at them. All imagined they saw gods not men.

Daedalus felt like a god. He was the inventor of human flight, the first mortal man to fly. He shouted to the air, the sun, the sea, exultantly.

"What say you mighty gods? You have changed men into birds to make them fly. Icarus remains a boy yet flies like an eagle through the air."

Icarus flew more like a gull than an eagle now, skimming low, delightfully, across the shimmer of sea so that his father had to shout and wave to him to keep the feathers dry. Then Icarus left the sea and flew higher in the air. Though annoyed at first to be taken from his game he was soon seized by still greater joy, moving his arms in more and more powerful strokes, swooping, soaring upwards in the sky like the eagle his father imagined him.

Daedalus returned to his godlike dreams and failed to watch the flight of Icarus.

"Other men need gods to make them fly. Icarus has only his mortal father Daedalus."

Higher and higher flew Icarus, towards the strengthening sun. The air grew hotter, the sun more brilliant, dazzling to his eyes. He had forgotten all warnings now, flying nearer as if drawn to it, like a moth towards a lamp.

And slowly the wax on his wings began to melt. It softened gently, then dripped a little, in slow, thick drops. A feather slipped from it, fell drifting, turning, down towards the sea. Other feathers followed, singly at first, but then more and more of them at once. And suddenly, though the ecstatic Icarus as confidently moved his wings, there were not enough feathers left to hold the air, to keep him up in flight.

His father looked back, to see his son plunge headlong, faster than the feathers, passing every one. Straight as a gull he fell towards the sea, but did not swerve in safety like a gull above the glittering waves. He plunged right into the heart of them, and their startled waters closed above his head. All that remained of Icarus were some feathers floating on the sea, while his father flew, weeping, in the sky, alone.

Reader's Response ～ What emotions do you think Daedalus might have felt after witnessing the death of his son?

Library Link ～ *Read Edith Hamilton's* Mythology *to learn more about ancient myths, legends, gods and heroes.*

# DAEDALUS SETS WORLD RECORD

SANTORINI, April 24, 1988 — A Greek Olympic bicyclist strode out of the water and onto the shore of this Greek island today, having just set a distance record for human-powered flight. The craft that he pedaled from the island of Crete, 74 miles across the Aegean Sea, weighed just 68 pounds. It had been designed by engineers at the Massachusetts Institute of Technology. The flight lasted three hours and 55 minutes. It covered a route similar to that taken by its namesake, Daedalus, the engineer of ancient mythology.

The pilot-cyclist, Kanellos Kanellopoulos, had been told today at 4 A.M. to prepare for the flight. He was just one of several competitive cyclists who had been in training as pilots. The Daedalus team rotated the cyclists through an exercise and diet schedule that ensured that one cyclist would be at peak strength and ready to go when the weather cleared. It seemed fitting that Kanellopoulos was the only Greek cyclist in the group.

Kanellopoulos was wired with electrodes that monitored his heart rate and condition. The Daedalus, with its wingspan of 112 feet and its skin of mylar, maintained an altitude of 15 feet and a speed of about 15 miles per hour. Everything went smoothly until the final moment, when a wind gust caused the Daedalus to drop suddenly and land not on shore but in the water. Kanellopoulos emerged smiling and was greeted with hugs and kisses by the waiting onlookers.

The Daedalus had made its record-breaking journey on human pedal-power alone.

# Landscape with the Fall of Icarus

According to Brueghel
when Icarus fell
it was spring

a farmer was plowing
his field
the whole pageantry

of the year was
awake tingling
near

the edge of the sea
concerned
with itself

sweating in the sun
that melted
the wings' wax

insignificantly
off the coast
there was

a splash quite unnoticed
this was
Icarus drowning

WILLIAM CARLOS WILLIAMS

LANDSCAPE WITH THE FALL OF ICARUS, *oil on canvas by Brueghel (elder), Flemish.*

# WINGS TO FLY

## BY JAY WILLIAMS
### from <u>Leonardo da Vinci</u>

*The dream of Daedalus lived on through the ages. During the Renaissance, this dream took hold in the imagination of Leonardo da Vinci, the great Italian artist and inventor.*

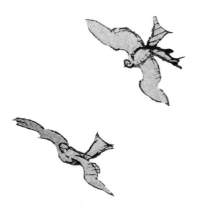

His passion for research and his respect for knowledge mark Leonardo unmistakably as a man of the Renaissance[1] and—even more, as a man of Florence. For it was in that rich and thriving Renaissance city, where old ways were being questioned and new ideas were coming into life, that Leonardo's artistic talent had flourished and his philosophical ideas had matured. It was there too that Leonardo's inventive genius began to assert itself. As he probed deeper into the mysteries of nature in order to understand them better as an artist and a thinker, he found he was spending more time on tinkering than on painting. Gradually, he abandoned art for technology and science and became specifically absorbed in a problem that had fascinated him for years—the problem of flight.

From his early youth he had dreamed of flying, and he was determined to make his dream a reality. Typically, he began by watching closely the flight of birds and then writing down his findings in his notebooks. After studying the structure of birds' wings, he made experiments with models and noted the results. He proposed to gather his observations into a book on the flight of birds. The book would be divided into four parts, the first of which "treats of their flight by beating their wings; the second of flight without beating their wings, and with the help of the wind; the third of flight in general, such as that of birds, bats, fishes, animals, and insects; the last of the mechanism of this movement." He watched the way birds used their tails as rudders and how they make gentle landings by stalling—lowering their tails and spreading the tailfeathers, flapping their wings quickly to cut down their speed, and changing their center of gravity by moving their heads. He dissected countless birds and bats to learn how the wing opens and closes and how its muscles move it. The end of all of his work was to be an attempt at actual flight.

[1]Renaissance (ren′ ə säns)

Leonardo's parachute, though pyramidal, operated in exactly the same way as the modern version; it was to be built of specially treated cloth.

Others, it happened, had made attempts before Leonardo. One, an Italian mathematician and engineer named Giovanni Danti, had made a short glide over—and into—Lake Trasimeno around 1490; later he made a second attempt at gliding, which resulted in a broken leg. Leonardo was certain he could succeed where Danti had failed.

"A bird," he wrote, "is an instrument working according to mathematical law, which instrument it is within the capacity of man to reproduce . . ." His investigations were spread over a long period of time, during which he watched and studied birds and invented various contraptions that would demonstrate how different surfaces are affected by the movement of air. Among his notes is a drawing of a parachute, made of starched linen, with which, wrote Leonardo, a man would be able "to throw himself down from any great height without sustaining any injury." Another drawing shows a kind of helicopter with a note that a model could be made of pasteboard with a steel-wire spring. "I find that if this instrument . . . be well made . . . and be turned swiftly . . . it will rise high."

His final plan was to build a great bird on which a man could ride, a device lacking, as he wrote, ". . . in nothing except the life of the bird, and this life must needs be supplied from that of man."

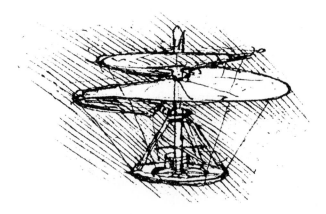

Leonardo's helicopter had a screw-shaped rotor operated by four men (to be workable, a powerful engine would, of course, have been necessary).

206

He knew that a bird's wings were moved by powerful chest muscles. The driving force for the wings of his bird machine, he felt, could be supplied by man's powerful leg muscles, which, he said, were twice as strong as was needed for bearing his weight. He never discovered, unfortunately, that in proportion to its size a bird's bones are much lighter than a man's, and thus he never realized how much power it would take to raise both a man and his machine into the air. He did, however, calculate fairly accurately how large a wing would be needed to support a man in glider flight, and he was far ahead of anyone of his own time—or for centuries to come—in recognizing the effect of air on the surfaces of wings.

Not realizing at first that man could never fly by muscle power, Leonardo tried to make his flying machine like a bird. He modeled his mechanical wing on that of a bat, noting that the frame (A) should be made of fir wood, the covering of fustion (B), a strong corduroy-like material, and starched taffeta (C), or, he cautiously added, "As a test, use thin pasteboard."

With particular care he studied the ways in which birds use the wind to rise and descend and their methods of balancing themselves in flight; how hawks rise on air currents, and the way in which they slant their wings and tails so as to take advantage of the wind. He wrote: "The man in a flying machine (has) to be free from the waist upward in order to be able to balance himself as he does in a boat, so that his center of gravity and that of his machine may . . . change where necessity requires . . ." Many of his notes show his startling powers of vision. He was able to observe, for instance, how a bird prevents itself from being turned over in the air when it is struck from underneath by the wind. He noted that "[the bird] lowers the right or left wing, for this will cause it to turn to the right or left, dropping down in a half circle."

Elsewhere he noted that "when the bird wishes suddenly to turn on one of its sides, it pushes out swiftly, toward its tail, the point of the wing on that side, and since every movement tends to maintain itself, or rather every body that is moved continues to move as long as the impression of the force of its mover is retained in it, therefore the movement of this wing . . . in the direction of the tail . . . will come to move the whole bird with it . . ."

On the basis of such close scrutiny and such precise piecing together of observations, Leonardo built many models, some of them fairly large. He worked on them in great secrecy, for he writes, "Close up with boards the large room above, and make the model large and high, and you will have space upon the roof above . . . if you stand upon the roof at the side of the tower, the men at work upon the cupola will not see you." Later, he made a note to himself to try a small model over the Arno, and he added, "See tomorrow to all these matters and the copies, and then efface the originals and leave them at Florence so that if you lose those that you take with you, the invention will not be lost." He tried all sorts of materials: light fir wood and cane for the framework of the wings, and starched cloth, paper, or parchment for the skin. Joints were padded with leather, springs were made of ox horn or steel wire, and bindings were of strong raw silk.

Leonardo drew plans for several different types of machines. His earliest device had the wings attached to the flier's body. Then, he developed a machine in which the pilot would lie flat on his face, pedaling at stirrups that made the wings rise and fall. Finally, he decided that the best position for the pilot was upright, both because it was more natural and because the machine would then never turn upside down. By this time the "bird" had become very complicated. It consisted of a kind of basket in which the pilot stood, pumping treadles with his feet, and with his hands turning a windlass to operate two pairs of huge wings. Each pair would move "crosswise after the manner of the gait of the horse." Two long retractable ladders were fastened under the machine to act as legs so that the wings could clear the ground when beating,

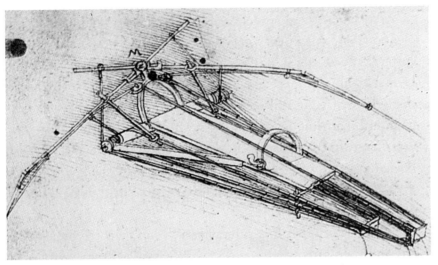

The "Orthopter" was designed so the pilot would lie flat, pedaling at stirrups that made the wings rise and fall.

and Leonardo mentions that some birds such as the martin, or swift, are not able to rise flying from the ground because their legs are so short.

Even while he was still in Milan, Leonardo seems to have tried out one of his inventions, probably a model of a larger machine, for among his records is an entry that speaks of making thongs of oxhide to hold the joints: "Tomorrow morning on the second day of January, 1496, I will make the thong and the attempt."

It is possible that some time in the year 1505 he put his "bird" to the test. Among his papers from about this time there is a page on which is written, "From the mountain which takes its name from the great bird, the famous bird will take its flight, which will fill the world with its great renown." The mountain is believed to be Mount Ceceri, not far from Florence, for the Italian word *cecero* means "swan." This is made surer by a sentence written on the cover of the same notebook: "The great bird will take its first flight upon the back of the great swan, filling the whole world with amazement and filling all records with its fame; and it will bring eternal glory to the nest where it was born."

209

And then there is silence. No one can say whether the complex machine with four wings was trundled up to a cliff on Mount Ceceri, or whether it was a kind of glider that was tried. Did Leonardo himself make the attempt, or some daring young apprentice? All that is known is summed up in the words of the philosopher and mathematician Geronimo Cardano, writing nearly fifty years later. In his book *De Subtilitate Rerum*, he remarks, "It has turned out badly for the two who have recently made a trial of it [flying]: Leonardo da Vinci also attempted to fly, but he was not successful."

Not for another four hundred years was man to conquer the air, and then only when a power source, the gasoline engine, had been developed which could give enough power to lift the weight of a man and his "bird"—and only when the principles of lateral balance and steering, first noted by Leonardo, had been rediscovered. Although Leonardo failed, his careful and inventive researches in aerodynamics make him the true forerunner of modern flying.

Reader's Response ∼ Leonardo da Vinci was both an artist and an architect. If you possessed his intellect and abilities, which career would you pursue? Why?

Library Link ∼ *You can learn more about the life of this fascinating genius by reading* Leonardo da Vinci *by Jay Williams.*

# A RENAISSANCE MAN

Perhaps you've heard someone referred to as a "Renaissance man" or a "Renaissance woman." Today we reserve that expression for someone who is unusually skilled and knowledgeable in many areas of the arts and sciences. The Renaissance was the revival of learning, literature and classical art that originated in Italy during the 14th century and reached its conclusion in Europe some two hundred years later. Of the leading thinkers of that important period, Leonardo da Vinci was perhaps the most notable.

Mona Lisa, DaVinci, The Louvre

Trained as a painter, Leonardo is considered one of the greatest artists of the Italian Renaissance. His *Mona Lisa*—with her beguiling smile—is possibly the best-known portrait ever painted.

As an artist Leonardo was an innovator; he experimented with new painting techniques and developed new pigments. He was also a military and civil engineer whose work involved planning the construction of guns and cannons, submarines, building devices, and bridges. His detailed plans for buildings and cities reflect his talent as an architectural designer.

An original thinker throughout his life, Leonardo believed in studying nature, which changed the way Europeans approached both art and science. Basing his work on corpses he dissected and examined, he made the first accurate drawings of human anatomy, showing how bones and muscles worked together. Interestingly, he also designed costumes and scenery for dramatic productions.

Clearly, Leonardo da Vinci was a Renaissance man.

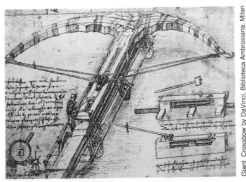

Giant Crossbow by DaVinci, Biblioteca Ambrosiana, Milan

Study of giant crossbow

211

# The People Could Fly

### told by Virginia Hamilton

"The People Could Fly" is one of the most extraordinary, moving tales in black folklore. It almost makes us believe that the people could fly. There are numerous separate accounts of flying Africans and slaves in the black folktale literature. Such accounts are often combined with tales of slaves disappearing. A plausible explanation might be the slaves running away from slavery, slipping away while in the fields or under cover of darkness. In code language murmured from one slave to another, "Come fly away!" might have been the words used. Another explanation is the wish-fulfillment motif.

The magic hoe variant is often combined with the flying-African tale. A magic hoe is left still hoeing in an empty field after all the slaves have flown away. Magic with the hoe and other farm tools, and the power of disappearing, are often attributed to Gullah (Angolan) African slaves. Angolan slaves were thought by other slaves to have exceptional powers.

"The People Could Fly" is a detailed fantasy tale of suffering, of magic power exerted against the so-called Master and his underlings. Finally, it is a powerful testament to the millions of slaves who never had the opportunity to "fly" away. They remained slaves, as did their children. "The People Could Fly" was first told and retold by those who had only their imaginations to set them free.

LEO DILLON ©85

212

213

They say the people could fly. Say that long ago in Africa, some of the people knew magic. And they would walk up on the air like climbin up on a gate. And they flew like black-birds over the fields. Black, shiny wings flappin against the blue up there.

Then, many of the people were captured for Slavery. The ones that could fly shed their wings. They couldn't take their wings across the water on the slave ships. Too crowded, don't you know.

The folks were full of misery, then. Got sick with the up and down of the sea. So they forgot about flyin when they could no longer breathe the sweet scent of Africa.

Say the people who could fly kept their power, although they shed their wings. They kept their secret magic in the land of slavery. They looked the same as the other people from Africa who had been coming over, who had dark skin. Say you couldn't tell anymore one who could fly from one who couldn't.

One such who could was an old man, call him Toby. And standin tall, yet afraid, was a young woman who once had wings. Call her Sarah. Now Sarah carried a babe tied to her back. She trembled to be so hard worked and scorned.

The slaves labored in the fields from sunup to sundown. The owner of the slaves callin himself their Master. Say he was a hard lump of clay. A hard, glinty coal. A hard rock pile, wouldn't be moved. His Overseer on horseback pointed out the slaves who were slowin down. So the one called Driver cracked his whip over the slow ones to make them move faster. That whip was a slice-open cut of pain. So they did move faster. Had to.

Sarah hoed and chopped the row as the babe on her back slept.

Say the child grew hungry. That babe started up bawlin too loud. Sarah couldn't stop to feed it. Couldn't stop to soothe and quiet it down. She let it cry. She didn't want to. She had no heart to croon to it.

"Keep that thing quiet," called the Overseer. He pointed his fingers at the babe. The woman scrunched low. The Driver cracked his whip across the babe anyhow. The babe hollered like any hurt child, and the woman fell to the earth.

214

The old man that was there, Toby, came and helped her to her feet.

"I must go soon," she told him.

"Soon," he said.

Sarah couldn't stand up straight any longer. She was too weak. The sun burned her face. The babe cried and cried, "Pity me, oh, pity me," say it sounded like. Sarah was so sad and starvin, she sat down in the row.

"Get up, you black cow," called the Overseer. He pointed his hand, and the Driver's whip snarled around Sarah's legs. Her sack dress tore into rags. Her legs bled onto the earth. She couldn't get up.

Toby was there where there was no one to help her and the babe.

"Now, before it's too late," panted Sarah. "Now, Father!"

"Yes, Daughter, the time is come," Toby answered. "Go, as you know how to go!"

He raised his arms, holding them out to her. "*Kum . . . yali, kum buba tambe*," and more magic words, said so quickly, they sounded like whispers and sighs.

The young woman lifted one foot on the air. Then the other. She flew clumsily at first, with the child now held tightly in her arms. Then she felt the magic, the African mystery. Say she rose just as free as a bird. As light as a feather.

The Overseer rode after her, hollerin. Sarah flew over the fences. She flew over the woods. Tall trees could not snag her. Nor could the Overseer. She flew like an eagle now, until she was gone from sight. No one dared speak about it. Couldn't believe it. But it was, because they that was there saw that it was.

Say the next day was dead hot in the fields. A young man slave fell from the heat. The Driver come and whipped him. Toby come over and spoke words to the fallen one. The words of ancient Africa once heard are never remembered completely. The young man forgot them as soon as he heard them. They went way inside him. He got up and rolled over on the air. He rode it awhile. And he flew away.

Another and another fell from the heat. Toby was there. He cried out to the fallen and reached his arms out to them. "*Kum kunka yali, kum . . . tambe!*" Whispers and sighs. And they too rose on the air. They rode the hot breezes. The ones flyin were black and shinin sticks, wheelin above the head of the Overseer. They crossed the rows, the fields, the fences, the streams, and were away.

"Seize the old man!" cried the Overseer. "I heard him say the magic *words*. Seize him!"

The one callin himself Master come runnin. The Driver got his whip ready to curl around old Toby and tie him up. The slaveowner took his hip gun from its place. He meant to kill old, black Toby.

But Toby just laughed. Say he threw back his head and said, "Hee, hee! Don't you know who I am? Don't you know some of us in this field?" He said it to their faces. "We are ones who fly!"

And he sighed the ancient words that were a dark promise. He said them all around to the others in the field under the whip, " . . . *buba yali . . . buba tambe.* . . ."

There was a great outcryin. The bent backs straighted up. Old and young who were called slaves and could fly joined hands. Say like they would ring-sing. But they didn't shuffle in a circle. They

didn't sing. They rose on the air. They flew in a flock that was black against the heavenly blue. Black crows or black shadows. It didn't matter, they went so high. Way above the plantation, way over the slavery land. Say they flew away to *Free-dom.*

And the old man, old Toby, flew behind them, takin care of them. He wasn't cryin. He wasn't laughin. He was the seer. His gaze fell on the plantation where the slaves who could not fly waited.

*"Take us with you!"* Their looks spoke it but they were afraid to shout it. Toby couldn't take them with him. Hadn't the time to teach them to fly. They must wait for a chance to run.

"Goodie-bye!" The old man called Toby spoke to them, poor souls! And he was flyin gone.

So they say. The Overseer told it. The one called Master said it was a lie, a trick of the light. The Driver kept his mouth shut.

The slaves who could not fly told about the people who could fly to their children. When they were free. When they sat close before the fire in the free land, they told it. They did so love firelight and *Free-dom,* and tellin.

They say that the children of the ones who could not fly told their children. And now, me, I have told it to you.

**Reader's Response** ∼ What most impressed you about this folktale?

**Library Link** ∼ *If you enjoyed* The People Could Fly, *you might like to read other books by Virginia Hamilton such as* The Planet of Junior Brown *and* Sweet Whispers, Brother Rush.

# Virginia Hamilton

## A Teller of Tales

"When I decide to write a story, I don't say to myself, now I'm going to write a Black story. But it happens that I know Black people better than any other people because I am one of them and I grew up knowing what it is we are about. I am at ease with being Black. More than anything, I write about emotions, which are part of all people."

Virginia Hamilton was born in 1936, the granddaughter of a fugitive slave. She grew up on an Ohio farm and often draws on her memories of that place and its people in her writings. Listening to the stories told by parents, aunts, uncles, and cousins, she became a teller of tales herself.

Now recognized as one of the nation's foremost authors of stories for young adults, Hamilton has written more than twenty books, many of which have won prestigious awards. Known for her versatility as a writer, she is also an explorer of language and genre. Her books include realistic fiction, folklore, science fiction, fantasy, historical fiction, and biography.

### A Hamilton Sampler

- *The House of Dies Drear*
- *The Mystery of Drear House: Book Two of Dies Drear*
- *The Mystery of Drear House: The Conclusion of the Dies Drear Chronicle*
- *Justice and Her Brother*
- *Dustland*
- *The Gathering*
- *In the Beginning: Creation Stories from Around the World*
- *M.C. Higgins, the Great*

# WEST WITH THE NIGHT

## BY BERYL MARKHAM

*There was hardly an adventure that the young British woman Beryl Markham did not attempt. As a young girl, she lived in the plains of East Africa, training horses on her family's ranch and hunting with native tribespeople. Then in the 1920s she met a veteran flier named Tom Black, and he helped her become the first professional woman pilot in all of Africa, delivering mail and supplies from cities like Cairo, Nairobi, and Kisumu to lonely outposts in the jungle.*

I have seldom dreamed a dream worth dreaming again, or at least none worth recording. Mine are not enigmatic dreams; they are peopled with characters who are plausible and who do plausible things, and I am the most plausible amongst them. All the characters in my dreams have quiet voices like the voice of the man who telephoned me at Elstree one morning in September of nineteen-thirty-six and told me that there was rain and strong head winds over the west of England and over the Irish Sea and that there were variable winds and clear skies in mid-Atlantic and fog off the coast of Newfoundland.

'If you are still determined to fly the Atlantic this late in the year,' the voice said, 'the Air Ministry suggests that the weather it is able to forecast for tonight, and for tomorrow morning, will be about the best you can expect.'

The voice had a few other things to say, but not many, and then it was gone, and I lay in bed half-suspecting that the telephone call and the man who made it were only parts of the mediocre dream I had been dreaming. I felt that if I closed my eyes the unreal quality of the message would be re-established, and that, when I opened them again, this would be another ordinary day with its usual beginning and its usual routine.

But of course I could not close my eyes, nor my mind, nor my memory. I could lie there for a few moments—remembering how it had begun, and telling myself, with senseless repetition, that by tomorrow morning I should either have flown the Atlantic to America—or I should not have flown it. In either case this was the day I would try.

I could stare up at the ceiling of my bedroom in Aldenham House, which was a ceiling undistinguished as ceilings go, and feel less resolute than anxious, much less brave than foolhardy. I could say to myself, 'You needn't do it, of course,' knowing at the same time that nothing is so inexorable as a promise to your pride.

I could ask, 'Why risk it?' as I have been asked since, and I could answer, 'Each to his element.' By his nature a sailor must sail, by his nature a flyer must fly. I could compute that I had flown a quarter of a million miles; and I could foresee that, so long as I had a plane and the sky was there, I should go on flying more miles.

There was nothing extraordinary in this. I had learned a craft and had worked hard learning it. My hands had been taught to seek the controls of a plane. Usage had taught them. They were at ease clinging to a stick, as a cobbler's fingers are in repose grasping an awl. No human pursuit achieves dignity until it can be called work, and when you can experience a physical loneliness for the tools of your trade, you see that the other things—the experiments, the irrelevant vocations, the vanities you used to hold—were false to you.

Record flights had actually never interested me very much for myself. There were people who thought that such flights were done for admiration and publicity, and worse. But of all the records—from Louis Blériot's first crossing of the English Channel in nineteen hundred and nine, through and beyond Kingsford Smith's flight from San Francisco to Sydney, Australia—none had been made by amateurs, nor by novices, nor by men or women less than hardened to failure, or less than masters of their trade. None of these was false. They were a company that simple respect and simple ambition made it worth more than an effort to follow.

The Carberrys (of Seramai) were in London and I could remember everything about their dinner party—even the menu. I could remember June Carberry and all her guests, and the man named McCarthy, who lived in Zanzibar, leaning across the table and saying, 'J. C., why don't you finance Beryl for a record flight?'

I could lie there staring lazily at the ceiling and recall J. C.'s dry answer: 'A number of pilots have flown the North Atlantic, west

to east. Only Jim Mollison has done it alone the other way—from Ireland. Nobody has done it alone from England—man or woman. I'd be interested in that, but nothing else. If you want to try it, Burl, I'll back you. I think Edgar Percival could build a plane that would do it, provided you can fly it. Want to chance it?'

'Yes.'

I could remember saying that better than I could remember anything—except J. C.'s almost ghoulish grin, and his remark that sealed the agreement: 'It's a deal, Burl. I'll furnish the plane and you fly the Atlantic—but, gee, I wouldn't tackle it for a million. Think of all that black water! Think how cold it is!'

And I had thought of both.

I had thought of both for a while, and then there had been other things to think about. I had moved to Elstree, half-hour's flight from the Percival Aircraft Works at Gravesend, and almost daily for three months now I had flown down to the factory in a hired plane and watched the Vega Gull they were making for me. I had watched her birth and watched her growth. I had watched her wings take shape, and seen wood and fabric moulded to her ribs to form her long, sleek belly, and I had seen her engine cradled into her frame, and made fast.

The Gull had a turquoise-blue body and silver wings. Edgar Percival had made her with care, with skill, and with worry—the care of a veteran flyer, the skill of a master designer, and the worry of a friend. Actually the plane was a standard sport model with a range of only six hundred and sixty miles. But she had a special undercarriage built to carry the weight of her extra oil and petrol tanks. The tanks were fixed into the wings, into the centre section, and into the cabin itself. In the cabin they formed a wall around my seat, and each tank had a petcock[1] of its own. The petcocks were important.

'If you open one,' said Percival, 'without shutting the other first, you may get an airlock. You know the tanks in the cabin have no gauges, so it may be best to let one run completely dry before opening the next. Your motor might go dead in the interval—but she'll start again. She's a De Havilland Gipsy—and Gipsys never stop.'

I had talked to Tom. We had spent hours going over the Atlantic chart, and I had realized that the tinker of Molo, now one of England's great pilots, had traded his dreams and had got in return a better thing. Tom had grown older too; he had jettisoned a deadweight of irrelevant hopes and wonders, and had left himself a realistic code that had no room for temporizing or easy sentiment.

'I'm glad you're going to do it, Beryl. It won't be simple. If you can get off the ground in the first place, with such an immense load of fuel, you'll be alone in that plane about a night and a day—mostly night. Doing it east to west, the wind's against you. In September, so is the weather. You won't have a radio. If you misjudge your course only a few degrees, you'll end up in Labrador or in the sea—so don't misjudge anything.'

Tom could still grin. He had grinned; he had said: 'Anyway, it ought to amuse you to think that your financial backer lives on a farm called "Place of Death" and your plane is being built at "Gravesend." If you were consistent, you'd christen the Gull "The Flying Tombstone."'

I hadn't been that consistent. I had watched the building of the plane and I had trained for the flight like an athlete. And now, as I lay in bed, fully awake, I could still hear the quiet voice of the man from the Air Ministry intoning, like the voice of a dispassionate court clerk: '. . . the weather for tonight and tomorrow . . . will be about the best

[1]petcock: valve

you can expect.' I should have liked to discuss the flight once more with Tom before I took off, but he was on a special job up north. I got out of bed and bathed and put on my flying clothes and took some cold chicken packed in a cardboard box and flew over to the military field at Abingdon, where the Vega Gull waited for me under the care of the R.A.F. I remember that the weather was clear and still.

Jim Mollison lent me his watch. He said: 'This is not a gift. I wouldn't part with it for anything. It got me across the North Atlantic and the South Atlantic too. Don't lose it—and, for God's sake, don't get it wet. Salt water would ruin the works.'

Brian Lewis gave me a life-saving jacket. Brian owned the plane I had been using between Elstree and Gravesend, and he had thought a long time about a farewell gift. What could be more practical than a pneumatic jacket that could be inflated through a rubber tube?

'You could float around in it for days,' said Brian. But I had to decide between the life-saver and warm clothes. I couldn't have both, because of their bulk, and I hate the cold, so I left the jacket.

And Jock Cameron, Brian's mechanic, gave me a sprig of heather. If it had been a whole bush of heather, complete with roots growing in an earthen jar, I think I should have taken it, bulky or not. The blessing of Scotland, bestowed by a Scotsman, is not to be dismissed. Nor is the well-wishing of a ground mechanic to be taken lightly, for these men are the pilot's contact with reality.

It is too much that with all those pedestrian centuries behind us we should, in a few decades, have learned to fly; it is too heady a thought, too proud a boast. Only the dirt on a mechanic's hands, the straining vise, the splintered bolt of steel underfoot on the hangar floor—only these and such anxiety as the face of a Jock Cameron can hold for a pilot and his plane before a flight, serve to remind us that, not unlike the heather, we too are earthbound. We fly, but we have not 'conquered' the air. Nature presides in all her dignity, permitting us the study and the use of such of her forces as we may understand. It is when we presume to intimacy, having been granted only tolerance, that the harsh stick falls across our impudent knuckles and we rub the pain, staring upward, startled by our ignorance.

'Here is a sprig of heather,' said Jock, and I took it and pinned it into a pocket of my flying jacket.

There were press cars parked outside the field at Abingdon, and several press planes and photographers, but the R.A.F. kept everyone away from the grounds except technicians and a few of my friends.

The Carberrys had sailed for New York a month ago to wait for me there. Tom was still out of reach with no knowledge of my decision to leave, but that didn't matter so much, I thought. It didn't matter because Tom was unchanging—neither a fairweather pilot nor a fair-weather friend. If for a month, or a year, or two years we sometimes had not seen each other, it still hadn't mattered. Nor did this. Tom would never say, 'You should have let me know.' He assumed that I had learned all that he had tried to teach me, and for my part, I thought of him, even then, as the merest student must think of his mentor. I could sit in a cabin overcrowded with petrol tanks and set my course for North America, but the knowledge of my hands on the controls would be Tom's knowledge. His words of caution and words of guidance, spoken so long ago, so many times, on bright mornings over the veldt or over a forest, or with a far mountain visible at the tip of our wing, would be spoken again, if I asked.

So it didn't matter, I thought. It was silly to think about.


You can live a lifetime and, at the end of it, know more about other people than you know about yourself. You learn to watch other people, but you never watch yourself because you strive against loneliness. If you read a book, or shuffle a deck of cards, or care for a dog, you are avoiding yourself. The abhorrence of loneliness is as natural as wanting to live at all. If it were otherwise, men would never have bothered to make an alphabet, nor to have fashioned words out of what were only animal sounds, nor to have crossed continents—each man to see what the other looked like.

Being alone in an aeroplane for even so short a time as a night and a day, irrevocably alone, with nothing to observe but your instruments and your own hands in semi-darkness, nothing to contemplate but the size of your small courage, nothing to wonder about but the beliefs, the faces, and the hopes rooted in your mind—such an experience can be as startling as the first awareness of a stranger walking by your side at night. You are the stranger.

It is dark already and I am over the south of Ireland. There are the lights of Cork and the lights are wet; they are drenched in Irish rain, and I am above them and dry. I am above them and the plane roars in a sobbing world, but it imparts no sadness to me. I feel the security of solitude, the exhilaration of escape. So long as I can see the lights and imagine the people walking under them, I feel selfishly triumphant, as if I have eluded care and left even the small sorrow of rain in other hands.

It is a little over an hour now since I left Abingdon. England, Wales, and the Irish Sea are behind me like so much time used up. On a long flight distance and time are the same. But there had been a moment when Time stopped—and Distance too. It was the moment I lifted the blue-and-silver Gull from the aerodrome, the moment the photographers aimed their cameras, the moment I felt the craft refuse its burden and strain toward the earth in sullen rebellion, only to listen at last to the persuasion of stick and elevators, the dogmatic argument of blueprints that said she *had* to fly because the figures proved it.

So she had flown, and once airborne, once she had yielded to the sophistry of a draughtsman's board, she had said, 'There: I have lifted the weight. Now, where are we bound?'—and the question had frightened me.

'We are bound for a place thirty-six hundred miles from here—two thousand miles of it unbroken ocean. Most of the way it will be night. We are flying west with the night.'

So there behind me is Cork; and ahead of me is Berehaven Lighthouse. It is the last light, standing on the last land. I watch it, counting the frequency of its flashes—so many to the minute. Then I pass it and fly out to sea.

The fear is gone now—not overcome nor reasoned away. It is gone because something else has taken its place; the confidence and the trust, the inherent belief in the security of land underfoot—now this faith is transferred to my plane, because the land has vanished and

there is no other tangible thing to fix faith upon. Flight is but momentary escape from the eternal custody of earth.

Rain continues to fall, and outside the cabin it is totally dark. My altimeter says that the Atlantic is two thousand feet below me, my Sperry Artificial Horizon says that I am flying level. I judge my drift at three degrees more than my weather chart suggests, and fly accordingly. I am flying blind. A beam to follow would help. So would a radio—but then, so would clear weather. The voice of the man at the Air Ministry had not promised storm.

I feel the wind rising and the rain falls hard. The smell of petrol in the cabin is so strong and the roar of the plane so loud that my senses are almost deadened. Gradually it becomes unthinkable that existence was ever otherwise.

At ten o'clock P.M. I am flying along the Great Circle Course for Harbour Grace, Newfoundland, into a forty-mile headwind at a speed of one hundred and thirty miles an hour. Because of the weather, I cannot be sure of how many more hours I have to fly, but I think it must be between sixteen and eighteen.

At ten-thirty I am still flying on the large cabin tank of petrol, hoping to use it up and put an end to the liquid swirl that has rocked the plane since my take-off. The tank has no gauge, but written on its side is the assurance: 'This tank is good for four hours.'

There is nothing ambiguous about such a guaranty. I believe it, but at twenty-five minutes to eleven, my motor coughs and dies, and the Gull is powerless above the sea.

I realize that the heavy drone of the plane has been, until this moment, complete and comforting silence. It is the actual silence following the last splutter of the engine that stuns me. I can't feel any fear; I can't feel anything. I can only observe with a kind of stupid disinterest that my hands are violently active and know that, while they move, I am being hypnotized by the needle of my altimeter.

I suppose that the denial of natural impulse is what is meant by 'keeping calm,' but impulse has reason in it. If it is night and you are sitting in an aeroplane with a stalled motor, and there are two thousand feet between you and the sea, nothing can be more reasonable than the impulse to pull back your stick in the hope of adding to that two thousand, if only by a little. The thought, the knowledge, the law that tells you that your hope lies not in this, but in a contrary act—the act of directing your impotent craft toward the water—seems a terrifying abandonment, not only of reason, but of sanity. Your mind and your heart reject it. It is your hands—your stranger's hands—that follow with unfeeling precision the letter of the law.

I sit there and watch my hands push forward on the stick and feel the Gull respond and begin its dive to the sea. Of course it is a simple thing; surely the cabin tank has run dry too soon. I need only to turn another petcock . . .

But it is dark in the cabin. It is easy to see the luminous dial of the altimeter and to note that my height is now eleven hundred feet, but it is not easy to see a petcock that is somewhere near the floor of the plane. A hand gropes and reappears with an electric torch, and fingers, moving with agonizing composure, find the petcock and turn it; and I wait.

At three hundred feet the motor is still dead, and I am conscious that the needle of my altimeter seems to whirl like the spoke of a spindle winding up the remaining distance between the plane and the

229

water. There is some lightning, but the quick flash only serves to emphasize the darkness. How high can waves reach—twenty feet, perhaps? Thirty?

It is impossible to avoid the thought that this is the end of my flight, but my reactions are not orthodox; the various incidents of my entire life do not run through my mind like a motion-picture film gone mad. I only feel that all this has happened before—and it has. It has all happened a hundred times in my mind, in my sleep, so that now I am not really caught in terror; I recognize a familiar scene, a familiar story with its climax dulled by too much telling.

I do not know how close to the waves I am when the motor explodes to life again. But the sound is almost meaningless. I see my hand easing back on the stick, and I feel the Gull climb up into the storm, and I see the altimeter whirl like a spindle again, paying out the distance between myself and the sea.

The storm is strong. It is comforting. It is like a friend shaking me and saying, 'Wake up! You were only dreaming.'

But soon I am thinking. By simple calculation I find that my motor had been silent for perhaps an instant more than thirty seconds.

I ought to thank God—and I do, though indirectly. I thank Geoffrey De Havilland who designed the indomitable Gipsy, and who, after all, must have been designed by God in the first place.

A lighted ship—the daybreak—some steep cliffs standing in the sea. The meaning of these will never change for pilots. If one day an ocean can be flown within an hour, if men can build a plane that so masters time, the sight of land will be no less welcome to the steersman of that fantastic craft. He will have cheated laws that the cunning of science has taught him how to cheat, and he will feel his guilt and be eager for the sanctuary of the soil.

I saw the ship and the daybreak, and then I saw the cliffs of Newfoundland wound in ribbons of fog. I felt the elation I had so long imagined, and I felt the happy guilt of having circumvented the stern authority of the weather and the sea. But mine was a minor triumph; my swift Gull was not so swift as to have escaped unnoticed. The night and the storm had caught her and we had flown blind for nineteen hours.

230

I was tired now, and cold. Ice began to film the glass of the cabin windows and the fog played a magician's game with the land. But the land was there. I could not see it, but I had seen it. I could not afford to believe that it was any land but the land I wanted. I could not afford to believe that my navigation was at fault, because there was no time for doubt.

South to Cape Race, west to Sydney on Cape Breton Island. With my protractor, my map, and my compass, I set my new course, humming the ditty that Tom had taught me: 'Variation West—magnetic best. Variation East—magnetic least.' A silly rhyme, but it served to placate, for the moment, two warring poles—the magnetic and the true. I flew south and found the lighthouse of Cape Race protruding from the fog like a warning finger, I circled twice and went on over the Gulf of Saint Lawrence.

After a while there would be New Brunswick, and then Maine— and then New York. I could anticipate. I could almost say, 'Well, if you stay awake, you'll find it's only a matter of time now' —but there was no question of staying awake. I was tired and I had not moved an inch since that uncertain moment at Abingdon when the Gull had elected to rise with her load and fly, but I could not have closed my eyes. I could sit there in the cabin, walled in glass and petrol tanks, and be grateful for the sun and the light, and the fact that I could see the water under me. They were almost the last waves I had to pass. Four hundred miles of water, but then the land again—Cape Breton. I would stop at Sydney to refuel and go on. It was easy now. It would be like stopping at Kisumu and going on.

Success breeds confidence. But who has a right to confidence except the Gods? I had a following wind, my last tank of petrol was more than three-quarters full, and the world was as bright to me as if it were a new world, never touched. If I had been wiser, I might have known that such moments are, like innocence, short-lived. My engine began to shudder before I saw the land. It died, it spluttered, it started again and limped along. It coughed and spat black exhaust toward the sea.

There are words for everything. There was a word for this— airlock, I thought. This had to be an airlock because there was petrol enough. I thought I might clear it by turning on and turning off all the empty tanks, and so I did that. The handles of the petcocks were sharp little pins of metal, and when I had opened and closed them a dozen times, I saw that my hands were bleeding and that the blood was dropping on my maps and on my clothes, but the effort wasn't any good. I coasted along on a sick and halting engine. The oil pressure and the oil temperature gauges were normal, the magnetos working, and yet I lost altitude slowly while the realization of failure seeped into my heart. If I made the land, I should have been the first to fly the North Atlantic from England, but from my point of view, from a pilot's point of view, a forced landing was failure because New York was my goal. If only I could land and then take off, I would make it still . . . if only, if only . . .

The engine cuts again, and then catches, and each time it spurts to life I climb as high as I can get, and then it splutters and stops and I glide once more toward the water, to rise again and descend again, like a hunting sea bird.

I find the land. Visibility is perfect now and I see land forty or fifty miles ahead. If I am on my course, that will be Cape Breton. Minute after minute goes by. The minutes almost materialize; they pass before my eyes like links in a long slow-moving chain, and each time the engine cuts, I see a broken link in the chain and catch my breath until it passes.

The land is under me. I snatch my map and stare at it to confirm my whereabouts. I am, even at my present crippled speed, only twelve minutes from Sydney Airport, where I can land for repairs and then go on.

The engine cuts once more and I begin to glide, but now I am not worried; she will start again, as she has done, and I will gain altitude and fly into Sydney.

But she doesn't start. This time she's dead as death; the Gull settles earthward and it isn't any earth I know. It is black earth stuck with boulders and I hang above it, on hope and on a motionless propeller. Only I cannot hang above it long. The earth hurries to meet me, I bank, turn, and sideslip to dodge the boulders, my wheels touch, and I feel them submerge. The nose of the plane is engulfed in mud, and I go forward striking my head on the glass of the cabin front, hearing it shatter, feeling blood pour over my face.

I stumble out of the plane and sink to my knees in muck and stand there foolishly staring, not at the lifeless land, but at my watch.

Twenty-one hours and twenty-five minutes.

Atlantic flight. Abingdon, England, to a nameless swamp — nonstop.

A Cape Breton Islander found me — a fisherman trudging over the bog saw the Gull with her tail in the air and her nose buried, and then he saw me floundering in the embracing soil of his native land. I had been wandering for an hour and the black mud had got up to my waist and the blood from the cut in my head had met the mud halfway.

From a distance, the fisherman directed me with his arms and with shouts toward the firm places in the bog, and for another hour I walked on them and came toward him like a citizen of Hades blinded by the sun, but it wasn't the sun; I hadn't slept for forty hours.

He took me to his hut on the edge of the coast and I found that built upon the rocks there was a little cubicle that housed an ancient telephone—put there in case of shipwrecks.

I telephoned to Sydney Airport to say that I was safe and to prevent a needless search being made. On the following morning I did step out of a plane at Floyd Bennett Field and there was a crowd of people still waiting there to greet me, but the plane I stepped from was not the Gull, and for days while I was in New York I kept thinking about that and wishing over and over again that it had been the Gull, until the wish lost its significance, and time moved on, overcoming many things it met on the way.

Reader's Response ∽ Do you think you would have had the courage to do what Beryl Markham did?

# FIRSTS IN FLIGHT

Louis Blériot

Amelia Earhart

Jeana Yeager & Dick Yutan

**1783**

Two adventurous Frenchmen become the first to fly in a hot-air balloon.

**1852**

The first steam-powered dirigible, built by a French engineer, reaches a speed of 6.7 mph.

**1891**

German inventor and airplane designer Otto Lilienthal builds the first piloted glider.

**1903**

The Wright Brothers make the first successful heavier-than-air machine flight, in Kitty Hawk, North Carolina.

**1909**

Louis Blériot makes the first flight across the English Channel.

**1919**

Two British pilots make the first nonstop transatlantic flight, from Newfoundland to Ireland.

**1926**

Navigator Richard Byrd and pilot Floyd Bennett make the first flight over the North Pole.

**1927**

Charles Lindbergh makes the first solo nonstop trans-atlantic flight.

**1932**

Amelia Earhart becomes the first woman to fly solo across the Atlantic.

**1939**

A German pilot makes the first successful flight of a jet-engine plane.

**1947**

Chuck Yeager, a pilot in the United States Air Force, makes the first piloted super-sonic flight.

**1986**

Dick Yutan and Jeana Yeager make the first nonstop around-the-world flight without refueling.

# DARK THEY WERE, AND GOLDEN-EYED

## by Ray Bradbury

*The Bittering family has traveled all the way from Earth to Mars.*
*They wonder how they will be affected by a world that is so different.*

The rocket metal cooled in the meadow winds. Its lid gave a bulging *pop*. From its clock interior stepped a man, a woman, and three children. The other passengers whispered away across the Martian meadow, leaving the man alone among his family.

The man felt his hair flutter and the tissues of his body draw tight as if he were standing at the center of a vacuum. His wife, before him, seemed almost to whirl away in smoke. The children, small seeds, might at any instant be sown to all the Martian climes.

The children looked up at him, as people look to the sun to tell what time of their life it is. His face was cold.

236

"What's wrong?" asked his wife.

"Let's get back on the rocket."

"Go back to Earth?"

"Yes! Listen!"

The wind blew as if to flake away their identities. At any moment the Martian air might draw his soul from him, as marrow comes from a white bone. He felt submerged in a chemical that could dissolve his intellect and burn away his past.

They looked at Martian hills that time had worn with a crushing pressure of years. They saw the old cities, lost in their meadows, lying like children's delicate bones among the blowing lakes of grass.

"Chin up, Harry," said his wife. "It's too late. We've come over sixty million miles."

The children with their yellow hair hollered at the deep dome of Martian sky. There was no answer but the racing hiss of wind through the stiff grass.

He picked up the luggage in his cold hands. "Here we go," he said—a man standing on the edge of a sea, ready to wade in and be drowned.

They walked into town.

Their name was Bittering. Harry and his wife Cora; Dan, Laura, and David. They built a small white cottage and ate good breakfasts there, but the fear was never gone. It lay with Mr. Bittering and Mrs. Bittering, a third unbidden partner at every midnight talk, at every dawn awakening.

"I feel like a salt crystal," he said, "in a mountain stream, being washed away. We don't belong here. We're Earth people. This is Mars. It was meant for Martians. For heaven's sake, Cora, let's buy tickets for home!"

But she only shook her head. "One day the atom bomb will fix Earth. Then we'll be safe here."

"Safe and insane!"

*Tick-tock, seven o'clock* sang the voice-clock; *time to get up.* And they did.

Something made him check everything each morning—warm hearth, potted blood-geraniums—precisely as if he expected something to be amiss. The morning paper was toast-warm from the 6 A.M. Earth rocket. He broke its seal and tilted it at his breakfast place. He forced himself to be convivial.

"Colonial days all over again," he declared. "Why, in ten years there'll be a million Earth Men on Mars. Big cities, everything! They said we'd fail. Said the Martians would resent our invasion. But did we find any Martians? Not a living soul! Oh, we found their empty cities, but no one in them. Right?"

A river of wind submerged the house. When the windows ceased rattling Mr. Bittering swallowed and looked at the children.

"I don't know," said David. "Maybe there're Martians around we don't see. Sometimes nights I think I hear 'em. I hear the wind. The sand hits my window. I get scared. And I see those towns way up in

237

the mountains where the Martians lived a long time ago. And I think I see things moving around those towns, Papa. And I wonder if those Martians *mind* us living here. I wonder if they won't do something to us for coming here."

"Nonsense!" Mr. Bittering looked out the windows. "We're clean, decent people." He looked at his children. "All dead cities have some kind of ghosts in them. Memories, I mean." He stared at the hills. "You see a staircase and you wonder what Martians looked like climbing it. You see Martian paintings and you wonder what the painter was like. You make a little ghost in your mind, a memory. It's quite natural. Imagination." He stopped. "You haven't been prowling up in those ruins, have you?"

"No, Papa." David looked at his shoes.

"See that you stay away from them. Pass the jam."

"Just the same," said little David, "I bet something happens."

Something happened that afternoon.

Laura stumbled through the settlement, crying. She dashed blindly onto the porch.

"Mother, Father—the war, Earth!" she sobbed. "A radio flash just came. Atom bombs hit New York! All the space rockets blown up. No more rockets to Mars, ever!"

"Oh, Harry!" The mother held onto her husband and daughter.

"Are you sure, Laura?" asked the father quietly.

Laura wept. "We're stranded on Mars, forever and ever!"

For a long time there was only the sound of the wind in the late afternoon.

Alone, thought Bittering. Only a thousand of us here. No way back. No way. No way. Sweat poured from his face and his hands and his body; he was drenched in the hotness of his fear. He wanted to strike Laura, cry, "No, you're lying! The rockets will come back!" Instead, he stroked Laura's head against him and said, "The rockets will get through someday."

"Father, what will we do?"

"Go about our business, of course. Raise crops and children. Wait. Keep things going until the war ends and the rockets come again."

The two boys stepped out onto the porch.

"Children," he said, sitting there, looking beyond them, "I've something to tell you."

"We know," they said.

In the following days, Bittering wandered often through the garden to stand alone in his fear. As long as the rockets had spun a silver web across space, he had been able to accept Mars. For he had always told himself: Tomorrow, if I want, I can buy a ticket and go back to Earth.

But now: The web gone, the rockets lying in jigsaw heaps of molten girder and unsnaked wire. Earth people left to the strangeness of Mars, the cinnamon dusts and wine airs, to be baked like gingerbread shapes in Martian summers, put into harvested storage by Martian winters. What would happen to him, the others? This was the moment Mars had waited for. Now it would eat them.

He got down on his knees in the flower bed, a spade in his nervous hands. Work, he thought, work and forget.

He glanced up from the garden to the Martian mountains. He thought of the proud old Martian names that had once been on those peaks. Earth Men, dropping from the sky, had gazed upon hills, rivers, Martian seas left nameless in spite of names. Once Martians had built cities, named cities; climbed mountains, named mountains; sailed seas, named seas. Mountains melted, seas drained, cities tumbled. In spite of this, the Earth Men had felt a silent guilt at putting new names to these ancient hills and valleys.

Nevertheless, man lives by symbol and label. The names were given.

Mr. Bittering felt very alone in his garden under the Martian sun, anachronism bent here, planting Earth flowers in a wild soil.

Think. Keep thinking. Different things. Keep your mind free of Earth, the atom war, the lost rockets.

He perspired. He glanced about. No one watching. He removed his tie. Pretty bold, he thought. First your coat off, now your tie. He hung it neatly on a peach tree he had imported as a sapling from Massachusetts.

He returned to his philosophy of names and mountains. The Earth Men had changed names. Now there were Hormel Valleys, Roosevelt Seas, Ford Hills, Vanderbilt Plateaus, Rockefeller Rivers, on Mars. It wasn't right. The American settlers had shown wisdom, using old Indian prairie names: Wisconsin, Minnesota, Idaho, Ohio, Utah, Milwaukee, Waukegan, Osseo. The old names, the old meanings.

Staring at the mountains wildly, he thought: Are you up there? All the dead ones, you Martians? Well, here we are, alone, cut off! Come down, move us out! We're helpless!

The wind blew a shower of peach blossoms.

He put out his sun-browned hand, gave a small cry. He touched the blossoms, picked them up. He turned them, he touched them again and again. Then he shouted for his wife.

"Cora!"

She appeared at a window. He ran to her.

"Cora, these blossoms!"

She handled them.

"Do you see? They're different. They've changed! They're not peach blossoms any more!"

"Look all right to me," she said.

"They're not. They're *wrong!* I can't

tell how. An extra petal, a leaf, something, the color, the smell!''

The children ran out in time to see their father hurrying about the garden, pulling up radishes, onions, and carrots from their beds.

"Cora, come look!''

They handled the onions, the radishes, the carrots among them.

"Do they look like carrots?''

"Yes . . . no.'' She hesitated. "I don't know.''

"They're changed.''

"Perhaps.''

"You know they have! Onions but not onions, carrots but not carrots. Taste: the same but different. Smell: not like it used to be.'' He felt his heart pounding, and he was afraid. He dug his fingers into the earth. "Cora, what's happening? What is it? We've got to get away from this.'' He ran across the garden. Each tree felt his touch. "The roses. The roses. They're turning green!''

And they stood looking at the green roses.

And two days later Dan came running. "Come see the cow. I was milking her and I saw it. Come on!''

They stood in the shed and looked at their one cow.

It was growing a third horn.

And the lawn in front of their house very quietly and slowly was coloring itself like spring violets. Seed from Earth but growing up a soft purple.

"We must get away,'' said Bittering.

"We'll eat this stuff and then we'll change— who knows to what? I can't let it happen. There's only one thing to do. Burn this food!"

"It's not poisoned."

"But it is. Subtly, very subtly. A little bit. A very little bit. We mustn't touch it."

He looked with dismay at their house. "Even the house. The wind's done something to it. The air's burned it. The fog at night. The boards, all warped out of shape. It's not an Earth Man's house any more."

"Oh, your imagination!"

He put on his coat and tie. "I'm going into town. We've got to do something now. I'll be back."

"Wait, Harry!" his wife cried.

But he was gone.

In town, on the shadowy step of the grocery store, the men sat with their hands on their knees, conversing with great leisure and ease.

Mr. Bittering wanted to fire a pistol in the air.

What are you doing, you fools! he thought. Sitting here! You've heard the news—we're stranded on this planet. Well, move! Aren't you frightened? Aren't you afraid? What are you going to do?

"Hello, Harry," said everyone.

"Look," he said to them. "You did hear the news, the other day, didn't you?"

They nodded and laughed. "Sure. Sure, Harry."

"What are you going to do about it?"

"Do, Harry, do? What *can* we do?"

"Build a rocket, that's what!"

"A rocket, Harry? To go back to all that trouble? Oh, Harry!"

"But you *must* want to go back. Have you noticed the peach blossoms, the onions, the grass?"

"Why, yes, Harry, seems we did," said one of the men.

"Doesn't it scare you?"

"Can't recall that it did much, Harry."

"Idiots!"

"Now, Harry."

Bittering wanted to cry. "You've got to work with me. If we stay here, we'll all change. The air. Don't you smell it? Something in the air. A Martian virus, maybe; some seed, or a pollen. Listen to me!"

They stared at him.

"Sam," he said to one of them.

"Yes, Harry?"

"Will you help me build a rocket?"

"Harry, I got a whole load of metal and some blueprints. You want to work in my metal shop on a rocket, you're welcome. I'll sell you that metal for five hundred dollars. You should be able to construct a right pretty rocket, if you work alone, in about thirty years."

Everyone laughed.

"Don't laugh."

Sam looked at him with quiet good humor.

"Sam," Bittering said. "Your eyes—"

"What about them, Harry?"

"Didn't they used to be grey?"

"Well now, I don't remember."

"They were, weren't they?"

"Why do you ask, Harry?"

"Because now they're kind of yellow-colored."

"Is that so, Harry?" Sam said, casually.

"And you're taller and thinner—"

"You might be right, Harry."

"Sam, you shouldn't have yellow eyes."

"Harry, what color eyes have *you* got?" Sam said.

"My eyes? They're blue, of course."

"Here you are, Harry." Sam handed him a pocket mirror. "Take a look at yourself."

Mr. Bittering hesitated, and then raised the mirror to his face.

There were little, very dim flecks of new gold captured in the blue of his eyes.

"Now look what you've done," said Sam a moment later. "You've broken my mirror."

Harry Bittering moved into the metal shop and began to build the rocket. Men stood in the open door and talked and joked without raising their voices. Once in a while they gave him a hand on lifting something. But mostly they just idled and watched him with their yellowing eyes.

"It's suppertime, Harry," they said.

His wife appeared with his supper in a wicker basket.

"I won't touch it," he said. "I'll eat only food from our Deepfreeze. Food that came from Earth. Nothing from our garden."

His wife stood watching him. "You can't build a rocket."

"I worked in a shop once, when I was twenty. I know metal. Once I get it started, the others will help," he said, not looking at her, laying out the blueprints.

"Harry, Harry," she said, helplessly.

"We've got to get away, Cora. We've *got* to!"

The nights were full of wind that blew down the empty moonlit sea meadows past the little white chess cities lying for their twelve-thousandth year in the shallows. In the Earth Men's settlement, the Bittering house shook with a feeling of change.

Lying abed, Mr. Bittering felt his bones shifted, shaped, melted like gold. His wife, lying beside him, was dark from many sunny afternoons. Dark she was, and golden-eyed, burnt almost black by the sun, sleeping, and the children metallic in their beds, and the wind roaring forlorn and changing through the old peach trees, the violet grass, shaking out green rose petals.

The fear would not be stopped. It had his throat and heart. It dripped in a wetness of the arm and the temple and the trembling palm.

A green star rose in the east.

A strange word emerged from Mr. Bittering's lips.

"*Iorrt. Iorrt.*" He repeated it.

It was a Martian word. He knew no Martian.

In the middle of the night he arose and dialed a call through to Simpson, the archaeologist.

"Simpson, what does the word *Iorrt* mean?"

"Why that's the old Martian word for our planet Earth. Why?"

"No special reason."

The telephone slipped from his hand.

"Hello, hello, hello, hello," it kept saying while he sat gazing out at the green star. "Bittering? Harry, are you there?"

The days were full of metal sound. He laid the frame of the rocket with the reluctant help of three indifferent men. He grew very tired in an hour or so and had to sit down.

"The altitude," laughed a man.

"Are you *eating*, Harry?" asked another.

"I'm eating," he said, angrily.

"From your Deepfreeze?"

"Yes!"

"You're getting thinner, Harry."

"I'm not!"

"And taller."

"Liar!"

His wife took him aside a few days later. "Harry, I've used up all the food in the Deepfreeze. There's nothing left. I'll have to make sandwiches using food grown on Mars."

He sat down heavily.

"You must eat," she said. "You're weak."

"Yes," he said.

He took a sandwich, opened it, looked at it, and began to nibble at it.

"And take the rest of the day off," she said. "It's hot. The children want to swim in the canals and hike. Please come along."

"I can't waste time. This is a crisis!"

"Just for an hour," she urged. "A swim'll do you good."

He rose, sweating. "All right, all right. Leave me alone. I'll come."

"Good for you, Harry."

The sun was hot, the day quiet. There was only an immense staring burn upon the land. They moved along the canal, the father, the mother, the racing children in their swim suits. They stopped and ate meat sandwiches. He saw their skin baking brown. And he saw the yellow eyes of his wife and his children, their eyes that were never yellow before. A few tremblings shook him, but were carried off in waves of pleasant heat as he lay in the sun. He was too tired to be afraid.

"Cora, how long have your eyes been yellow?"

She was bewildered. "Always, I guess."

"They didn't change from brown in the last three months?"

She bit her lips. "No. Why do you ask?"

"Never mind."

They sat there.

"The children's eyes," he said. "They're yellow, too."

"Sometimes growing children's eyes change color."

"Maybe *we're* children, too. At least to Mars. That's a thought." He laughed. "Think I'll swim."

They leaped into the canal water, and he let himself sink down and down to the bottom like a golden statue and lie there in green silence. All was water-quiet and deep, all was peace. He felt the steady, slow current drift him easily.

If I lie here long enough, he thought, the water will work and eat away my flesh until the bones show like coral. Just my skeleton left. And then the water can build on that skeleton—green things, deep water things, red things, yellow things. Change. Change. Slow, deep, silent change. And isn't that what it is up *there*?

He saw the sky submerged above him, the sun made Martian by atmosphere and time and space.

Up there, a big river, he thought, a Martian river, all of us lying deep in it, in our pebble houses, in our sunken boulder houses, like crayfish hidden, and the water washing away our old bodies and lengthening the bones and—

He let himself drift up through the soft light.

Dan sat on the edge of the canal, regarding his father seriously.

"*Utha,*" he said.

"What?" asked his father.

The boy smiled. "You know. *Utha's* the Martian word for 'father.' "

"Where did you learn it?"

"I don't know. Around. *Utha!*"

"What do you want?"

The boy hesitated. "I—I want to change my name."

"Change it?"

"Yes."

His mother swam over. "What's wrong with Dan for a name?"

Dan fidgeted. "The other day you called Dan, Dan, Dan. I didn't even hear. I said to myself, That's not my name. I've a new name I want to use."

Mr. Bittering held to the side of the canal, his body cold and his heart pounding slowly. "What is this new name?"

"Linnl. Isn't that a good name? Can I use it? Can't I, please?"

Mr. Bittering put his hand to his head. He thought of the silly rocket, himself working alone, himself alone even among his family, so alone.

He heard his wife say, "Why not?"

He heard himself say, "Yes, you can use it."

"Yaaa!" screamed the boy. "I'm Linnl, Linnl!"

Racing down the meadowlands, he danced and shouted.

Mr. Bittering looked at his wife. "Why did we do that?"

"I don't know," she said. "It just seemed like a good idea."

They walked into the hills. They strolled on old mosaic paths, beside still pumping fountains. The paths were covered with a thin film of cool water all summer long. You kept your bare feet cool all the day, splashing as in a creek, wading.

They came to a small deserted Martian villa with a good view of the valley. It was on top of a hill. Blue marble halls, large murals, a swimming pool. It was refreshing in this hot summertime. The Martians hadn't believed in large cities.

"How nice," said Mrs. Bittering, "if we could move up here to this villa for the summer."

"Come on," he said. "We're going back to town. There's work to be done on the rocket."

But as he worked that night, the thought of the cool blue marble villa entered his mind. As the hours passed, the rocket seemed less important.

In the flow of days and weeks, the rocket receded and dwindled. The old fever was gone. It frightened him to think he had let it slip this way. But somehow the heat, the air, the working conditions—

He heard the men murmuring on the porch of his metal shop.

"Everyone's going. You heard?"

"All going. That's right."

Bittering came out. "Going where?" He saw a couple of trucks, loaded with children and furniture, drive down the dusty street.

"Up to the villas," said the man.

"Yeah, Harry. I'm going. So is Sam. Aren't you, Sam?"

"That's right, Harry. What about you?"

"I've got work to do here."

"Work! You can finish that rocket in the autumn, when it's cooler."

He took a breath. "I got the frame all set up."

"In the autumn is better." Their voices were lazy in the heat.

"Got to work," he said.

"Autumn," they reasoned. And they sounded so sensible, so right.

"Autumn would be best," he thought. "Plenty of time, then."

No! cried part of himself, deep down, put away, locked tight, suffocating. No! No!

"In the autumn," he said.

"Come on, Harry," they all said.

"Yes," he said, feeling his flesh melt in the hot liquid air. "Yes, in the autumn. I'll begin work again then."

"I got a villa near the Tirra Canal," said someone.

"You mean the Roosevelt Canal, don't you?"

"Tirra. The old Martian name."

"But on the map—"

"Forget the map. It's Tirra now. Now I found a place in the Pillan mountains—"

"You mean the Rockefeller range," said Bittering.

"I mean the Pillan mountains," said Sam.

"Yes," said Bittering, buried in the hot, swarming air. "The Pillan mountains."

Everyone worked at loading the truck in the hot, still afternoon of the next day.

Laura, Dan, and David carried packages. Or, as they preferred to be known, Ttil, Linnl, and Werr carried packages.

The furniture was abandoned in the little white cottage.

"It looked just fine in Boston," said

the mother. "And here in the cottage. But up at the villa? No. We'll get it when we come back in the autumn."

Bittering himself was quiet.

"I've some ideas on furniture for the villa," he said after a time. "Big, lazy furniture."

"What about your encyclopedia? You're taking it along, surely?"

Mr. Bittering glanced away. "I'll come and get it next week."

They turned to their daughter. "What about your New York dresses?"

The bewildered girl stared. "Why, I don't want them any more."

They shut off the gas, the water, they locked the doors and walked away. Father peered into the truck.

"Gosh, we're not taking much," he said. "Considering all we brought to Mars, this is only a handful!"

He started the truck.

Looking at the small white cottage for a long moment, he was filled with a desire to rush to it, touch it, say good-by to it, for he felt as if he were going away on a long journey, leaving something to which he could never quite return, never understand again.

Just then Sam and his family drove by in another truck.

"Hi, Bittering! Here we go!"

The truck swung down the ancient highway out of town. There were sixty others traveling the same direction. The town filled with a silent, heavy dust from their passage. The canal waters lay blue in the sun, and a quiet wind moved in the strange trees.

"Good-by, town!" said Mr. Bittering.

"Good-by, good-by," said the family, waving to it.

They did not look back again.

Summer burned the canals dry. Summer moved like flame upon the meadows. In the empty Earth settlement, the painted houses flaked and peeled. Rubber tires upon which children had swung in back yards hung suspended like stopped clock pendulums in the blazing air.

At the metal shop, the rocket frame began to rust.

In the quiet autumn Mr. Bittering stood, very dark now, very golden-eyed, upon the slope above his villa, looking at the valley.

"It's time to go back," said Cora.

"Yes, but we're not going," he said quietly. "There's nothing there any more."

"Your books," she said. "Your fine clothes.

"Your *llles* and your fine *ior uele rre*," she said.

"The town's empty. No one's going back," he said. "There's no reason to, none at all."

The daughter wove tapestries and the sons played songs on ancient flutes and pipes, their laughter echoing in the marble villa.

Mr. Bittering gazed at the Earth settlement far away in the low valley. "Such odd, such ridiculous houses the Earth people built."

246

"They didn't know any better," his wife mused. "Such ugly people. I'm glad they've gone."

They both looked at each other, startled by all they had just finished saying. They laughed.

"Where did they go?" he wondered. He glanced at his wife. She was golden and slender as his daughter. She looked at him, and he seemed almost as young as their eldest son.

"I don't know," she said.

"We'll go back to town maybe next year, or the year after, or the year after that," he said, calmly. "Now—I'm warm. How about taking a swim?"

They turned their backs to the valley. Arm in arm they walked silently down a path of clear-running spring water.

Five years later a rocket fell out of the sky. It lay steaming in the valley. Men leaped out of it, shouting.

"We won the war on Earth! We're here to rescue you! Hey!"

But the American-built town of cottages, peach trees, and theaters was silent. They found a flimsy rocket frame rusting in an empty shop.

The rocket men searched the hills. The captain established headquarters in an abandoned bar. His lieutenant came back to report.

"The town's empty, but we found native life in the hills, sir. Dark people. Yellow eyes. Martians. Very friendly. We talked a

bit, not much. They learn English fast. I'm sure our relations will be most friendly with them, sir."

"Dark, eh?" mused the captain. "How many?"

"Six, eight hundred, I'd say, living in those marble ruins in the hills, sir. Tall, healthy. Beautiful women."

"Did they tell you what became of the men and women who built this Earth-settlement, Lieutenant?"

"They hadn't the foggiest notion of what happened to this town or its people."

"Strange. You think those Martians killed them?"

"They look surprisingly peaceful. Chances are a plague did this town in, sir."

"Perhaps. I suppose this is one of those mysteries we'll never solve. One of those mysteries you read about."

The captain looked at the room, the dusty windows, the blue mountains rising beyond, the canals moving in the light, and he heard the soft wind in the air. He shiv-ered. Then, recovering, he tapped a large fresh map he had thumbtacked to the top of an empty table.

"Lots to be done, Lieutenant." His voice droned on and quietly on as the sun sank behind the blue hills. "New settlements. Mining sites, minerals to be looked for. Bacteriological specimens taken. The work, all the work. And the old records were lost. We'll have a job of remapping to do, renaming the mountains and rivers and such. Calls for a little imagination.

"What do you think of naming those mountains the Lincoln Mountains, this canal the Washington Canal, those hills—we can name those hills for you, Lieutenant. Diplomacy. And you, for a favor, might name a town for me. Polishing the apple. And why not make this the Einstein Valley, and further over . . . are you *listening*, Lieutenant?"

The lieutenant snapped his gaze from the blue color and the quiet mist of the hills far beyond the town.

"What? Oh, *yes*, sir!"

Reader's Response ∾ Do you think the Bitterings were happier as settlers from earth or as "Martians?"

Library Link ∾ *If you're interested in other stories by Ray Bradbury, look for* S Is for Space *in your school or local library.*

# IS THERE LIFE ON MARS?

When early astronomers looked at our neighboring planet Mars, they detected Earthlike features. Polar ice caps grew and shrank; there appeared to be open seas; a Mars day was just over 24 hours long; and its tilted axis gave it four seasons. Since Mars was so like Earth, they supposed it too must be inhabited.

In 1877 the Italian astronomer Giovanni Schiaparelli observed lines on Mars' surface, which he called *canali*, or channels. He drew no conclusions about what caused them, but *canali* was translated into English as "canals." The only canals on Earth were built by humans. It stood to reason, then, that the canals on Mars had been built by Martians.

In 1898 the writer H.G. Wells published *The War of the Worlds*, in which he describes technologically advanced Martians invading Earth with deadly weapons. One Sunday evening forty years later, the American actor Orson Welles and the *Mercury Theatre on the Air* broadcast a radio play based on Wells's book. The broadcast made it seem as though the invasion were actually taking place in a New Jersey town called Grovers Mill. Of the millions who listened, many never heard the announcement that the broadcast was "only a play," and thought that the Martians had, in fact, landed. People ran screaming into the streets, called police stations and armories for protection, and gathered in churches to pray. The mass panic made history.

In 1911 Edgar Rice Burroughs published the first of his very popular books about life on Mars, called "Barsoom" by its inhabitants.

One child who was fascinated by the books was Ray Bradbury. As an adult, Bradbury wrote his own stories about Mars. His book *The Martian Chronicles* is now a science-fiction classic.

Twenty-five years after Bradbury's tales of Earth colonists and Martians were published, an unmanned spacecraft from Earth landed on Mars.

What did it discover?

# I Shot an Arrow

## by Rod Serling

## Characters

*In the Monitor Control Room*
LANGFORD, *chief of the control room*
BRANDT, *technician in the television
control room*

MEMBERS OF THE STAFF

NARRATOR

*The Aircraft Crew*
COLONEL R. G. DONLIN, *commander of*
Arrow One *airship*
FLIGHT OFFICER COREY, *member of flight
crew*
FLIGHT OFFICER PIERSON, *member of
flight crew*
NAVIGATOR HUDAK, *crew member,
hurt in the crash landing*

## ACT ONE

FADE IN: *Shot of the sky: the various neb-
ulae and the planet bodies stand out in
sharp, sparkling relief. The camera pans
down and we see a huge rocket poised
for launching, on it the lettering, "Arrow
One."*

NARRATOR'S VOICE. *(Offscreen.)* There is
a fifth dimension beyond that which is
known to man. It is a dimension as vast as
space and as timeless as infinity. It is the
middle ground between light and shadow, between science and superstition.
And it lies between the pit of his fears and
the summit of his knowledge. This is the
dimension of imagination. It is an area we
call The Twilight Zone.

DISSOLVE TO: *Interior of the Launching
Control Room. It is night. The launching
team is now busily engaged in the final
seconds of the countdown. The room
consists mainly of television monitors,
automatic controls, receivers and a large
plotting chart.*

BRANDT'S VOICE. *(Offscreen.)* Minus fifteen. Minus fourteen. Minus thirteen . . .

NARRATOR'S VOICE. Her name is *Arrow
One.* She represents four and a half years
of planning, preparation and training; and
a thousand years of science and mathematics and the projected dreams and
hopes of not only a nation but a world.
She is the first manned aircraft into space.
And this is the countdown, the last five
seconds before man shot an arrow into
the air.

BRANDT'S VOICE. Minus three. Minus
two. Minus one. Minus zero.

The camera pulls back to where a man wearing a head set and speaker is writing in the word "unreported" across the incomplete vector-path of an object labeled "Arrow One." Brandt is sitting at his paper-littered desk, confronted by Langford, obviously the man in authority.

LANGFORD. *(Excited.)* Well, what do you mean we've lost it? I mean, with all the monitors we have going . . .

BRANDT. *(Cutting in.)* We could have fifteen thousand monitors, but the situation would be the same. We've lost contact. She's off her vector-path, off the radar screen. Just gone, completely gone.

LANGFORD. *(Turns away, rubbing his jaw reflectively. He walks over to a radar screen, reaches out and flicks at it nervously with a finger.)* So an aircraft with an eight-man crew just disappears like a puff of smoke. One moment she's there; the next moment she's gone. *(Musingly and softly.)* I shot an arrow into the air.
It landed I know not where.
An old rhyme for the age of space.
Gentlemen, wherever you are . . .
God help you!

FADE TO BLACK

FADE TO: *The barren, rocky face of a blistering desert. The mountains in the background are pure bedrock, jagged shapes from another world. The upper portion of a space aircraft comes into view, gradually taking shape through a cloud of smoke. A*
side panel of the ship shows the lettering, "Arrow One." The ship is nose down in the sand. In the foreground we see men carrying bodies of fellow crew members. Donlin, Pierson and Corey are pulling various crew members as far away from the ship as they can and laying them in the sand. Corey is the farthest away from the group, pulling another crew member across the sand by the armpits, stumbling, falling with semi-exhaustion, then rising to pull him again.

PIERSON. *(Shouting.)* Come on, Corey. Get him away from there, quick!

DONLIN. *(Urgently.)* That all of them, Pierson?

PIERSON. *(Looking up with a grimy, sweaty face.)* That's all of them, Colonel. They're all dead, sir, except Hudak.

*Donlin walks over toward them. He looks from one body to the other, then kneels down beside Hudak, wipes the sweat from the man's face, takes his jacket and bunches it up as a pillow, gently puts it under the man's head.*

DONLIN. *(Rises, to Pierson, softly.)* Let's cover them up, Pierson. We'll take fifteen or twenty minutes and then we'll bury them.

*As Pierson covers each of the men in turn, Donlin sits down in the sand and pulls out a ledger book. Very slowly and deliberately he writes in it. Over the action we hear his voice.*

253

DONLIN'S VOICE. First entry. Log. *Arrow One*. Colonel R. G. Donlin commanding. We have crash-landed on what appears to be an uncharted asteroid. Cause of the malfunction and ultimate crash— unknown. There was an explosion. The electrical system went out. And that's all any of us can remember, "any of us" being Flight Officers Corey and Pierson and Navigator Hudak, who has been seri- ously hurt, and myself. The rest of the crew is dead. There is very little left of the aircraft. The radio is gone, the bulk of the supplies have been destroyed in the crash and, as of this moment, there is little cer- tainty that we have been tracked and our whereabouts known.

COREY. *(He rips the book out of Donlin's hand. His eyes are wide, blazing; his face white.)* Begging the Colonel's pardon. This is no time to write your memoirs!

DONLIN. Corey, we're in bad shape and that's no mistake, but we're still a crew. As long as we're a crew there'll be discipline and there'll be protocol. And until I'm lying in a hole like the rest of those devils, we'll operate from the book! Now go over there and sit down.

COREY. *(Picks up the ledger and shakes it.)* Captain Donlin, it's hot, see? It's very hot and it makes it hard to think. So if you're going to expend all that energy, use it to figure a way out of here. A way to get back. A way to let them know where we are.

PIERSON. *(Shouting.)* Corey! *(He walks over to him and pulls him away.)* You heard the Captain. Get over there and sit down.

*Corey turns away, walks over a few yards, sinks to his knees close to the prostrate form of Hudak. He studies the stricken man's face, then sinks down into a heap and just stares lifelessly across the desert.*

PIERSON. Something's wrong with Corey, sir. The bump on his head, or whatever it was. He's not acting right.

*Donlin nods, picks up the ledger, opens it, stares at it, then closes it and tosses it aside. He walks over to look down at Hudak. He takes out a canteen, kneels beside the man, tilts his head up and puts a little water into his mouth. We see Corey in the background watching.*

COREY. How much water is there?

DONLIN. A five gallon can and what we have on us.

COREY. *(Pointing toward Hudak's figure.)* Then why waste it? He won't live through the day.

DONLIN. You the consulting surgeon, Corey?

COREY. *(Slowly rises.)* I'm one man out of three who's going to need water. And five gallons isn't gonna last very long.

DONLIN. If the situation were reversed, Corey, if that was you lying there, I'll give you good odds you wouldn't want to get written off, five gallons of water or no.

COREY. *(On his feet, close to Donlin.)* He's going to die, Captain.

DONLIN. *(Lashes out and grabs him.)* If he dies, he dies, Corey! But nobody gets behind to push. If he's thirsty, he gets water. If he's hot, we move him in the shade. And then if he goes, we'll give him a prayer or two. *(Without turning his eyes from Corey's face.)* Pierson!

PIERSON. Sir?

DONLIN. There's half a shovel near the packs. Let's start digging the graves. I'll relieve you in five minutes. Then Corey will relieve me.

*He lets go of Corey's tunic. Corey turns to look toward Hudak on the ground.*

PIERSON. *(Picks up the half a shovel.)* What's the matter, Corey. You want him on detail too?

*Corey doesn't answer him. He walks over toward the gear that's been stowed in a circle in the sand. He stares down at the five gallon water can and wets his lips. He looks up to see Pierson staring at him and he turns away.*

PIERSON. Colonel? That's odd. The size of the sun, I mean.

DONLIN. *(Nods.)* I noticed.

COREY. The size of the sun?

DONLIN. It's hardly any different than we knew it on Earth.

PIERSON. Which means whatever asteroid we've landed on is close to the Earth.

COREY. How close?

DONLIN. (Shrugs.) Pick a number.

PIERSON. (Softly.) Like that, huh?

DONLIN. (Nods.) Fifty thousand miles. A hundred thousand miles. Who knows? (He looks up toward the sun and closes his eyes and wipes his face.) Wherever we are, it's a cinch it isn't Heaven. We can count on that. (He turns to look from Pierson to Corey.) We can count on this, too. We've got maybe six, seven gallons of water and food concentrates for maybe four days. And that's it. So we might as well make our plans with this in mind.

COREY. What kind of plans?

DONLIN. We'll use this as a base and spread out in two man patrols. One man to stay behind and watch Hudak. (He jerks his head toward the direction of the mountains.) Maybe see what lies on the other side. We've got one thing in our favor. The air is perfect and there's no radiation count to speak of. (He bends down and picks up a fragment of metal from the ship.) It took four and a half years to build that ship. There wasn't any prototype. Just the one ship. The only one of its kind. And it took four and a half years to

build her. So if they know where we are and want to come and get us, they've got to build another ship. (He takes a deep breath. His eyes go down toward the sandy floor of the desert. He scrabbles it with his boot then looks up at the two men.) So get comfortable, gentlemen. We've got a devil of a long wait.

DISSOLVE TO: Four graves obviously freshly covered. The camera pans up until we're looking down on Pierson, who stands close to Hudak, shading his eyes against the sun. Donlin and Corey walk slowly back toward the area.

DONLIN. (Nods toward Hudak.) How is he?

PIERSON. The same. Breathing seems shallower though. Did you see anything, Captain?

Donlin shakes his head. Corey, in the process of finishing a drink out of his canteen, takes it out of his mouth, wipes his face with his sleeve, screws on the top of the canteen.

COREY. Yeah, we saw something. Sand. Sand, rocks and those scrubby mountains over there. This isn't an asteroid; it's an eight ball. (He shakes his head slowly, sinks to a sitting position on the sand.) And hot, Pierson. Hot like nothing you've ever felt before.

PIERSON. (Looks over to Donlin.) It'll be cooler at night, sir. I'll head south toward the mountains. I'll look in that direction. (A pause.) If there is a night here!

Donlin nods, takes out a canteen, starts to unscrew it. Corey grabs his wrist.

COREY. Not this time, Colonel. Not this time. I want an even shake. I want a chance.

DONLIN. You're alive, Corey. That's a better shake than those four got.

COREY. I want to *stay* alive. So don't give him *my* water.

Donlin reaches over and firmly takes Corey's hand from his wrist and pushes it aside. Then he carries the canteen over toward Hudak's mouth. Corey bats the canteen out of his hand. Donlin, enraged, is on his feet and throws himself at Corey. The two men start to grapple in the sand.

PIERSON. (In a strained voice.) Colonel Donlin? (As Donlin turns, Pierson is hunched over the body of Hudak.) You'll be pleased to hear, Corey, he won't drink any more of your water! (He reaches over to a crumpled top of a uniform that lies on the sand, picks it up and covers Hudak's face. Donlin walks over, stares down at the body, shakes his head slowly from side to side.)

DONLIN. You died a long way from home, boy. A long way from home. (He turns to look at the other two.) We'll wait till dark. Then we'll start taking some treks over the mountain and down to the flats in all four directions. This is home now, gentlemen. Such as it is.

PIERSON. (Sees Corey cutting the water canteen from Hudak's belt.) Corey!

Corey reacts as if burnt and scrambles backwards. Pierson takes three steps over to him, his voice shaking with anger.

PIERSON. For the record, Corey, there's just three of us now. And the big problem is going to be to stay alive. I mean the three of us! Something may be wrong with you, Corey. Something happened to you when you hit your head. I don't think you're responsible any more. But if I catch you filching just once, just once, Corey . . .

DONLIN. (Quietly, but with authority.) Pierson, let's forget it.

PIERSON. This dirty little grave robbing . . .

DONLIN. (Shouts.) Pierson!

PIERSON. (Very quietly turning away.) Yes, sir!

He goes over and sits down. Donlin does the same thing, stretching himself out in the sand, half covering his face with a jacket collar. Corey just remains there squatting, staring across at Pierson. Their eyes lock and there is a mutual challenge in the look.

FADE OUT

**END ACT ONE**

## ACT TWO

FADE IN: *The desert at night. There is a campfire. The silence is almost incredible, a total cessation of noise. Donlin sits staring at the fire, rises, stirs it with a stick, then looks around the darkness trying to probe with his eyes. He looks up at the sky for a moment, then looks at his watch. He starts as he hears the sound of what appears to be the crunching of footsteps on sand.*

DONLIN. *(Calling out.)* Pierson? *(His eyes are narrow with suspicion and concern as he goes back to the fire and picks up his rifle.)*

*Suddenly a figure, at first just a shrouded silhouette, appears in the gloom and then takes on a gradual dimension until we see Corey appear in the light. He looks totally bushed, bearded, sweaty. He walks on into the light of the campfire, half stumbles to his knees, then turns himself over so that he's lying on his back.*

DONLIN. *(Staring down at him.)* Well?

COREY. *(Shakes his head.)* Nothing. Not a thing. I must have gone twelve, fifteen miles anyway. Sand flats, that's all there was. Just sand flats. I thought I could get some kind of a fix using the stars. But it's overcast.

DONLIN. *(Nods.)* I know. I thought of the same thing. *(A pause.)* What about Pierson?

*Corey doesn't answer. He busily unscrews the top of his canteen, takes a long, long gulp, then very slowly and methodically screws the top back on, looks at Donlin again.*

COREY. What about him?

DONLIN. You didn't see him? You didn't hear him at all?

COREY. He went south toward the mountains. I went west toward . . . *(he grins ruefully)* I went west toward nothing. What time is it?

*Donlin walks back toward the light and stares out into the dark desert beyond. Once again he checks his watch. He speaks with his back toward Corey.*

DONLIN. He's been gone six hours. He should have been back by now.

*He turns to stare at Corey, who is once again drinking from the canteen. He screws back the top and throws the canteen on the ground. It lands with a heavy thud. Donlin stares at him; something freezes on his face. He runs to Corey, stops, stands above him, his voice quiet but shaking.*

DONLIN. Corey?

COREY. *(Looking up.)* Yeah?

DONLIN. You didn't hear Pierson or see him or anything?

COREY. *(Unflinching.)* I already told you, Captain. We went in different directions.

258

259

DONLIN. *(Leaning close to Corey.)* Corey, was it hot out there?

COREY. *(Nods.)* You know it.

DONLIN. Made you thirsty, didn't it.

COREY. *(Wary, now.)* I'm getting accustomed to it, Captain.

DONLIN. *(Slowly reaches over and picks up the canteen.)* Obviously. *Very* accustomed to it. So accustomed to it, Corey, that you didn't drink any water. You were out three hours and you didn't touch a drop.

COREY. Put me in for a medal.

*Donlin lashes out with both hands and grabs him, pulling him so that their faces are only an inch apart.*

DONLIN. Buddy, what I'm gonna give you can't be pinned on a uniform. I want to know why you started out three hours ago with half a canteen. *(He releases him, picks up the canteen and shakes it.)* And then come back with it three quarters full. Come on, Corey. I want to know where you left Pierson and what you did to him. *(Shouting in his face.)* Come on. Corey, Come on!

COREY. *(As his head goes down, Donlin pulls him upright by the hair.)* I found him. Face down. He must have . . . he must have fallen and hit his head on a rock. He was dead.

DONLIN. Where did this happen?

COREY. At the foot of the mountain. The sand was too deep heading west. I had to change directions.

DONLIN. You better change your story.

COREY. Captain, I swear, I didn't touch him. I found him. He was dead. I saw his canteen and I poured his water into mine. I knew you wouldn't believe me. That's why I told you I hadn't seen him.

*Donlin releases him, their eyes locking. Then Donlin slowly gets to his feet, goes over to the fire and picks up his rifle. He points toward Corey.*

DONLIN. Up on your feet. We're going to bring him back.

COREY. You're out of your mind. It's seven or eight miles out there. I can't make it again. I'm dead, Captain.

DONLIN. Correction! You're almost dead. But you're not quite yet. Let's go, Corey. I want a conducted tour to Pierson's body. I want to see for myself. Let's move out!

DISSOLVE TO: *Shots of the two men clambering over sand dunes and down again. Corey is in the foreground. Behind him we see Donlin with the gun. Corey stops dead, staring down, his eyes wide with surprise and shock. Donlin comes up alongside. Corey turns to him.*

COREY. This is where he was. I swear, this is where he was.

DONLIN. *(Tersely.)* But he's not here now.

260

*The camera pans over the ground. We can see a furrow as if a man had dragged himself across the sand.*

COREY. Captain, look. He must have crawled away.

DONLIN. You said he was dead!

COREY. I was wrong. I must have been wrong.

DONLIN. *(Holds the gun up.)* Where are the rocks, Corey? The rocks he hit his head on.

COREY. *(Takes a step backwards.)* I don't know. But I swear . . . it was an accident or something. I didn't do anything to him. I swear to you, Captain. You've got to believe me. I didn't touch him.

DONLIN. *(Stares around him and shouts.)* Pierson? *(A pause.)* Pierson, it's Captain Donlin. Pierson, answer me.

*Donlin stumbles as he half runs in the direction of the furrow. Corey stands alone; his face suddenly looks set and determined. He hears Donlin's voice fading off as he calls, "Pierson, Pierson, Pierson." Then Corey slowly reaches into his pocket. He takes out a small wrench, grips it in his fist and starts out in the direction of Donlin's voice.*

DISSOLVE TO: *The base of one of the small rocky hills that loom up. We see the prostrate body of Pierson on the sand. He is propped up against the side of a rock, his eyes open, his breathing shallow. He's close to death. He looks up and weakly reacts to the men approaching him. Donlin runs to Pierson, throws himself down close to him, takes out his canteen, tilts the wounded man's head back and pours water through parched, cracked lips. Pierson, with desperation, weakly pounds on Donlin's sleeve, and his head half turns to look toward the mountain behind them.*

DONLIN. What, Pierson, what? *(He looks in the direction of the mountain.)* Did you go up there, Pierson,? You went up there, is that the idea?

*Pierson nods.*

DONLIN. And what, Pierson? What did you see?

*Pierson's lips move and his eyes dart around agonizingly. He calls on the strength that he no longer possesses; then his eyes close. He's obviously unable to vocalize. Then his face takes on a set, determined look. Slowly, with a shaking hand, he draws a line in the sand, then crisscrosses it with two other horizontal lines. He turns to stare into Donlin's face, a pleading look, as though silently begging the Colonel to understand what he means. Suddenly his fingers convulse, pull back into a fist, then the hand falls to one side, limp. Donlin's face shows his agonized reaction to the death. Then he looks questioningly over to the symbol in the sand. As he looks up, he sees Corey standing there.*

DONLIN. He drew this. Some kind of a sign or symbol of something. *(He looks up toward Corey.)* He was trying to tell us something. What do you suppose he . . .

*Donlin's eyes travel up toward the mountain. He puts the carbine aside and starts to climb. As he starts to scramble up, Corey picks up the gun and holds it at his hip, pointing up toward Donlin.*

COREY. Colonel!

*Donlin turns to stare down at him.*

COREY. Colonel, two men can live maybe five days. One man can live ten. You'll forgive me, Colonel . . .

DONLIN. You killed Pierson, didn't you, Corey? You killed him.

*Corey nods.*

DONLIN. *(shakes his head slowly from side to side, in a whisper.)* Corey, you're demented. You're out of your mind. You've already killed once, you've already . . .

*He's interrupted by the explosion of the carbine. He totters for a moment and then pitches forward on his face. He lands, lifeless. Corey stands there with a smoking gun.*

COREY. *(Very softly.)* Sorry, Colonel. Real sorry *(Shakes his head).* No choice. No alternatives. Just had to be.

*Then he slowly puts the carbine down and looks up toward the mountain, wipes his face, blinks his eyes, sits down with his back against the rock wall and slowly falls asleep.*

DISSOLVE TO: *The foot of the mountain. It is day. The camera pans across the bodies of Pierson and Donlin to the huddled, sleeping figure of Corey who suddenly awakens with a start. He looks around him, startled, then gets to his feet, looks briefly at Donlin's body and walks a few feet to where Pierson lies. He kneels down and studies the imprint that Pierson has made in the sand, the three lines. He reacts thoughtfully and reflectively. He rises again slowly and looks up toward the mountain and begins a slow climb toward the peak.*

DISSOLVE TO: *Corey is climbing hand over hand, scrambling at the rock and the outgrowths. He hoists himself onto a small flat rock and lies there for a long moment panting heavily. His eyes narrow suddenly. He listens to something and then gradually we hear it. It's the sound of engines. Corey jerks himself upright staring around wildly and then suddenly stops dead, staring down and ahead to the other side of the mountain, his mouth wide open, his eyes bugged.*

COREY. Pierson. Pierson, now I know what you meant. Now I know what you were trying to describe. *(A pause.)* Telephone poles. Pierson, you were trying to draw a telephone pole!

*The camera begins a giant sweep down the other side of the mountain until we see a four-lane, concrete highway. A sign in the foreground reads: "Reno, Nevada, 97 miles." Beyond that a sign which reads "Nelson's Motel just up ahead. Gas-oil-eats." Then down the highway rolls a big truck and after a few moments in the opposite direction a big flashy convertible. The camera sweeps back and we are* looking up at Corey, who starts to cry and laugh at the same time.

COREY. *(Shouts.)* Hey! Oh, no! Captain Donlin. Pierson. Hudak.

*He whirls around and all the names die in his throat as he looks at the distant crumpled figures of the two dead men. He closes his eyes and the tears roll down his cheeks.*

COREY. I know what happened. We never left the Earth. That's why nobody tracked us. We never left the Earth. We just . . . we just crashed back into it. *(He is lying on his face, sobbing.)* Donlin . . . Pierson . . . Hudak . . . I'm sorry. Please forgive me. I'm sorry.

NARRATOR'S VOICE. Practical joke perpetrated by mother nature and a combination of improbable events. Practical joke wearing the trappings of nightmare, terror, desperation. Small human drama played out in a desert a hundred miles from Reno, Nevada, U.S.A., Continent of North America, the Earth and, of course, The Twilight Zone.

**Reader's Response** ∾ How might you react if you found yourself in the same situation as the crew of the *Arrow One*?

**Library Link** ∾ *If you enjoyed* I Shot an Arrow, *you might like to read Rod Serling's* Night Gallery 2, *a collection of science fiction and horror stories upon which his television series* Night Gallery *was based.*

# The Genius of Rod Serling

Rod Serling, the creator of "The Twilight Zone," is considered by many to have been one of the great writers and directors of early television. While other TV programs of the early sixties followed a simple, predictable plot line, Serling's "Twilight Zone" episodes often explored the darker side of human behavior, as "I Shot an Arrow" illustrates. Serling's characters, unlike those of most other programs, often display the cowardice, prejudice and greed that exists in society. Perhaps it is this willingness to address such unpleasant qualities that makes "The Twilight Zone" as popular today as it was when it first appeared.

But it is not simply the issues Serling addressed that make "The Twilight Zone" superior to other programs. It is the genius of his writing—his ability to show how average people react when faced with uncomfortable situations or their own preconceptions. And rather than present his dramas within the confines of reality, Serling chose to place his characters in, as he called it, "another dimension," which was nothing more than the dimension of imagination. His settings included both distant planets and small towns. Once there, the viewer could examine the paranoia of one man or the prejudice of an entire community, depending on the particular message Serling wanted to convey to his audience.

Although Serling wrote his material for "The Twilight Zone" approximately 30 years ago, many of the issues he addressed are still relevant today. This is not surprising when one considers that human behavior has changed little over the course of time. But Serling did more than bring the dark side of humanity to light. He essentially forced his audience to grapple with the fears and biases of our society. That is the true genius of Rod Serling.

265

# THE WIND FROM THE SUN

## by Arthur C. Clarke

*John Merton, the captain of the ship* Diana, *is in a race from the Earth to the Moon. He is racing against six other ships:* Gossamer, Santa Maria, Sunbeam, Woomera, Lebedev, *and* Arachne. *These unique vehicles are equipped with fifty million square feet of sails that capture energy from the sun.*

It seemed a strange thing to do, what with the race having just started, but he thought it might be a good idea to get some sleep. The two-man crews on the other boats could take it in turns, but Merton had no one to relieve him. He must rely on his own physical resources, like that other solitary seaman, Joshua Slocum, in his tiny *Spray*. The American skipper had sailed *Spray* singlehanded around the world; he could never have dreamed that, two centuries later, a man would be sailing singlehanded from Earth to Moon—inspired, at least partly, by his example.

Merton snapped the elastic bands of the cabin seat around his waist and legs, then placed the electrodes of the sleep-inducer on his forehead. He set the timer for three hours, and relaxed. Very gently, hypnotically, the electronic pulses throbbed in the frontal lobes of his brain. Colored spirals of light expanded beneath his closed eyelids, widening outward to infinity. Then nothing . . .

The brazen clamor of the alarm dragged him back from his dreamless sleep. He was instantly awake, his eyes scanning the instrument panel. Only two hours had passed—but above the accelerometer, a red light was flashing. Thrust was falling; *Diana* was losing power.

Merton's first thought was that something had happened to the sail; perhaps the antispin devices had failed, and the rigging had become twisted. Swiftly, he checked the meters that showed the tension of the shroud lines. Strange—on one side of the sail they were reading normally, but on the other the pull was dropping slowly, even as he watched.

In sudden understanding, Merton grabbed the periscope, switched to wide-angle vision, and started to scan the edge of the sail. Yes—there was the trouble, and it could have only one cause.

A huge, sharp-edged shadow had begun to slide across the gleaming silver of the sail. Darkness was falling upon *Diana,* as if a cloud had passed between her and the Sun. And in the dark, robbed of the rays that drove her, she would lose all thrust and drift helplessly through space.

But, of course, there were no clouds here, more than twenty thousand miles above the Earth. If there was a shadow, it must be made by man.

Merton grinned as he swung the periscope toward the Sun, switching in the filters that would allow him to look full into its blazing face without being blinded.

"Maneuver 4a," he muttered to himself. "We'll see who can play best at *that* game."

It looked as if a giant planet was crossing the face of the Sun; a great black disc had bitten deep into its edge. Twenty miles astern, *Gossamer* was trying to arrange an artificial eclipse, specially for *Diana*'s benefit.

The maneuver was a perfectly legitimate one. Back in the days of ocean racing, skippers had often tried to rob each other of the wind. With any luck, you could leave your rival becalmed, with his sails collapsing around him—and be well ahead before he could undo the damage.

Merton had no intention of being caught so easily. There was plenty of time to take evasive action; things happened very slowly when you were running a solar sailboat. It would be at least twenty minutes before *Gossamer* could slide completely across the face of the Sun, and leave him in darkness.

*Diana*'s tiny computer—the size of a matchbox, but the equivalent of a thousand human mathematicians— considered the problem for a full second and then flashed the answer. He'd have to open control panels three and four, until the sail had developed an extra twenty degrees of tilt; then the radiation pressure would blow him out of *Gossamer*'s dangerous shadow, back into the full blast of the Sun. It was a pity to interfere with the autopilot, which had been carefully programed to give the fastest possible run—but that, after all, was why he was here. This was what made solar yachting a sport, rather than a battle between computers.

Out went control lines one and six, slowly undulating like sleepy snakes as they momentarily lost their tension. Two miles away, the triangu-lar panels began to open lazily, spill-ing sunlight through the sail. Yet, for a long time, nothing seemed to happen. It was hard to grow accustomed to this slow-motion world, where it took minutes for the effects of any action to become visible to the eye. Then Merton saw that the sail was indeed tipping toward the Sun—and that *Gossamer*'s shadow was sliding harmlessly away, its cone of darkness lost in the deeper night of space.

Long before the shadow had vanished, and the disc of the Sun had cleared again, he reversed the tilt and brought *Diana* back on course. Her new momentum would carry her clear of the danger; no need to overdo it, and upset his calculations by side-stepping too far. That was another rule that was hard to learn: the very moment you had started something happening in space, it was already time to think about stopping it.

He reset the alarm, ready for the next natural or manmade emergency. Perhaps *Gossamer*, or one of the other contestants, would try the same trick again. Meanwhile, it was time to eat, though he did not feel particularly hungry. One used little physical energy in space, and it was easy to forget about food. Easy—and dangerous; for when an emergency arose, you might not have the reserves needed to deal with it.

He broke open the first of the meal packets, and inspected it without enthusiasm. The name on the label—SPACETASTIES—was enough to put him off. And he had grave doubts about the promise printed underneath: "Guaranteed crumbless." It had been said that crumbs were a greater danger to space vehicles than meteorites; they could drift into the most unlikely places, causing short circuits, blocking vital jets, and getting into instruments that were supposed to be hermetically sealed.

Still, the liverwurst went down pleasantly enough; so did the chocolate and the pineapple purée. The plastic coffee bulb was warming on the electric heater when the outside world broke in upon his solitude, as the radio operator on the Commodore's launch routed a call to him.

"Dr. Merton? If you can spare the time, Jeremy Blair would like a few words with you." Blair was one of the more responsible news commentators, and Merton had been on his program many times. He could refuse to be interviewed, of course, but he liked Blair, and at the moment he could certainly not claim to be too busy. "I'll take it," he answered.

"Hello, Dr. Merton," said the commentator immediately. "Glad you can spare a few minutes. And congratulations—you seem to be ahead of the field."

"Too early in the game to be sure of *that*," Merton answered cautiously.

"Tell me, Doctor, why did you decide to sail *Diana* by yourself? Just because it's never been done before?"

"Well, isn't that a good reason? But it wasn't the only one, of course." He paused, choosing his words carefully. "You know how critically the performance of a sun yacht depends on its mass. A second man, with all his supplies, would mean another five hundred pounds. That could easily be the difference between winning and losing."

"And you're quite certain that you can handle *Diana* alone?"

"Reasonably sure, thanks to the automatic controls I've designed. My main job is to supervise and make decisions."

"But—two square miles of sail! It just doesn't seem possible for one man to cope with all that."

Merton laughed. "Why not? Those two square miles produce a maximum pull of just ten pounds. I can exert more force with my little finger."

"Well, thank you, Doctor. And good luck. I'll be calling you again."

As the commentator signed off, Merton felt a little ashamed of himself. For his answer had been only part of the truth; and he was sure that Blair was shrewd enough to know it.

There was just one reason why he was here, alone in space. For almost forty years he had worked with teams of hundreds or even thousands of men, helping to design the most complex vehicles that the world had ever seen. For the last twenty years he had led one of those teams, and watched his creations go soaring to the stars. (Sometimes . . . There *were* failures, which he could never forget, even though the fault had not been his.) He was famous, with a successful career behind him. Yet he had never done anything by himself; always he had been one of an army.

This was his last chance to try for individual achievement, and he would share it with no one. There would be no more solar yachting for at least five years, as the period of the Quiet Sun ended and the cycle of bad weather began, with radiation storms bursting through the solar system. When it was safe again for these frail, unshielded craft to venture aloft, he would be too old. If, indeed, he was not too old already . . .

He dropped the empty food containers into the waste disposal and turned once more to the periscope. At first he could find only five of the other yachts; there was no sign of *Woomera*. It took him several minutes to locate her—a dim, star-eclipsing phantom, neatly caught in the shadow of *Lebedev*. He could imagine the frantic efforts the Australasians were making to extricate themselves, and wondered how they had fallen into the trap. It suggested that *Lebedev* was unusually maneuverable. She would bear watching, though she was too far away to menace *Diana* at the moment.

Now the Earth had almost vanished; it had waned to a narrow, brilliant bow of light that was moving steadily toward the Sun. Dimly outlined within that burning bow was the night side of the planet, with the phosphorescent gleams of great cities showing here and there through gaps in the clouds. The disc of darkness had already blanked out a huge section of the Milky Way. In a few minutes, it would start to encroach upon the Sun.

The light was fading; a purple, twilight hue—the glow of many sunsets, thousands of miles below—was falling across the sail as *Diana* slipped silently into the shadow of Earth. The Sun plummeted below that invisible horizon; within minutes, it was night.

Merton looked back along the orbit he had traced, now a quarter of the way around the world. One by one he saw the brilliant stars of the other yachts wink out, as they joined him in the brief night. It would be an hour before the Sun emerged from that enormous black shield, and through all that time they would be completely helpless, coasting without power.

He switched on the external spotlight, and started to search the now-darkened sail with its beam. Already the thousands of acres of film were beginning to wrinkle and become flaccid. The shroud lines were slackening, and must be wound in lest they become entangled. But all this was expected; everything was going as planned.

Fifty miles astern, *Arachne* and *Santa Maria* were not so lucky. Merton learned of their troubles when the radio burst into life on the emergency circuit.

"Number Two and Number Six, this is Control. You are on a collision course; your orbits will intersect in sixty-five minutes! Do you require assistance?"

There was a long pause while the two skippers digested this bad news. Merton wondered who was to blame. Perhaps one yacht had been trying to shadow the other, and had not completed the maneuver before they were both caught in darkness. Now there was nothing that either could do. They were slowly but inexorably converging, unable to change course by a fraction of a degree.

Yet—sixty-five minutes! That would just bring them out into sunlight again, as they emerged from the shadow of the Earth. They had a slim chance, if their sails could snatch enough power to avoid a crash. There must be some frantic calculations going on aboard *Arachne* and *Santa Maria*.

*Arachne* answered first. Her reply was just what Merton had expected.

"Number Six calling Control. We don't need assistance, thank you. We'll work this out for ourselves."

I wonder, thought Merton; but at least it will be interesting to watch. The first real drama of the race was approaching, exactly above the line of midnight on the sleeping Earth.

For the next hour, Merton's own sail kept him too busy to worry about *Arachne* and *Santa Maria*. It was hard to keep a good watch on that fifty million square feet of dim plastic out there in the darkness, illuminated only by his narrow spotlight and the rays of the still-distant Moon. From now on, for almost half his orbit around the Earth, he must keep the

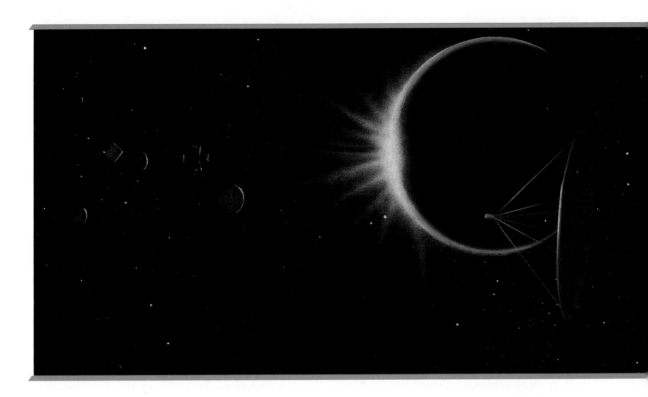

whole of this immense area edge-on to the Sun. During the next twelve or fourteen hours, the sail would be a useless encumbrance; for he would be heading *into* the Sun, and its rays could only drive him backward along his orbit. It was a pity that he could not furl the sail completely, until he was ready to use it again; but no one had yet found a practical way of doing this.

Far below, there was the first hint of dawn along the edge of the Earth. In ten minutes the Sun would emerge from its eclipse. The coasting yachts would come to life again as the blast of radiation struck their sails. That would be the moment of crisis for

*Arachne* and *Santa Maria*—and, indeed, for all of them.

Merton swung the periscope until he found the two dark shadows drifting against the stars. They were very close together—perhaps less than three miles apart. They might, he decided, just be able to make it . . .

Dawn flashed like an explosion along the rim of Earth as the Sun rose out of the Pacific. The sail and shroud lines glowed a brief crimson, then gold, then blazed with the pure white light of day. The needles of the dynamometers began to lift from their zeroes—but only just. *Diana* was still almost completely weightless, for with the sail pointing toward the Sun, her acceleration was now only a few millionths of a gravity.

But *Arachne* and *Santa Maria* were crowding on all the sail that they could manage, in their desperate attempt to keep apart. Now, while there was less than two miles between them, their glittering plastic clouds were unfurling and expanding with agonizing slowness as they felt the first delicate push of the Sun's rays. Almost every TV screen on Earth would be mirroring this protracted drama; and even now, at this last minute, it was impossible to tell what the outcome would be.

The two skippers were stubborn men. Either could have cut his sail and fallen back to give the other a chance; but neither would do so. Too much prestige, too many millions, too many reputations were at stake. And so, silently and softly as snowflakes falling on a winter night, *Arachne* and *Santa Maria* collided.

The square kite crawled almost imperceptibly into the circular spider web. The long ribbons of the shroud lines twisted and tangled together with dreamlike slowness. Even aboard *Diana*, Merton, busy with his own rigging, could scarcely tear his eyes away from this silent, long-drawn-out disaster.

For more than ten minutes the billowing, shining clouds continued to merge into one inextricable mass. Then the crew capsules tore loose and went their separate ways, missing each other by hundreds of yards. With a flare of rockets, the safety launches hurried to pick them up.

That leaves five of us, thought Merton. He felt sorry for the skippers who had so thoroughly eliminated each other, only a few hours after the start of the race, but they were young men and would have another chance.

Within minutes, the five had dropped to four. From the beginning, Merton had had doubts about the slowly rotating *Sunbeam*; now he saw them justified.

The Martian ship had failed to tack properly. Her spin had given her too much stability. Her great ring of a sail was turning to face the Sun, instead of being edge-on to it. She was being blown back along her course at almost her maximum acceleration.

That was about the most maddening thing that could happen to a skipper—even worse than a collision, for he could blame only himself. But no one would feel much sympathy for the frustrated colonials, as they dwindled slowly astern. They had made too many brash boasts before the race,

275

and what had happened to them was poetic justice.

Yet it would not do to write off *Sunbeam* completely; with almost half a million miles still to go, she might yet pull ahead. Indeed, if there were a few more casualties, she might be the only one to complete the race. It had happened before.

The next twelve hours were uneventful, as the Earth waxed in the sky from new to full. There was little to do while the fleet drifted around the unpowered half of its orbit, but Merton did not find the time hanging heavily on his hands. He caught a few hours of sleep, ate two meals, wrote his log, and became involved in several more radio interviews. Sometimes, though rarely, he talked to the other skippers, exchanging greetings and friendly taunts. But most of the time he was content to float in weightless relaxation, beyond all the cares of Earth, happier than he had been for many years. He was—as far as any man could be in space—master of his own fate, sailing the ship upon which he had lavished so much skill, so much love, that it had become part of his very being.

The next casualty came when they were passing the line between Earth and Sun, and were just begin-

ning the powered half of the orbit. Aboard *Diana*, Merton saw the great sail stiffen as it tilted to catch the rays that drove it. The acceleration began to climb up from the microgravities, though it would be hours yet before it would reach its maximum value.

It would never reach it for *Gossamer*. The moment when power came on again was always critical, and she failed to survive it.

Blair's radio commentary, which Merton had left running at low volume, alerted him with the news: "Hello, *Gossamer* has the wriggles!" He hurried to the periscope, but at first could see nothing wrong with the great circular disc of *Gossamer*'s sail. It was difficult to study it because it was almost edge-on to him and so appeared as a thin ellipse; but presently he saw that it was twisting back and forth in slow, irresistible oscillations. Unless the crew could damp out these waves, by properly timed but gentle tugs on the shroud lines, the sail would tear itself to pieces.

They did their best, and after twenty minutes it seemed that they had succeeded. Then, somewhere near the center of the sail, the plastic film began to rip. It was slowly driven outward by the radiation pressure, like smoke coiling upward from a fire. Within a quarter of an hour, nothing was left but the delicate tracery of the radial spars that had supported the great web. Once again there was a flare of rockets, as a launch moved in to retrieve the *Gossamer*'s capsule and her dejected crew.

"Getting rather lonely up here, isn't it?" said a conversational voice over the ship-to-ship radio.

"Not for you, Dimitri," retorted Merton. "You've still got company back there at the end of the field. I'm the one who's lonely, up here in front." It was not an idle boast; by this time *Diana* was three hundred miles ahead of the next competitor, and her lead should increase still more rapidly in the hours to come.

Aboard *Lebedev*, Dimitri Markoff gave a good-natured chuckle. He did not sound, Merton thought, at all like a man who had resigned himself to defeat.

"Remember the legend of the tortoise and the hare," answered the Russian. "A lot can happen in the next quarter-million miles."

It happened much sooner than that, when they had completed their first orbit of Earth and were passing the starting line again—though thousands of miles higher, thanks to the extra energy the Sun's rays had given

them. Merton had taken careful sights on the other yachts, and had fed the figures into the computer. The answer it gave for *Woomera* was so absurd that he immediately did a recheck.

There was no doubt of it—the Australasians were catching up at a completely fantastic rate. No solar yacht could possibly have such an acceleration, unless . . .

A swift look through the periscope gave the answer. *Woomera*'s rigging, pared back to the very minimum of mass, had given way. It was her sail alone, still maintaining its shape, that was racing up behind him like a handkerchief blown before the wind. Two hours later it fluttered past, less than twenty miles away; but long before that, the Australasians had joined the growing crowd aboard the Commodore's launch.

So now it was a straight fight between *Diana* and *Lebedev*—for though the Martians had not given up, they were a thousand miles astern and no longer counted as a serious threat. For that matter, it was hard to see what *Lebedev* could do to overtake *Diana*'s lead; but all the way around the second lap, through eclipse again and the long, slow drift against the Sun, Merton felt a growing unease.

He knew the Russian pilots and designers. They had been trying to win this race for twenty years—and, after all, it was only fair that they should, for had not Pyotr Nikolaevich Lebedev been the first man to detect the pressure of sunlight, back at the very beginning of the twentieth century? But they had never succeeded.

And they would never stop trying. Dimitri was up to something— and it would be spectacular.

Aboard the official launch, a thousand miles behind the racing yachts, Commodore van Stratten looked at the radiogram with angry dismay. It had traveled more than a hundred million miles, from the chain of solar observatories swinging high above the blazing surface of the Sun; and it brought the worst possible news.

The Commodore—his title was purely honorary, of course; back on Earth he was Professor of Astrophysics at Harvard—had been half expecting it. Never before had the race been arranged so late in the season. There had been many delays; they had gambled—and now, it seemed, they might all lose.

Deep beneath the surface of the Sun, enormous forces were gathering. At any moment the energies of a million hydrogen bombs might burst forth in the awesome explosion

known as a solar flare. Climbing at millions of miles an hour, an invisible fireball many times the size of Earth would leap from the Sun and head out across space.

The cloud of electrified gas would probably miss the Earth completely. But if it did not, it would arrive in just over a day. Spaceships could protect themselves, with their shielding and their powerful magnetic screens; but the lightly built solar yachts, with their paper-thin walls, were defenseless against such a menace. The crews would have to be taken off, and the race abandoned.

John Merton knew nothing of this as he brought *Diana* around the Earth for the second time. If all went well, this would be the last circuit, both for him and for the Russians. They had spiraled upward by thousands of miles, gaining energy from the Sun's rays. On this lap, they should escape from Earth completely, and head outward on the long run to the Moon. It was a straight race now; *Sunbeam*'s crew had finally withdrawn exhausted, after battling valiantly with their spinning sail for more than a hundred thousand miles.

Merton did not feel tired; he had eaten and slept well, and *Diana* was behaving herself admirably. The

278

autopilot, tensioning the rigging like a busy little spider, kept the great sail trimmed to the Sun more accurately than any human skipper could have. Though by this time the two square miles of plastic sheet must have been riddled by hundreds of micrometeorites, the pinhead-sized punctures had produced no falling off of thrust.

He had only two worries. The first was shroud line number eight, which could no longer be adjusted properly. Without any warning, the reel had jammed; even after all these years of astronautical engineering, bearings sometimes seized up in a vacuum. He could neither lengthen nor shorten the line, and would have to navigate as best he could with the others. Luckily, the most difficult maneuvers were over; from now on, *Diana* would have the sun behind her as she sailed straight down the solar wind. And as the old-time sailors had often said, it was easy to handle a boat when the wind was blowing over your shoulder.

His other worry was *Lebedev*, still dogging his heels three hundred miles astern. The Russian yacht had shown remarkable maneuverability, thanks to the four great panels that could be tilted around the central sail. Her flipovers as she rounded the Earth had been carried out with superb precision. But to gain maneuverability she must have sacrificed speed. You could not have it both ways; in the long, straight haul ahead, Merton should be able to hold his own. Yet he could not be certain of victory until, three or four days from now, *Diana* went flashing past the far side of the Moon.

And then, in the fiftieth hour of the race, just after the end of the second orbit around Earth, Markoff sprang his little surprise.

"Hello, John," he said casually over the ship-to-ship circuit. "I'd like you to watch this. It should be interesting."

Merton drew himself across to the periscope and turned up the magnification to the limit. There in the field of view, a most improbable sight against the background of the stars, was the glittering Maltese cross of *Lebedev*, very small but very clear. As he watched, the four arms of the cross slowly detached themselves from the central square, and went drifting away, with all their spars and rigging, into space.

Markoff had jettisoned all unnecessary mass, now that he was coming up to escape velocity and need no longer plod patiently around the Earth, gaining momentum on each circuit. From now on, *Lebedev* would be almost unsteerable—but that did not matter; all the tricky navigation lay behind her. It was as if an old-time yachtsman had deliberately thrown away his rudder and heavy keel, knowing that the rest of the race would be straight downwind over a calm sea.

"Congratulations, Dimitri," Merton radioed. "It's a neat trick. But it's not good enough. You can't catch up with me now."

"I've not finished yet," the Russian answered. "There's an old winter's tale in my country about a sleigh being chased by wolves. To save himself, the driver has to throw off the passengers one by one. Do you see the analogy?"

Merton did, all too well. On this final straight lap, Dimitri no longer needed his copilot. *Lebedev* could really be stripped down for action.

"Alexis won't be very happy about this," Merton replied. "Besides, it's against the rules."

"Alexis isn't happy, but I'm the captain. He'll just have to wait around for ten minutes until the Commodore picks him up. And the regulations say nothing about the size of the crew—*you* should know that."

Merton did not answer; he was too busy doing some hurried calculations, based on what he knew of *Lebedev*'s design. By the time he had finished, he knew that the race was still in doubt. *Lebedev* would be

catching up with him at just about the time he hoped to pass the Moon.

But the outcome of the race was already being decided, ninety-two million miles away.

On Solar Observatory Three, far inside the orbit of Mercury, the automatic instruments recorded the whole history of the flare. A hundred million square miles of the Sun's surface exploded in such blue-white fury that, by comparison, the rest of the disc paled to a dull glow. Out of that seething inferno, twisting and turning like a living creature in the magnetic fields of its own creation, soared the electrified plasma of the great flare. Ahead of it, moving at the speed of light, went the warning flash of ultraviolet and X rays. That would reach Earth in eight minutes, and was relatively harmless. Not so the charged atoms that were following behind at their leisurely four million miles an hour—and which, in just over a day, would engulf *Diana*, *Lebedev*, and their accompanying little fleet in a cloud of lethal radiation.

The Commodore left his decision to the last possible minute. Even when the jet of plasma had been tracked past the orbit of Venus, there was a chance that it might miss the

Earth. But when it was less than four hours away, and had already been picked up by the Moon-based radar network, he knew that there was no hope. All solar sailing was over, for the next five or six years—until the Sun was quiet again.

A great sigh of disappointment swept across the solar system. *Diana* and *Lebedev* were halfway between Earth and Moon, running neck and neck—and now no one would ever know which was the better boat. The enthusiasts would argue the result for years; history would merely record: "Race canceled owing to solar storm."

When John Merton received the order, he felt a bitterness he had not known since childhood. Across the years, sharp and clear, came the memory of his tenth birthday. He had been promised an exact scale model of the famous spaceship *Morning Star,* and for weeks had been planning how he would assemble it, where he would hang it in his bedroom. And then, at the last moment, his father had broken the news. "I'm sorry, John—it cost too much money. Maybe next year . . ."

Half a century and a successful lifetime later, he was a heartbroken boy again.

For a moment, he thought of disobeying the Commodore. Suppose he sailed on, ignoring the warning? Even if the race was abandoned, he could make a crossing to the Moon that would stand in the record books for generations.

But that would be worse than stupidity; it would be suicide—and a very unpleasant form of suicide. He had seen men die of radiation poisoning, when the magnetic shielding of their ships had failed in deep space. No—nothing was worth that . . .

He felt as sorry for Dimitri Markoff as for himself. They had both deserved to win, and now victory would go to neither. No man could argue with the Sun in one of its rages, even though he might ride upon its beams to the edge of space.

Only fifty miles astern now, the Commodore's launch was drawing alongside *Lebedev*, preparing to take off her skipper. There went the silver sail, as Dimitri—with feelings that he would share—cut the rigging. The tiny capsule would be taken back to Earth, perhaps to be used again; but a sail was spread for one voyage only.

He could press the jettison button now, and save his rescuers a few minutes of time. But he could not do it; he wanted to stay aboard to the very end, on the little boat that had been for so long a part of his dreams and his life. The great sail was spread now at right angles to the Sun, exerting its utmost thrust. Long ago it had torn him clear of Earth, and *Diana* was still gaining speed.

Then, out of nowhere, beyond all doubt or hesitation, he knew what must be done. For the last time, he sat down before the computer that had navigated him halfway to the Moon.

When he had finished, he packed the log and his few personal belongings. Clumsily, for he was out of practice, and it was not an easy job to do by oneself, he climbed into the emergency survival suit. He was just sealing the helmet when the Commodore's voice called over the radio.

"We'll be alongside in five minutes, Captain. Please cut your sail, so we won't foul it."

John Merton, first and last skipper of the sun yacht *Diana*, hesitated a moment. He looked for the last time around the tiny cabin, with its shining instruments and its neatly arranged controls, now all locked in their final positions. Then he said into the microphone: "I'm abandoning ship. Take your time to pick me up. *Diana* can look after herself."

There was no reply from the Commodore, and for that he was grateful. Professor van Stratten would have guessed what was happening—and would know that, in these final moments, he wished to be left alone.

He did not bother to exhaust the air lock, and the rush of escaping gas blew him gently out into space. The thrust he gave her then was his last gift to *Diana*. She dwindled away from him, sail glittering splendidly in the sunlight that would be hers for centuries to come. Two days from now she would flash past the Moon; but the Moon, like the Earth, could never catch her. Without his mass to slow her down, she would gain two thousand miles an hour in every day of sailing. In a month, she would be traveling faster than any ship that man had ever built.

As the Sun's rays weakened with distance, so her acceleration would fall. But even at the orbit of Mars, she would be gaining a thousand miles an hour in every day. Long before then, she would be moving too swiftly for the Sun itself to hold her. Faster than a comet had ever streaked in from the stars, she would be heading out into the abyss.

The glare of rockets, only a few miles away, caught Merton's eye. The launch was approaching to pick him up—at thousands of times the acceleration that *Diana* could ever attain. But its engines could burn for a few minutes only, before they exhausted

their fuel—while *Diana* would still be gaining speed, driven outward by the Sun's eternal fires, for ages yet to come.

"Good-by, little ship," said John Merton. "I wonder what eyes will see you next, how many thousand years from now?"

At last he felt at peace, as the blunt torpedo of the launch nosed up beside him. He would never win the race to the Moon; but his would be the first of all man's ships to set sail on the long journey to the stars.

**Reader's Response** ∽ If you had the chance, would you sail alone into space?

# Whispers from the Past

**P**erhaps nothing is so lost that it can never be found. What motivates people to dig into the past?

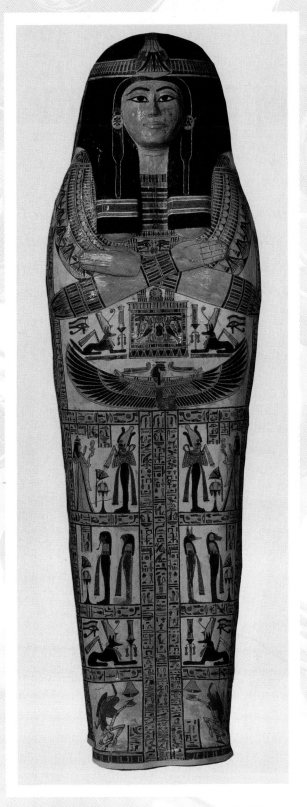

WOODEN MUMMY CASE OF HENETTAWY, *Egyptian, ca. 1039–922 B.C.,*
*25.3.182, © The Metropolitan Museum of Art, New York*

# Theme Books for

# Whispers from the Past

**W**hat will motivate you to reach through time and space to discover former cultures and past civilizations? What will you find if you travel there? Adventure, intrigue . . . Read on!

❋ Buried treasure, a gallery of scoundrels, and a perilous sea journey . . . these are the makings for a rousing adventure aboard the *Hispaniola*, where mutiny, deceit, and greed abound. Who will survive to reap the cache of gold in Robert Louis Stevenson's *Treasure Island*?

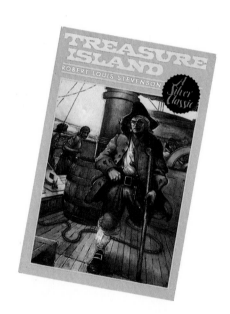

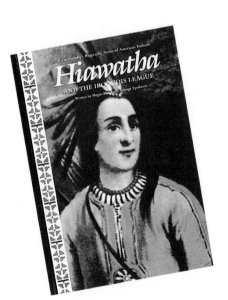

❋ How did Hiawatha survive the trickery of the loathsome Atotarho and become the founder of the world's first republic? In *Hiawatha and the Iroquois League*, Megan McClard tells the story of this famous Native American's quest for peace and unity in the 1500s, and of his impact on today's world.

✼ In Rosemary Sutcliff's ***Dragon Slayer***, honor and peril await Beowulf as he faces Grendel, the monstrous Night-Stalker who brings death and horror to the Danes.

✼ The future of a lost civilization depends on Lian Webster in ***The Lost Star*** by H. M. Hoover. Join Lian and other galactic travelers on a futuristic archae-ological dig aboard a grounded starship that is home to extraordinary creatures with an agonizing past.

## *More Books to Enjoy*

***In Search of Tutankhamen*** by Piero Ventura
***Country of Broken Stone*** by Nancy Bond
***Pyramid*** by David Macaulay
***The Illyrian Adventure*** by Lloyd Alexander

289

# THE DOG OF POMPEII

FROM <u>THE DONKEY OF GOD</u>
BY LOUIS UNTERMEYER

Tito and his dog Bimbo lived (if you could call it living) under the wall where it joined the inner gate. They really didn't live there; they just slept there. They lived anywhere. Pompeii was one of the gayest of old Latin towns, but although Tito was never an unhappy boy, he was not exactly a merry one. The streets were always lively with shining chariots and bright red trappings; the open-air theatres rocked with laughing crowds; sham-battles and athletic sports were free for the asking in the great stadium. Once a year the Caesar visited the pleasure-city and the fire-works lasted for days; the sacrifices in the Forum were better than a show. But Tito saw none of these things. He was blind—had been blind from birth. He was known to every one in the poorer quarters. But no one could say how old he was, no one remembered his parents, no one could tell where he came from. Bimbo was another mystery. As long as people could remember seeing Tito—about twelve or thirteen years—they had seen Bimbo. Bimbo had never left his side. He was not only dog, but nurse, pillow, playmate, mother and father to Tito.

Did I say Bimbo never left his master? (Perhaps I had better say comrade, for if anyone was the master, it was

291

Bimbo.) I was wrong. Bimbo did trust Tito alone exactly three times a day. It was a fixed routine, a custom understood between boy and dog since the beginning of their friendship, and the way it worked was this: Early in the morning, shortly after dawn, while Tito was still dreaming, Bimbo would disappear. When Tito woke, Bimbo would be sitting quietly at his side, his ears cocked, his stump of a tail tapping the ground, and a fresh-baked bread—more like a large round roll—at his feet. Tito would stretch himself; Bimbo would yawn; then they would breakfast. At noon, no matter where they happened to be, Bimbo would put his paw on Tito's knee and the two of them would return to the inner gate. Tito would curl up in the corner (almost like a dog) and go to sleep, while Bimbo, looking quite important (almost like a boy) would disappear again. In half an hour he'd be back with their lunch. Sometimes it would be a piece of fruit or a scrap of meat, often it was nothing but a dry crust. But sometimes there would be one of those flat rich cakes, sprinkled with raisins and sugar, that Tito liked so much. At supper-time the same thing happened, although there was a little less of everything, for things were hard to snatch in the evening with the streets full of people. Besides, Bimbo didn't approve of too much food before going to sleep. A heavy supper made boys too restless and dogs too stodgy—and it was the business of

a dog to sleep lightly with one ear open and muscles ready for action.

But, whether there was much or little, hot or cold, fresh or dry, food was always there. Tito never asked where it came from and Bimbo never told him. There was plenty of rainwater in the hollows of soft stones; the old egg-woman at the corner sometimes gave him a cupful of strong goat's milk; in the grape-season the fat wine-maker let him have drippings of the mild juice. So there was no danger of going hungry or thirsty. There was plenty of everything in Pompeii, if you knew where to find it—and if you had a dog like Bimbo.

As I said before, Tito was not the merriest boy in Pompeii. He could not romp with the other youngsters and play Hare-and-Hounds and I-spy and Follow-your-Master and Ball-against-the-Building and Jack-stones and Kings-and-Robbers with them. But that did not make him sorry for himself. If he could not see the sights that delighted the lads of Pompeii he could hear and smell things they never noticed. He could really see more with his ears and nose than they could with their eyes. When he and Bimbo went out walking he knew just where they were going and exactly what was happening.

"Ah," he'd sniff and say, as they passed a handsome villa, "Glaucus Pansa is giving a grand dinner tonight. They're going to have three kinds of bread, and roast pigling, and stuffed goose, and a great stew—I think bear-stew—and a fig-pie." And Bimbo would note that this would be a good place to visit tomorrow.

Or, "H'm," Tito would murmur, half through his lips, half through his nostrils. "The wife of Marcus Lucretius is expecting her mother. She's shaking out every piece of goods in the house; she's going to use the best clothes—the ones she's been keeping in pine-needles and camphor—and there's an extra girl in the kitchen. Come, Bimbo, let's get out of the dust!"

Or, as they passed a small but elegant dwelling opposite the public-baths, "Too bad! The tragic poet is ill again. It must be a bad fever this time, for they're trying smoke-fumes instead of medi-cine. Whew! I'm glad I'm not a tragic poet!"

Or, as they neared the Forum, "Mm-m! What good things they have in the Macellum today!" (It really was a sort of butcher-grocer-market-place, but Tito didn't know any better. He called it the Macellum.) "Dates from Africa, and salt oysters from sea-caves, and cuttlefish, and new honey, and sweet onions, and—ugh—water-buffalo steaks. Come, let's see what's what in the Forum." And Bimbo, just as curious as his comrade, hurried on. Being a dog, he trusted his ears and nose (like Tito) more than his eyes. And so the two of them entered the center of Pompeii.

The Forum was the part of the town to which everybody came at least once during each day. It was the Central Square and everything happened here. There were no private houses; all was public—the chief temples, the gold and red bazaars, the silk-shops, the town-hall, the booths belonging to the weavers and jewel-merchants, the wealthy woolen market, the shrine of the household gods. Everything glittered here. The buildings looked as if they were new—which, in a sense, they were. The earthquake of twelve years ago had brought down all the old structures and, since the citizens of Pompeii were ambitious to rival Naples and even Rome, they had seized the opportunity to rebuild the whole town. And they had done it all within a dozen years. There was scarcely a building that was older than Tito.

Tito had heard a great deal about the earthquake, though being about a year old at the time, he could scarcely remember it. This particular quake had been a light one—as earthquakes go. The weaker houses had been shaken down, parts of the out-worn wall had been wrecked; but there was little loss of life, and the brilliant new Pompeii had taken the place of the old. No one knew what caused these earthquakes. Records showed they had happened in the neighborhood since the beginning of time. Sailors said that it was to teach the lazy city-folk a lesson and make them appreciate those who risked the dangers of the sea to bring them luxuries and protect their town from invaders. The priests said that the gods took this way of showing their anger to those who refused to worship properly and who failed to bring enough sacrifices to the altars and (though they didn't say it in so many words) presents to the priests. The tradesmen said that the foreign merchants had corrupted the ground and it was no longer safe to traffic in imported goods that came from strange places and carried a curse with them. Every one had a different explanation—and every one's explanation was louder and sillier than his neighbors'.

They were talking about it this afternoon as Tito and Bimbo came out of the side-street into the public square. The Forum was the favorite promenade for rich and poor. What with the priests arguing with the politicians, servants doing the day's shopping, tradesmen crying their wares, women displaying the latest fashions from Greece and Egypt, children playing hide-and-seek among the marble columns, knots of soldiers, sailors, peasants from the provinces—to say nothing of those who merely came to lounge and look on—the square was crowded to its last inch. His ears even more than his nose guided Tito to the place where the talk was the loudest. It was in front of the Shrine of the Household Gods that, naturally enough, the householders were arguing.

"I tell you," rumbled a voice which Tito recognized as bathmaster Rufus, "there won't be another earthquake in my lifetime or yours. There may be a tremble or two, but earthquakes, like lightnings, never strike twice in the same place."

"Do they not?" asked a thin voice Tito had never heard. It had a high, sharp ring to it and Tito knew it as the accent of a stranger. "How about the two towns of Sicily that have been ruined three times within fifteen years by the eruptions of Mount Etna? And were they not warned? And does that column of smoke above Vesuvius mean nothing?"

"That?" Tito could hear the grunt with which one question answered another.

"That's always there. We use it for our weather-guide. When the smoke stands up straight we know we'll have fair weather; when it flattens out it's sure to be foggy; when it drifts to the east—"

"Yes, yes," cut in the edged voice. "I've heard about your mountain barometer. But the column of smoke seems hundreds of feet higher than usual and it's thickening and spreading like a shadowy tree. They say in Naples—"

"Oh, Naples!" Tito knew this voice by the little squeak that went with it. It was Attilio, the cameo-cutter. "*They* talk while we suffer. Little help we got from them last time. Naples commits the crimes and Pompeii pays the price. It's become a proverb with us. Let them mind their own business."

"Yes," grumbled Rufus, "and others, too."

"Very well, my confident friends," responded the thin voice which now sounded curiously flat. "We also have a proverb—and it is this: Those who will not listen to men must be taught by the gods. I say no more. But I leave a last warning. Remember the holy ones. Look to your temples. And when the smoke-tree above Vesuvius grows to the shape of an umbrella-pine, look to your lives."

Tito could hear the air whistle as the speaker drew his toga about him and the quick shuffle of feet told him the stranger had gone.

"Now what," said the cameo-cutter, "did he mean by that?"

"I wonder," grunted Rufus, "I wonder."

Tito wondered, too, and Bimbo, his head at a thoughtful angle, looked as if he had been doing a heavy piece of pondering. By nightfall the argument had been forgotten. If the smoke had increased no one saw it in the dark. Besides, it was Caesar's birthday and the town was in a holiday mood. Tito and Bimbo were among the merry-makers, dodging the charioteers who shouted at them. A dozen times they almost upset baskets of sweets and jars of Vesuvian wine, said to be as fiery as the streams inside the volcano, and a dozen times they were cursed and cuffed. But Tito never missed his footing. He was thankful for his keen ears and quick instinct—most thankful of all for Bimbo.

They visited the uncovered theatre and, though Tito could not see the faces of the actors, he could follow the play better than most of the audience, for their attention wandered—they were distracted by the scenery, the costumes, the by-play, even by themselves—while Tito's whole attention was centered in what he heard. Then to the city-walls, where the people of Pompeii watched a mock naval-battle in which the city was attacked by the sea and saved after thousands of flaming arrows had been exchanged and countless colored torches had been burned. Though the thrill of flaring ships and lighted skies was lost to Tito, the shouts and cheers excited him as much as any and he cried out with the loudest of them.

The next morning there were *two* of the beloved raisin and sugar cakes for his breakfast. Bimbo was unusually active and thumped his bit of a tail until Tito was afraid he would wear it out. The boy could not imagine whether Bimbo was urging him to some sort of game or trying to tell something. After a while, he ceased to notice Bimbo. He felt drowsy. Last night's late hours had tired him. Besides, there was a heavy mist in the air—no, a thick fog rather than a mist—a fog that got into his throat and scraped it and made him cough. He walked as far as the marine gate to get a breath of the sea. But the blanket of haze had spread all over the bay and even the salt air seemed smoky.

He went to bed before dusk and slept. But he did not sleep well. He had too many dreams—dreams of ships lurching in the Forum, of losing his way in a screaming crowd, of armies marching across his chest, of being pulled over every rough pavement of Pompeii.

He woke early. Or, rather, he was pulled awake. Bimbo was doing the pulling. The dog had dragged Tito to his feet and was urging the boy along. Somewhere. Where, Tito did not know. His feet stumbled uncertainly; he was still half asleep. For a while he noticed nothing except the fact that it was hard to breathe. The air was hot. And heavy. So heavy that he could taste it. The air, it seemed, had turned to powder, a warm powder that stung his nostrils and burned his sightless eyes.

Then he began to hear sounds. Peculiar sounds. Like animals under the earth. Hissings and groanings and muffled cries that a dying creature might make dislodging the stones of his underground cave. There was no doubt of it now. The noises came from underneath. He not only heard them—he could feel them. The earth twitched; the twitching changed into an uneven shrugging of the soil. Then, as Bimbo half-pulled, half-coaxed him across, the ground jerked

away from his feet and he was thrown against a stone-fountain.

The water—hot water—splashing his face revived him. He got to his feet, Bimbo steadying him, helping him on again. The noises grew louder; they came closer. The cries were even more animal-like than before, but now they came from human throats. A few people, quicker of foot and more hurried by fear, began to rush by. A family or two—then a sec-tion—then, it seemed, an army broken out of bounds. Tito, bewildered though he was, could recognize Rufus as he bel-lowed past him, like a water-buffalo gone mad. Time was lost in a nightmare.

It was then the crashing began. First a sharp crackling, like a monstrous snap-ping of twigs; then a roar like the fall of a whole forest of trees; then an explosion that tore earth and sky. The heavens, though Tito could not see them, were shot through with continual flickerings of fire. Lightnings above were answered by thunders beneath. A house fell. Then another. By a miracle the two compan-ions had escaped the dangerous side-streets and were in a more open space. It was the Forum. They rested here awhile—how long he did not know.

Tito had no idea of the time of day. He could *feel* it was black—an unnatural blackness. Something inside—perhaps the lack of breakfast and lunch—told him it was past noon. But it didn't matter. Nothing seemed to matter. He was get-ting drowsy, too drowsy to walk. But walk he must. He knew it. And Bimbo knew it; the sharp tugs told him so. Nor was it a moment too soon. The sacred ground of the Forum was safe no longer. It was beginning to rock, then to pitch, then to split. As they stumbled out of the square, the earth wriggled like a caught snake and all the columns of the temple of Jupi-ter came down. It was the end of the world—or so it seemed.

To walk was not enough now. They must run. Tito was too frightened to know what to do or where to go. He had lost all sense of direction. He started to go back to the inner gate; but Bimbo, strain-ing his back to the last inch, almost pulled his clothes from him. What did the crea-ture want? Had the dog gone mad?

Then, suddenly, he understood. Bimbo was telling him the way out—urging him there. The sea-gate of course. The sea-gate—and then the sea. Far from the falling buildings, heaving ground. He turned, Bimbo guiding him across open pits and dangerous pools of bubbling mud, away from buildings that had caught fire and were dropping their burning beams. Tito could no longer tell whether the noises were made by the shrieking sky or the agonized people. He and Bimbo ran on—the only silent beings in a howling world.

New dangers threatened. All Pom-peii seemed to be thronging toward the marine gate and, squeezing among the crowds, there was the chance of being trampled to death. But the chance had to be taken. It was growing harder and harder to breathe. What air there was choked him. It was all dust now—dust and pebbles, pebbles as large as beans. They fell on his head, his hands—pumice stones from the black heart of Vesuvius. The mountain was turning itself inside out. Tito remembered a phrase that the stranger had said in the Forum two days ago: "Those who will not listen to men must be taught by the gods." The people of Pompeii had refused to heed the warnings; they were being taught now—if it was not too late.

Suddenly it seemed too late for Tito. The red hot ashes blistered his skin, the stinging vapors tore his throat. He could not go on. He staggered toward a small tree at the side of the road and fell. In a moment Bimbo was beside him. He coaxed. But there was no answer. He licked Tito's hands, his feet, his face. The boy did not stir. Then Bimbo did the last thing he could—the last thing he wanted to do. He bit his comrade, bit him deep in the arm. With a cry of pain, Tito jumped to his feet, Bimbo after him. Tito was in despair, but Bimbo was determined. He drove the boy on, snapping at his heels, worrying his way through the crowd; barking, baring his teeth, heedless of kicks or falling stones. Sick with hunger, half-dead with fear and sulphur-fumes, Tito pounded on, pursued by Bimbo. How

long he never knew. At last he staggered through the marine-gate and felt soft sand under him. Then Tito fainted . . .

Some one was dashing sea-water over him. Some one was carrying him toward a boat.

"Bimbo," he called. And then louder, "Bimbo!" But Bimbo had disappeared.

Voices jarred against each other. "Hurry—hurry!" "To the boats!" "Can't you see the child's frightened and starving!"

"He keeps calling for some one!" "Poor boy, he's out of his mind." "Here, child—take this!"

They tucked him in among them. The oar-locks creaked; the oars splashed; the boat rode over toppling waves. Tito was safe. But he wept continually.

"Bimbo!" he wailed. "Bimbo! Bimbo!" He could not be comforted.

Eighteen hundred years passed. Scientists were restoring the ancient city; excavators were working their way through the stones and trash that had buried the entire town. Much had already been brought to light—statues, bronze instruments, bright mosaics, household articles; even delicate paintings had been preserved by the fall of ashes that had taken over two thousand lives. Columns were dug up and the Forum was beginning to emerge.

It was at a place where the ruins lay deepest that the Director paused.

"Come here," he called to his assistant. "I think we've discovered the remains of a building in good shape. Here are four huge mill-stones that were most likely turned by slaves or mules—and here is a whole wall standing with shelves inside it. Why! It must have been a bakery. And here's a curious thing. What do you think I found under this heap where the ashes were thickest? The skeleton of a dog!"

"Amazing!" gasped his assistant.

"You'd think a dog would have had sense enough to run away at the time. And what is that flat thing he's holding between his teeth? It can't be a stone."

"No. It must have come from this bakery. You know it looks to me like some sort of cake hardened with the years. And, bless me, if those little black pebbles aren't raisins. A raisin-cake almost two thousand years old! I wonder what made him want it at such a moment?"

"I wonder," murmured the assistant.

Reader's Response ∾ As you read this story, what puzzled you? What questions would you have liked to ask the author?

Library Link ∾ *If you enjoyed this selection you might enjoy Louis Untermeyer's* The Donkey of God, *from which this story is excerpted.*

# SPECTACULAR CATASTROPHES

*Between Australia and the Asian mainland lie the many islands of Indonesia. On these islands are volcanoes that rumble and smoke —and sometimes erupt.*

**Volcano:** Mount Tambora
**Location:** on the island of Sumbawa, east of Java
**Date of eruption:** April 7, 1815
**Description:** The mountain, which was about 13,000 feet high, had 4,000 feet of its top blown off. About 36 cubic miles of debris exploded into the air.
**Effects:** Ash circled the earth and rains fell steadily from England to eastern Canada. The famous "year without a summer" occurred in New England, with snow in June and crop-killing frosts in July and August.

**Volcano:** Krakatoa
**Location:** a volcanic island between Java and Sumatra
**Date of eruption:** August 27, 1883
**Description:** A series of explosions began on August 26 and reached ear-shattering proportions. The final explosion was heard 2,200 miles away in Australia.
**Effects:** Over two-thirds of Krakatoa vanished. For two days, the sun could not penetrate the ash in the atmosphere, and the region was in darkness. The eruption caused a tidal wave that killed thousands of people on nearby islands.

Mount Pinatubo in the Philippines, which erupted in June of 1991, spewed smoke and ash into the sky for weeks and caused much devastation to surrounding areas.

# THE CAVE NEAR TIKAL

## by Luz Nuncio Schick

It might have been the strain and hurry of the plane trips that day, first from Mexico City to Guatemala City, and then on to Tikal in the lowlands of northern Guatemala. Or it might have been the heat and humidity of the Tikal rain forest in August. Or maybe it was just happiness. Fourteen-year-old Elena Torres thought about the reasons she might be feeling so lightheaded this evening. She was sitting on a low wooden bench outside Don Miguel's thatched house in Tikal, watching darkness take over the rain forest. Little by little, the cries of parrots and howler monkeys were giving way to the haunting noises of the night creatures, hidden overhead and all around the dense vegetation.

It was probably just happiness, Elena thought. At long last she was here, in Tikal, Guatemala! Here the ancient Maya had flourished a thousand years ago and then mysteriously vanished, leaving their glorious city to be swallowed up by the rain forest. For Elena, student of archaeology and most especially of the ancient Maya, to be here was happiness enough. But to be here to discover something that nobody knew about the ancient Maya, to solve the mystery, maybe, of what had made them leave this place—*that* was enough to make anyone lightheaded. As the night settled in the rain forest, Elena thought back to the day when she and her parents first learned of the cave near Tikal with its beautiful, strange inscriptions that nobody could read. Although it had only been a week ago, it seemed like hundreds of years,

as far away in time as this rain forest was in distance from her home in the rush and commotion of Mexico City. . . .

"I have wonderful news, Elenita!" Luisa Torres came into the living room to find her daughter absorbed in the sports section of the newspaper.

"What is it, mother?" asked Elena, looking up surprised. Although her mother usually came home with interesting news from her job as an archaeologist at the National Museum of Anthropology, she seldom came home in the middle of the day, and she seldom sounded as excited and happy as she was sounding now.

"Dr. Portales called me this morning from Tikal," explained Mrs. Torres. He told me that a huge cave with ancient Maya glyphs painted all over its walls was discovered there just last week. It seems a young Maya boy found it while he was looking for his dog in the rain forest.

"Dr. Portales went into the cave yesterday, thinking that the glyphs were probably like the ones he's deciphered on the ruins at Tikal National Park. But it turns out they're not like anything he knows, and he thinks maybe your father and you and I should go down there to see if we can help figure them out. I told him—"

"Oh, mother, that sounds wonderful!" shouted Elena happily.

"Well, that's what I told him!" Mrs. Torres exclaimed, laughing, "Now the only question is your father. I'll have to call him to see if he can leave his project in Chichén Itzá and join us down there."

Elena's father was also an archaeologist at the National Museum of Anthropology in Mexico City. Like his wife, Roberto Torres was a specialist in deciphering the glyphs, or picture writing, of the highly developed Indian civilizations that had flourished throughout Mexico and Central America as many as two thousand years before the Spanish conquest. It was not difficult for Mrs. Torres and Elena to persuade him to fly down to Tikal.

"It'll be good to be in Tikal again," said Mr. Torres. "I've always loved the feeling the rain forest there gives me, like it's full of secrets, some of which we'll never know . . . you'll see what I mean when we get there, Elenita. . . ."

Suddenly Elena sat up straight on the wooden bench, her lightheadedness gone. Somewhere nearby, in the darkness of the rain forest all around her, a creature was moving. Was it a jaguar, or a boa constrictor, or some fierce crocodile that would creep stealthily out of the still, hot gloom and attack her? She looked back at the thatched house just a few feet behind her. Everyone was in there, accounted for—her parents and Dr. Portales were laughing and chatting with their hosts, Don Miguel and Doña Tila Uuc. Would there be time to call them for help when the creature attacked, she wondered?

"Balam, get over here!" shouted a voice right behind Elena, causing her to stifle a scream. Don Miguel, a slight, agile Maya peasant in his late fifties, had come silently out of the house with a lantern in his hand. At the sound of his voice, a skinny, brown-spotted mutt trotted meekly out of the darkness. Elena sighed with relief.

"That dog is always wandering off!" complained Don Miguel to Elena.

"I thought it was a jaguar or something coming out of the rain forest," said Elena sheepishly.

"What, Balam?" asked Don Miguel, surprised. "Well, *Balam* means 'jaguar' in our language, but the only reason we call him that is because my grandson thought he would grow up to be big and scary. But he just grew up, that's all, poor little Balam!"

At that moment, Elena's parents and Dr. Portales stepped to the doorway of the house. Dr. Portales had been Mr. and Mrs. Torres's archaeology professor when they were students at the excavation project in Tikal. He was a short, stout, distinguished-looking man with graying hair and beard. It was very rarely that Dr. Portales looked as serious and preoccupied as he did now. Usually, he was a cheerful, amiable man, in love with his work and as excited and awed by it as any beginning archaeology student.

"How nice of you to come out to join us," said Don Miguel to Dr. Portales and Elena's parents. "The little one and I were just talking about the ferocious jaguars in the rain forest." Don Miguel winked at Elena.

"I wish the jaguars were all we had to worry about," said Dr. Portales sadly.

"For me, the most frightening, most destructive beast of all walks on two legs and calls himself civilized. He comes into beautiful, wild places like this to vandalize and loot and, maybe, even to kill."

"That's why I tell you we have no time to lose," continued Dr. Portales, turning again to Elena's parents. His tone was urgent. "Looters have found out about the cave, and they've already done some terrible damage to the walls and columns in there. Even the most expert reader of Maya script could not read around the holes and scratches they've made to cut out whatever they can sell to foreign galleries and museums."

"I feel sad to say it, but I thought that would happen," sighed Mrs. Torres. "I remember when we were first here, working on the project to clear the rain forest away from Tikal," added Mr. Torres. "I was scarcely older than Elena. One night I made the mistake of going by a part of the site that we hadn't started working on yet. There was so much to do, we couldn't watch every part of the site, even though we knew that all around us, hidden by the rain forest, there were precious artifacts. I surprised a gang of men who were sawing apart an ancient stone monument. Luckily, they got scared when they saw me and ran away. But things could have turned out much worse—these looters have a big business going and they're not happy when you get in their way."

"Yes, that's so," said Dr. Portales, shaking his head. "But it's our business to not even let them have a way, or if you want to be cynical, to at least learn as much as we can from the ruins and now from these cave walls and columns before they get to them."

"Please don't worry, my friends," said Don Miguel consolingly. "Tomorrow morning, very early, I will take you to the cave and show you the pictures."

Dr. Portales relaxed and put his arm around Don Miguel's shoulders. "Yes," he said, smiling, "tomorrow morning we'll get going. Right now we should all get some sleep."

"Actually, before we go to sleep," said Don Miguel, "I have something to show you that was given to me at the market the other day." Don Miguel went inside the house and came back out with a tattered, three-year-old issue of an American sports magazine. He turned to an article full of photographs of baseball players.

"I was hoping you could look at it and tell me what it says sometime. I've been looking at it for days now, and I think I know what the pictures are about, but I would be most grateful if you could tell me what the words say."

"I can help you, Don Miguel," said Elena. "I've been studying English at school and I can read it pretty well."

"And she also knows a little bit about baseball," teased Mr. Torres.

"Yes," said Elena shyly. In fact, she knew a great deal about baseball. The summer she was twelve, her parents had worked on a dig of Maya ruins in Belize. Every day, Elena would help them in the morning, and head back to the hotel in the afternoon to watch a North American team, the Chicago Cubs, on television. Little by little, Elena had figured out the game and developed a passionate interest in playing and watching it.

"Ah, then, it is not only a pleasure, but good fortune as well to have you here," said Don Miguel happily to Elena.

An hour later, everything was still at Don Miguel's house. As she fell asleep, Elena listened to the rain forest, dark and secret and alive with the rustle of its night creatures. Balam was not one of them— he was curled up peacefully in a corner of the room. But out there real jaguars might be lurking, thought Elena—and other beasts, too.

The following day, the Torres family, Dr. Portales, and Don Miguel set out shortly after dawn. The day was hotter than usual in the already steamy rain forest, and everybody except Don Miguel kept tripping on the muddy trail over huge fallen trees and climbing vines.

As they advanced, Elena tried to conjure up an image of the time when the first archaeologists made their way through the wild green press of trees and vines to uncover the ruins at Tikal. They had come at a time when nobody, including the descendants of the ancient Maya themselves, had been willing to place much importance on the stone structures that were barely visible under the moss and fallen trees of the rain forest. Now, everybody recognized the importance of these ruins. "Maybe too many people recognize it now," Elena thought worriedly, remembering the looters.

"Just a little more, we're almost there," called Don Miguel, as the group laboriously followed his trail. Then, just when Elena thought she needed to stop again to rest, the spry old gentleman cried out, "Here it is!"

The visitors looked up in astonishment. Suddenly, the rain forest had given way to the huge black entrance of a cave, perhaps sixty feet high and forty feet wide. The white stalactites hanging down in irregular lengths made the entrance seem like the enormous jaws of some monstrous, ancient Maya deity. For a moment, the visitors stood still and marveled at this magnificent work of nature. No wonder the Maya had come here to confide the record of their lives! The cave entrance seemed to be an opening into a hallowed, timeless place, a place where secrets could be kept forever.

Before they entered the cave, Dr. Portales reached into his knapsack and pulled out flashlights for himself and the Torres family. Don Miguel had brought his own flashlight, which had been a gift from Dr. Portales. The flashlights of the group

barely pierced the dark, steep slope beyond the cave entrance. Their path took them through narrow, sharply winding tunnels and along slender ledges in the limestone walls of cave chambers unfathomably deep.

"Careful!" shouted Don Miguel. The group came to a standstill, clinging to the niches and ridges in the cavern wall. A few moments later, they heard the loud, echoing splash of a large rock falling into the water in the black depths of the cave. A piece of the ledge ahead of Don Miguel had fallen away.

"There is enough space left on the ledge for us to go ahead," said Don Miguel softly and slowly. "We will just have to move even more carefully. We're very close now . . . just watch for the ledge to grow smaller, then right where it ends, there will be a crack in the wall leading into the room

with the pictures, . . . just feel the wall for the crack, . . . let your hands be your eyes."

Suddenly, Elena noticed that she could no longer see the outline of Don Miguel's body ahead of her. Her heart began to pound as she felt along the wall to find him.

"I am here, little one," she heard from the other side of the wall. "Give me your hand and I'll pull you through."

Elena inched along the ledge until she felt the long, jagged edge of the crack in the wall. The strong grip of Don Miguel's hand pulled her off what was now just a strip of ledge and into a chamber of glistening white columns and walls.

The room became brighter as the rest of the members of the group entered the chamber and turned their flashlights on its walls.

"How beautiful!" exclaimed Mrs. Torres, as she played the beam of her flashlight along delicately painted columns of glyphs.

"Wait, there's a date there." Mr. Torres bent closer towards the glyph at the beginning of one of the columns. "It's 3 Ahau 3 Mol in the Maya calendar—"

Elena checked the Maya calendar tables her mother had brought. "That's June 30, A.D. 741!" she exclaimed.

"Elenita is indeed her parent's daughter!" laughed Dr. Portales. "Yes, the paintings and glyphs here span about three decades—from A.D. 733 to 762, a time when the civilization at Tikal was at its highest point. Over here, we have drawings of Maya ballplayers with their full uniform on. As you can see, they are very similar to the style and content of drawings that we've found at Tikal and elsewhere in what used to be Maya territory."

"I like these the best of all," announced Don Miguel after looking closely at the pictures of Maya ballplayers wearing the conventional torso armor, jaguar skin, and kneepads.

"They *are* beautifully done," agreed Mrs. Torres, "but I wonder what the glyphs next to them can mean. Please, all of you, shine your lights on the walls while I photograph them. These glyphs could be very important . . . they could tell us what happened to the Maya who lived at Tikal."

Elena could scarcely contain her excitement as her mother photographed the neat drawings and columns of symbols. If they could read these glyphs, and if the glyphs were indeed about specific events in Maya history, they might be able to solve the riddle of the collapse of Tikal little more than a century after scribes had painted in this cave. This was perhaps the greatest mystery surrounding the civilization at Tikal—how it had vanished so suddenly and completely. Two hundred years after these glyphs had been drawn, squatters were occupying the already crumbling temples and palaces at Tikal and looting the graves of the rulers buried in them. One hundred years later, Tikal had been completely deserted, and the rain forest had grown over it for nearly a thousand years.

"I think I've got it all now," said Mrs. Torres, packing her camera gear and the Maya calendar tables back in her knapsack. "We really should head back now."

As slowly and carefully as they had come into the chamber, the group made their way out. The feeling of anticipation among them was even greater now that they had the photographs of the glyphs. Soon they would be able to study them closely, and later they would return to the cave to see if they could excavate pottery or artifacts from the chamber floor.

Inch by inch, the group retraced their steps behind Don Miguel. They were past the narrow ledge and slipping on the wet clay floor of a small tunnel when they heard a low, distant rumble that seemed to come from the depths of the cave.

"It's an earthquake!" shouted Don Miguel as the rumble became louder and the ground beneath them started to shake even more violently.

They had barely gotten beyond the white fringe of stalactites at the cave entrance when they heard a loud crash behind them. Then came utter silence. The tremor had stopped.

"Mother, are you all right?" cried Elena.

"I'm fine, Elena," answered her mother, "just a little bruised." Then, after a moment, Mrs. Torres continued tearfully, "But I lost my knapsack in the cave. I had to let go of it when I tried to protect myself from the rocks."

"We can go back and find it another day," said Elena comfortingly, but Dr. Portales placed a gentle hand on her shoulder.

"I'm afraid not, Elenita. Look behind you."

What Elena saw when she turned around made her eyes also fill with tears. A huge row of stalactites had fallen across the cave entrance, completely blocking the path beyond the slope. The jaws of the monstrous Maya deity that had permitted access into the cave to scribe, looter, and archaeologist alike had snapped shut forever.

For a few minutes, the group rested in mournful silence outside the cave. Then they started their trek back through the hushed rain forest.

Elena did not look back at the cave. As she walked through the difficult trail back to Don Miguel's house, she thought about the glyphs and drawings she had seen in the cave, and tried to remember what they looked like so that she could draw them as soon as possible.

Elena thought of the looters, too. Perhaps that was the way it was meant to be. Perhaps nature was reclaiming the cave, hiding its contents once again, as it had done for more than one thousand years, to keep them from the unscrupulous people who wanted to profit from them. And per-haps the price that archaeologists had to pay of never knowing what was in the cave near Tikal was really a small price, since they could at least rest assured that the glyphs and drawings of the ancient Maya would remain undisturbed. The musicians on the walls would play their unknown song, the ballplayers would continue their mysterious, ritualistic game, with no wit-nesses—benevolent or otherwise—ever again.

That evening, Don Miguel, Doña Tila and the Torres family were all invited to dinner at Dr. Portales's house. On the way there, they drove past Tikal National Park and stopped to gaze at the ruins of the palaces, temples, and ballcourts the ancient Maya had somehow built and decorated in the hostile rain forest around them. For the moment, until another discovery came along, and until looters could be kept from it, this was all that people could know about the ancient civilization at Tikal. It was a great deal, but there was a great deal more hidden—enough to make Elena a little lightheaded just at the thought of it.

Reader's Response ∿ How do you think Elena's experience changed her?

# MAYAN MYSTERIES

The Guatemalan Indians of the region had long known about the site at Tikal. Non-Indian explorers made visits beginning in the nineteenth century, though it wasn't until 1956 that archaeologists began to excavate Tikal systematically. A thousand-year growth of forest covered the ancient city; only its tallest structures rose above the trees. But as the archaeologists exposed more and more of Tikal, their excitement—and their questions—grew.

Tikal was a major center by about A.D. 300. Its citizens included experts in architecture, weaving, woodcarving, pottery, writing, astronomy, mathematics, and art. But by A.D. 900 all building at Tikal stopped, and eventually the city and its temples vanished into the Guatemalan jungle.

How did Tikal rise as a center of Mayan civilization? And where did this complex civilization come from? The pyramid-temples of Tikal soar to the sky, yet they were constructed by a people who had no knowledge of the wheel, beasts of burden, or metal tools. How were these enormous structures built?

# The Tomb of King Tutankhamen

from *Sphinx* by Robin Cook

*Because the ancient Egyptians were buried with many of their household goods and personal possessions, the excavation of their tombs has told us much about how they lived. For any archaeologist, the most exciting find is the tomb of a king, or pharaoh. Since these men had great wealth, there is always the hope that their tombs will turn up splendid treasures. All too often, however, the tombs have been found empty—stripped by looters hundreds of years before.*

*Howard Carter, an English archaeologist, had spent about ten years searching for the tomb of King Tutankhamen. Now he had found it. But would there be anything of value beyond the sealed door?*

## NOVEMBER 26, 1922

*t*he excitement was infectious. Even the Sahara sun knifing through the cloudless sky could not diminish the suspense. The fellahin quickened their pace as they brought basket after basket of limestone chips from the entrance to Tutankhamen's tomb. They had reached a second door thirty feet down a corridor from the first. It too had been sealed for three thousand years. What lay beyond? Would the tomb be empty like all the others robbed in antiquity? No one knew.

Sarwat Raman, the beturbaned foreman, climbed the sixteen steps to ground level with a layer of dust clinging to his features like flour. Clutching his galabia, he strode across to the tent marquee, which provided the only bit of shade in the remorselessly sunny valley.

"Beg to inform your Excellency that the entrance corridor has been cleared of rubble," said Raman, bowing slightly. "The second door is now fully exposed."

Howard Carter looked up from his lemonade, squinting from under the black homburg he insisted on wearing despite the shimmering heat. "Very good, Raman. We will inspect the door as soon as the dust settles."

"I will await your honorable instructions." Raman turned and retreated.

"You are a cool one, Howard," said Lord Carnarvon, christened George Edward Stanhope Molyneux Herbert. "How can you sit here and finish your lemonade without knowing what is behind that door?" Carnarvon smiled and winked at his daughter, Lady Evelyn Herbert. "Now I can understand why Belzoni employed a battering ram when he found Seti I's tomb."

"My methods are diametrically opposed to those of Belzoni," said Carter defensively. "And Belzoni's methods were appropriately rewarded with an empty tomb, save for the sarcophagus." Carter's gaze moved involuntarily toward the nearby opening of Seti I's tomb. "Carnarvon, I'm not really certain what we've found here. I don't think we should allow ourselves to get too excited. I'm not even sure it's a tomb. The design is not typical for an eighteenth-dynasty pharaoh. It could be just a cache of Tutankhamen's belongings brought from Akhetaten. Besides, tomb robbers have preceded us, not once but twice. My only hope is that it was robbed in antiquity and someone thought it important enough to reseal the doors. So I truly have no idea what we are going to find."

Maintaining his English aplomb, Carter allowed his eyes to roam about the desolate Valley of the Kings. But his stomach was in knots. He had never been so excited in all of his forty-nine years. In the previous six barren seasons of excavation, he had found nothing. Two hundred thousand tons of gravel and sand had been moved and sifted, for absolutely nothing. Now the suddenness of the find after only five days of excavating was overwhelming. Swirling his lemonade, he tried not to think or hope. They waited. The whole world waited.

*t*he larger dust particles settled in a fine layer on the sloping corridor floor. The group made an effort not to stir the air as they entered. Carter was first, followed by Carnarvon, then his daughter, and finally A. R. Callender, Carter's assistant. Raman waited at the entrance after giving Carter a crowbar. Callender carried a large flashlight and candles.

"As I said, we are not the first to broach this tomb," said Carter, nervously pointing to the upper-left-hand corner. "The door was entered and then resealed in that small area." Then he traced a larger circular area in the middle. "And again in this much larger area here. It is very strange." Lord Carnarvon bent over to look at the royal necropolis seal, a jackal with nine bound prisoners.

"Along the base of the door are examples of the original Tutankhamen seal," continued Carter. The beam of the flashlight reflected the fine dust still suspended in the air, before illuminating the ancient seals in the plaster.

"Now, then," said Carter as coolly as if he were suggesting afternoon tea, "let's see what is behind this door." But his stomach contorted into a tight mass, aggravating his ulcer, and his hands were damp, not so much from the heat as from the unexpressed tension. His body quivered as he lifted the crowbar and made a few preliminary cuts into the ancient plaster. The bits and pieces rained down about his feet. The exertion gave expression to his pent-up emotions, and each lunge was more vigorous than the last. Suddenly the crowbar broke through the plaster, causing Carter to stumble up against the door. Warm air issued from the tiny hole, and Carter fumbled with the matches, lighting a candle and holding a flame to the opening. It was a crude test for the presence of oxygen. The candle continued to burn.

No one dared to speak as Carter gave the candle to Callender and continued working with the crowbar. Carefully he enlarged the hole, making certain that the plaster and stone blocking fell into the corridor and not into the room beyond. Taking the candle again, Carter thrust it through the hole. It burned contentedly. He then put his head to the hole, his eyes straining in the darkness.

In a moment time stood still. As Carter's eyes adjusted, three thousand years disappeared as in a minute. Out of the blackness emerged a golden head of Amnut, ivory teeth bared. Other gilded beasts loomed, the flickering candlelight throwing their exotic silhouettes on the wall.

"Can you see anything?" asked Carnarvon excitedly.

"Yes, wonderful things," answered Carter finally, his voice for the first time betraying emotion. Then he replaced the candle with his flashlight, and those behind him could see the chamber filled with unbelievable objects. The golden heads were part of three funerary beds. Moving the light to the left, Carter gazed at a jumble of gilded and inlaid chariots heaped in the corner. Tracing back to the right, he began to ponder the curiously chaotic state of the room. Instead of the prescribed stately order, objects appeared to have been thrown about without thought. Immediately to the right were two life-size statues of Tutankhamen, each with a kilt of gold, wearing gold sandals, and armed with mace and staff.

Between the two statues was another sealed door.

Carter left the opening so the others could have a better look. Like Belzoni, he was tempted to crash down the wall and dive into the room. Instead, he calmly announced that the rest of the day would be devoted to photographing the sealed door. They would not attempt to enter what was obviously an antechamber until morning.

## NOVEMBER 27, 1922

It took more than three hours for Carter to dismantle the ancient blocking of the door to the antechamber. Raman and a few other fellahin helped during this stage. Callender had laid in temporary electric wires, so the tunnel was brightly lit. Lord Carnarvon and Lady Evelyn entered the corridor when the job was almost complete. The last baskets of plaster and stone were hauled away. The moment of entry had arrived. No one spoke. Outside, at the mouth of the tomb, hundreds of reporters from newspapers around the world tensely waited for their first view.

*Howard Carter and Lord Carnarvon at the entrance to the burial chamber*

For a brief second Carter hesitated. As a scientist he was interested in the minutest detail inside the tomb; as a human being he was embarrassed by his intrusion into the sacred realm of the dead; and as an explorer he was experiencing the exhilaration of discovery. But, British to the core, he merely straightened his bow tie and stepped over the threshold, keeping his eye on the objects below.

Without a sound he pointed at a beautiful lotiform cup of translucent alabaster on the threshold, so Carnarvon could avoid it. Carter then made his way over to the sealed door between the two life-size statues of Tutankhamen. Carefully he began to examine the seals. His heart sank as he realized that this door had also been opened by the ancient tomb robbers and then resealed.

Carnarvon stepped into the antechamber, his mind reeling with the beauty of the objects so carelessly scattered around him. He turned to take his daughter's hand as she prepared to enter, and in the process noticed a rolled papyrus leaning against the wall to the right of the alabaster cup. To the left was a garland of dead flowers, as if Tutankhamen's funeral had been only yesterday, and beside it a blackened oil lamp. Lady Evelyn entered, holding her father's hand, followed by Callender. Raman leaned into the antechamber but did not enter for lack of space.

"Unfortunately, the burial chamber has been entered and resealed," said Carter, pointing toward the door in front of him. Carefully Carnarvon, Lady Evelyn, and Callender moved over to the archaeologist, their eyes following his finger. Raman stepped into the antechamber.

"Curiously, though," continued Carter, "it has been entered only once, instead of twice, like the doors into the antechamber. So there is hope that the thieves did not reach the mummy." Carter turned, seeing Raman for the first time. "Raman, I did not give you permission to enter the antechamber."

"I beg your Excellency's pardon. I thought that I could be of assistance."

"Indeed. You can be of assistance by making sure no one enters this chamber without my personal approval."

"Of course, your Excellency." Raman silently slipped from the room.

"Howard," said Carnarvon, "Raman is undoubtedly as enchanted as we with the find. Perhaps you could be a little more generous."

"The workers will all be allowed to view this room, but I will designate the time," said Carter. "Now, as I was saying, the reason I feel hopeful about the mummy is that I think the tomb robbers were surprised in the middle of their sacrilege. There is something mysterious about the way these priceless objects are haphazardly thrown about. It appears as if someone spent a little time rearranging things after the thieves, but not enough to put everything back in its original state. Why?"

Carnarvon shrugged.

"Look at that beautiful cup on the threshold," continued

Carter. "Why wasn't that replaced? And that gilded shrine with its door ajar. Obviously a statue was stolen, but why wasn't the door even closed?" Carter stepped back to the door. "And this ordinary oil lamp. Why was it left within the tomb? I tell you, we'd better record the positioning of each object in this room very carefully. These clues are trying to tell us something. It is very strange indeed."

Sensing Carter's tension, Carnarvon tried to look about the tomb through his friend's trained eyes. Indeed, leaving an oil lamp within the tomb was surprising, and so was the disarray of the objects. But Carnarvon was so overwhelmed by the beauty of the pieces he could think of nothing else. Gazing at the translucent alabaster cup abandoned so casually on the threshold, he yearned to pick it up and hold it in his hands. It was so enticingly beautiful. Suddenly he noticed a subtle change in its orientation with regard to the garland of dried flowers and the oil lamp. He was about to say something when Carter's excited voice rang out in the chamber.

"There's another room. Everyone take a look." Carter was squatting down, shining his flashlight beneath one of the

*Howard Carter examines the sarcophagus of Tutankhamen.*

funerary beds. Carnarvon, Lady Evelyn, and Callender hurried over to him. There, glittering in the circle of light from the torch, another chamber took form, filled with gold and jeweled treasure. As in the anteroom, the precious objects had been chaotically scattered, but for the moment the Egyptologists were too awed by their find to question what had happened three thousand years in the past.

Later, when they would be ready to explore the mystery, Carnarvon was already fatally ill with blood poisoning. At 2 A.M. on April 5, 1923, less than twenty weeks after the opening of Tutankhamen's tomb and during an unexplainable five-minute power failure throughout Cairo, Lord Carnarvon died. His illness reputedly was started by the bite of an insect, but questions were raised.

Within months four other people associated with the opening of the tomb died under mysterious circumstances. One man disappeared from the deck of his own yacht lying at anchor in the placid Nile. Interest in the ancient robbery of the tomb waned and was replaced by a reassertion of the reputation of the ancient Egyptians in the occult sciences. The specter of the "Curse of the Pharaohs" rose from the shadows of the past. *The New York Times* was moved to write about the deaths: "It is a deep mystery, which it is all too easy to dismiss by skepticism." A fear began to infiltrate the scientific community. There were just too many coincidences.

Reader's Response ⤳ Do you think it's right to excavate ancient treasures, or should they be left undisturbed forever?

Library Link ⤳ *To find out more about ancient Egypt, read Robin Cook's* Sphinx, *the book from which this selection is excerpted.*

# Who Was King Tut?

**t**he tomb of King Tutankhamen yielded magnificent riches. So famous is his tomb that whenever Egyptian pharaohs are mentioned, the name that most often comes to mind is King Tut. Yet very little is known about him.

King Tutankhamen was an Egyptian ruler of the Eighteenth Dynasty, during the New Kingdom period. Approximately nine years old when he became king, Tutankhamen reigned for fewer than ten years.

King Tut succeeded to the throne of his father, the pharaoh Akhenaten. During the years of his reign, Akhenaten set about destroying the old temples and the traditional religion in order to introduce a new religion: the worship of the sun god Aten. These sudden changes brought much disruption to Egyptian society.

Tutankhamen, being a boy king, did not have real power. The empire was really run by two men, a leading official named Ay and a general named Horemheb. They quickly began restoring the old forms of worship when Tut became king.

King Tut died suddenly in his late teens and his burial chamber was prepared hurriedly. An X-ray of his skull shows a bone fragment. Was he hit over the head? And if he was murdered, who did it? Ay or Horemheb? Could it be that King Tut began to seek power for himself when he reached manhood? No one knows.

After King Tut died, the aged Ay took over the throne. At his death, Horemheb became pharaoh. He replaced the recorded names of Tutankhamen and Ay with his own, and King Tut was soon forgotten, only to be discovered many centuries later.

COLOSSUS OF RAMSES II, *statue, Egyptian.*

# OZYMANDIAS

PERCY BYSSHE SHELLEY

I met a traveller from an antique land
Who said: "Two vast and trunkless legs of stone
Stand in the desert. Near them, on the sand,
Half sunk, a shattered visage lies, whose frown,
And wrinkled lip, and sneer of cold command,
Tell that its sculptor well those passions read
Which yet survive, stamped on these lifeless things,
The hand that mocked them, and the heart that fed:
And on the pedestal these words appear:
*My name is Ozymandias, King of Kings:*
*Look on my works, ye Mighty, and despair*!
Nothing beside remains. Round the decay
Of that colossal wreck, boundless and bare
The lone and level sands stretch far away."

# HANDS

Robinson Jeffers

Inside a cave in a narrow canyon near Tassajara
The vault of rock is painted with hands,
A multitude of hands in the twilight, a cloud of men's palms,
   no more,
No other picture.  There's no one to say
Whether the brown shy quiet people who are dead intended
Religion or magic, or made their tracings
In the idleness of art; but over the division of years these
   careful
Signs-manual are now like a sealed message
Saying: "Look: we also were human; we had hands, not paws.
   All hail
You people with the cleverer hands, our supplanters
In the beautiful country; enjoy her a season, her beauty and
   come down
And be supplanted; for you also are human."

CAVE PAINTINGS, *Spain.*

# MANHOLE COVERS

KARL SHAPIRO

The beauty of manhole covers—what of that?
Like medals struck by a great savage khan,
Like Mayan calendar stones, unliftable, indecipherable,
Not like old electrum, chased and scored,
Mottoed and sculptured to a turn,
But notched and whelked and pocked and smashed
With the great company names:
Gentle Bethlehem, smiling United States.
This rustproof artifact of my street,
Long after roads are melted away, will lie
Sidewise in the graves of the iron-old world,
Bitten at the edges,
Strong with its cryptic American,
Its dated beauty.

AZTEC SUN DISK, *used to calculate*
*day and year, Mexico.*

# THE MOON AND THE YEAR

## FROM THE MAYA

The moon and the year
travel and pass away:
also the day, also the wind.
Also the flesh passes away
to the place of its quietness.

# THE TREASURES OF
# TOMB
# 26

**from Motel of the Mysteries**
**written and illustrated by**
## David Macaulay

*In the year 4020, a great mystery surrounded the continent of North America. Its civilization had disappeared thousands of years before under the weight of heavy pollution and third- and fourth-class mail. There were signs that a complex civilization with skilled artisans had once thrived, but little was actually known of how these fascinating people lived. Little, that is, until Howard Carson's amazing discovery.*

**B**efore his forty-second birthday, Howard Carson had accomplished nothing of interest. Of obscure parentage, he spent his first four decades untroubled by public attention. In fact, it was not until the autumn of his life that Carson achieved the unprecedented mediocrity that was to make him, by the time of his death, unique among amateurs.

WINNING

Author

During his early forties, while rapidly consuming the remnants of a trust fund, Carson's interests were divided between his collection of antique space shuttles and a number of questionable, albeit visionary, experiments relating to increased camel-hump productivity. He must also have had some interest in history, because we know that he possessed at this time a fairly up-to-date translation of the writings of the ancient scholar Hoving and a rather dog-eared facsimile of the *Michelin Fragments*, and that he was a subscriber to the *National Geographic Magazine*.

In 4022 pressure brought on by the anticipated failure of yet another of his experiments led the desperate Carson to seek a change. He entered the 116th Cross-Continental North American Catastrophe Memorial Marathon. Little did he know when he set sail for East Usa what lay in store. Less than a month later, and already well behind the rest of the pack, Carson found himself crossing the great rubble heaps along the perimeter of a deserted excavation site.

The ground below his feet suddenly gave way. He was precipitated headlong downward. When the dust had settled and he had recovered his spectacles, he found himself at the bottom of an ancient shaft, facing the entrance of a long-forgotten tomb. The shaft, probably dug by tomb robbers shortly after the tomb was sealed, had been covered initially by the natural vegetation of the surface. More recently, the whole area had been buried under vast quantities of soil from the adjacent excavation.

Unimpressed and rather annoyed at this inconvenience, Carson's first thought was to call out for assistance, but, before he could utter a sound, light from the shaft caught the area around the handle on the tomb door. Upon closer inspection, he discovered that the sacred seal which was traditionally placed on the door following the burial rites was still in place. Staff artists' reconstructions of similar, but always defiled, tombs that had appeared in his most recent *National Geographic* flooded his mind. Thunderstruck, he realized he was on the threshold of history. His entire body trembled as he contemplated the possible significance of his find. The mysterious burial customs of the late twentieth-century North Americans were finally (and as it turned out, magnificently) to be revealed.

Less than a month later, aided by his companion, Harriet Burton, who "enjoyed sketching," and a dedicated group of volunteers, Carson began the first of seven years' work on the excavation of the Motel of the Mysteries complex, and most specifically on the removal and recording of the treasures from Tomb 26.

While Carson paced back and forth in a supervisory manner, Harriet numbered each of the items surrounding the entrance as well as those on the great door. Descriptions of the most significant discoveries are to be found in her diary:

Number 21, "the gleaming Sacred Seal, which had first caught Howard's attention, was placed on the door by the officials after the burial to protect the tomb and its inhabitant for eternity."

Number 28, "the Sacred Eye, which was believed to ward off evil spirits."

Number 18, "the partially exposed Plant That Would Not Die. One of these exquisite plants, which had apparently been grown in separate pieces and then joined together, was placed on each side of the entrance."

Numbers 19 and 20, "containers in which the sacrificial meal was offered to the gods of eternal life."

Once the exterior of the tomb had been recorded in detail, preparations for entering it were begun. With a steady hand, Carson, who had presumably picked up a few tricks in his time, jimmied the lock. With his helpers peering nervously from a safe distance, he cautiously pried open the door. The creaking of the ancient hinges, in Miss Burton's own words, "cut through the silence like the scream of a ghostly fleeing spirit." Suddenly, to Carson's astonishment, the door stopped dead. A frantic but successful search for the obstruction revealed a beautifully crafted chain about two thirds up the inside of the door, linking it with the sturdy frame. Clearly this stood as the final barrier between the present and the past. Once the workers had sawed through the chain, they withdrew, and Carson continued to open the great door.

At first, everything was dark. Carson lit a match. Still everything was dark. Carson lit two matches. Still, everything was dark. Attempting to avoid a rather protracted delay, Harriet eased the large spotlight toward the entrance with her foot. As the blanket of darkness was stripped away from the treasures within the tomb, Carson's mouth fell open. Everywhere was the glint of plastic. Impatiently, the others waited for a response. "Can you see anything, Howard?" they asked in unison.

"Yes," he replied . . .

"WONDERFUL THINGS!"

*The cataloging of each item in the tomb and the excavation of the surrounding area took many years and was accompanied by sensational press coverage. When the Treasures were finally moved to a major museum for exhibition, thousands of people lined up— each hoping for at least a glimpse of these marvels from the past.*

## THE TREASURES

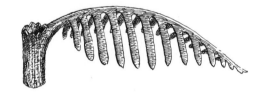

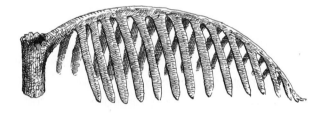

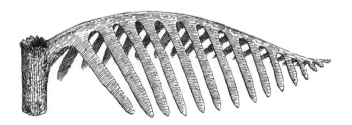

## Three Fragments from the Plant That Would Not Die

This plant, developed by the ancients specifically for eternal life, was grown in separate pieces through a now lost biological process. The proportion and size of each plant could then be perfectly matched to its ultimate location. Many such plants were found throughout the complex.

## The Sacred Seal

Constructed of *plasticus eternicus*, this particular treasure has proportions of classic beauty. It was placed upon the handle of the great outer door by the necropolis officials following the closing of the tomb.

## The Great Altar

This magnificent structure, toward which everything in the outer chamber was directed, represents the essence of religious communication as practiced by the ancient North Americans. Although it was capable of communication with a large number of gods, the altar seems to have been intended primarily for communion with the gods MOVIEA and MOVIEB. Judging by impact marks on the top and sides of the upper altar, some aspect of this communication was dependent upon pounding the surface. Communication with the altar was symbolically continued into eternal life by placing the communicator box in the hand of the deceased. Below the exquisite glass face of the upper altar are a number of sealed spaces for offerings.

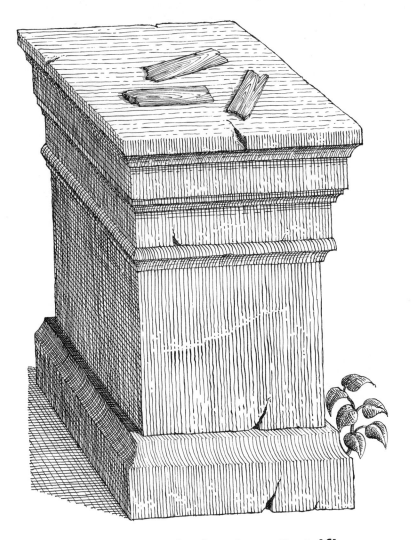

## Fragments of *Plasticus Petrificus*

Called simply "Formica" by the ancients (MICA being the god of craftsmanship), these three priceless fragments from the front of the Great Altar represent an unequaled degree of aesthetic sophistication and almost superhuman technical skill. The richness of the coloring and the intricacy of the linear engraving can only be approximated today by using the finest woods.

## The Bell System

This highly complex percussion instrument was found near the statue of WATT. Markings similar to those on the face of the upper altar imply a symbolic connection to the gods. The Bell System was played by holding one half of the instrument in each hand and banging them together in some pre-established rhythmic pattern. The impact would cause a small bell inside the larger of the two pieces to ring. Both halves were connected by a beautifully crafted coil which would miraculously reform itself into the identical number of loops after each playing.

## The Internal Component Enclosure

This exquisitely fashioned container, a twentieth-century adaptation of the ancient Canopic[1] jar, stood on a specially designed table in the outer chamber. The exterior surface of the container was fashioned out of *plasticus petrificus*, while the interior was lined with a priceless translucent substance. Since no trace of an internal organ was found in the ICE its function as a Canopic jar is considered to have been merely symbolic.

[1]Canopic (kə nō′ pik): A jar in which the ancient Egyptians preserved the internal organs of a deceased person, usually for burial with a mummy.

## Small Relief

This extremely fine piece of workmanship served as a portable shrine which was to be carried through life and into eternal life. Its delicate inscriptions were intended to identify an individual's religious preference along with the burial site to which the body should be delivered when necessary. Matching inscriptions were found on the main doors of the great sanctuary. Because the ancients were unable to predict the exact time of death, each of the shrines had to last for an entire year.

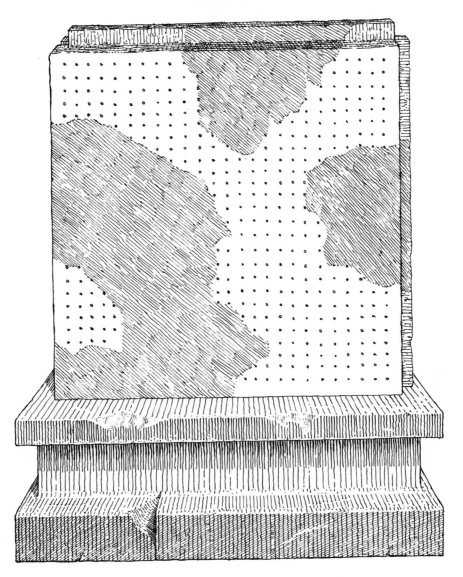

## A Mosaic Tile (restored)

Unlike their predecessors, the ancient North Americans covered the ceilings of their buildings, rather than the floors, with intricate mosaics. Each tile was decorated with a series of parallel perforations, and then a color was added by applying the occasional and always subtle watermark.

# Epilogue

*In the years to come, hundreds of people would travel to the Motel of the Mysteries to view the vast complex of tombs—complete with ceremonial pool.*

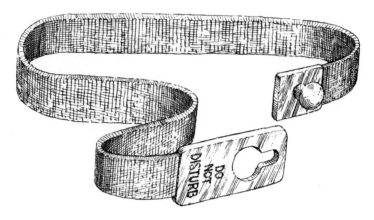

SACRED SEAL BELT

This attractive all-leather belt is made especially for THE MUSEUM SHOP by a famous Italian belt maker. The beautiful two-piece buckle is based on the Sacred Seal and the handle from the outer door. Great care has been taken to accurately reproduce the inscription and the proportions of the original. Both pieces are available in either silver or 24-karat gold.

**Reader's Response** ∽ Of all the treasures listed, which did you find the most amusing? Why?

**Library Link** ∽ *To find more of Howard Carson's hilarious interpretations of twentieth-century life, look for* Motel of the Mysteries *by David Macaulay.*

# DAVID MACAULAY

David Macaulay is the author-illustrator of books noted for their accuracy of detail, intriguing content, and appeal to both children and adults. In award-winning books such as *Cathedral: The Story of Its Construction,* and *City: A Story of Roman Planning and Construction,* Macaulay lays bare the inner workings of structures. *The Way Things Work* is a best-seller, satisfying people's desire to understand the machines around them.

A teacher of drawing and illustration, Macaulay has strong ideas about the importance of understanding what we see. He expressed some of those ideas in a speech he made while accepting the prestigious Caldecott Medal for his book *Black and White.*

"Seeing necessitates looking and thinking. When I teach drawing, I must constantly remind my students to distinguish between what they see and what they think they see. Thinking—at least the lazy, day-to-day kind of thinking—often gets in the way of the drawing process, which requires a stubborn curiosity about why things look the way they do.

"The problem of not really seeing sounds inoffensive enough; after all, we can't be expected to see everything. But as soon as not seeing becomes a habit, we start accepting our visual environment without question. As technology becomes increasingly more complex, we are less and less able to actually see how things work. Switches and buttons are hidden behind plates. Just flip or push, but don't ask questions. Visual complacency rears its ugly head, and each time it does we humans lose a little ground."

*Yonder in the north . . . Cloud maidens dance . . . There we take our being.*
—TEWA PUEBLO CHANT

Ancestors of today's Pueblo peoples pecked out images of a kachina,
an arrow-swallower, and a shield near Galisteo, New Mexico, about A.D. 1400.
Photograph by Ira Block

THROUGH TEWA EYES

by ALFONSO ORTIZ

I do not remember the day, of course, but I know what happened. Four days after I was born in the Pueblo Indian village of San Juan in the Rio Grande Valley in New Mexico, the "umbilical cord-cutting mother" and her assistant came to present me to the sun and to give me a name. They took me from the house just as the sun's first rays appeared over the Sangre de Cristo Mountains. The cord-cutting mother proffered me and two perfect ears of corn, one blue and one white, to the six sacred directions. A prayer was said:

> *Here is a child who has been given to us. Let us bring him to*
> *manhood. . . . You who are dawn youths and dawn maidens.*
> *You who are winter spirits. You who are summer spirits . . .*
> *Take therefore. . . . Give him good fortune, we ask of you.*

Now the name was given. It was not the name at the head of this story. It was my Tewa name, a thing of power. Usually such a name evokes either nature—the mountains or the hills or the season—or a ceremony under way at the time of the birth. By custom such a name is shared only within the community, and with those we know well. Thus, in the eyes of my Tewa people, I was "brought in out of the darkness," where I had no identity. Thus I became a child of the Tewa. My world is the Tewa world. It is different from your world.

Consider the question of the origin of Native American peoples. Archaeologists will tell you that we came at least 12,000 years ago from Asia, crossing the Bering land bridge, then spreading over the two American continents. These archaeologists have dug countless holes in the earth looking for spearpoints, bones, traces of fires; they have subjected these objects to sophisticated dating analysis—seeking to prove or disprove a hypothesis or date. I know of their work. I too have been to Soviet Asia and seen cave art and an old ceremonial costume remarkably similar to some found in America. But a Tewa is not so interested in the work of archaeologists.

A Tewa is interested in our own story of our origin, for it holds all that we need to know about our people, and how one should live as a human. The story defines our society. It tells me who I am, where I came from, the boundaries of my world, what kind of order exists within it; how suffering, evil, and death came into this world; and what is likely to happen to *me* when I die.

Let me tell you that story:

*Yonder in the north there is singing on the lake. Cloud
    maidens dance on the shore. There we take our being.
Yonder in the north cloud beings rise. They ascend onto
    cloud blossoms. There we take our being.
Yonder in the north rain stands over the land ... Yonder
    in the north stands forth at twilight the arc of a rainbow.
There we have our being.*

Our ancestors came from the north. Theirs was not a journey to be measured in centuries, for it was as much a journey of the spirit as it was a migration of a people. The Tewa know not when the journey southward began or when it ended, but we do know where it began, how it proceeded, and where it ended. We are unconcerned about time in its historical dimensions, but we will recall in endless detail the features of the 12 places our ancestors stopped.

We point to these places to show that the journey did indeed take place. This is the only proof a Tewa requires. And each time a Tewa recalls a place where they paused, for whatever length of time, every feature of the earth and sky comes vividly to life, and the journey itself lives again.

At the beginning of all beginnings our ancestors came up out of the earth, until they were living beneath Sandy Place Lake to the north. The world under the lake was like this one, but dark. Spirits, people, and animals lived together; death was unknown.

Among the spirits were the first mothers of all the Tewa, known as Blue Corn Woman Near to Summer and White Corn Maiden Near to Ice. These mothers asked one of the men present

In a distant time and place—a lake "far to the north"—our ancestors originated, the Tewa tell their children. Artist Felipe Davalos transformed the vivid oral tradition into this imaginative painting.

The story proceeds: In the dark within earth, Blue Corn Woman Near to Summer and White Corn Maiden Near to Ice ask a man to explore how the people might emerge. When he travels to the "above," predatory birds and animals attack but then befriend him. With their gifts of weapons and clothing, he returns to his people as the Hunt Chief and creates a Summer (Blue Corn) Chief and a Winter (White Corn) chief, here flanked by war gods. Each chief will lead the people part of the year. (And so it is today.)

Next, pairs of brothers are sent to explore in all directions: The two who move upward find a rainbow and guide their people to the light. But the people must return to the lake for essential help: a medicine man to counter evil, sacred painted clowns to banish sadness, and a scalp chief for success in war, with a women's society to assist him.

345

to go forth and explore the way by which the people might leave the lake.

After many adventures and struggles he returned to the people, announcing his arrival with the call of a fox. He came now as Mountain Lion or Hunt Chief. The people rejoiced, saying, "We have been accepted."

They left the lake and entered the land.

That the Tewa see all life as beginning within the earth, like the corn plant that has sustained us for centuries, is manifest in our sacred places: The kiva, the ceremonial center, which represents the primordial home under the lake; the "earth mother earth navel middle place" in every village; and our mountaintop shrines— "earth navels"—shaped of stones or boulders.

These trace back to the first permanent habitations of the Pueblo people.

The canyons, cliffs, and mesa tops of the Four Corners area of the Southwest hold evidence that, at least by the fifth century anno Domini (as the white man reckons time), the Pueblo people did, indeed, begin life within the earth. The habitations they constructed were circular pit houses, dug wholly or mostly underground and covered with branches and dirt. Entrance ramps opened to the southeast, the direction of the rising sun during the colder months of the year. To enter the pit house, then, was to enter the earth, and to enter the earth was to return to one of the two sources of all life through the opening that connected it with the other source, the sun.

These pit-house people lived within the womb of mother earth while also drawing sustenance from the sun father. A small round hole was also dug and carefully protected on the floor of their pit house to remind them of their original emergence from within the earth. They termed such a hole "earth germinating mother earth navel middle place"— the origin of the sacred place in the plazas of our villages today.

From the outside these pit houses resembled nothing more than giant rounded anthills. Yet their form would take on profound meaning.

The kiva is central to Pueblo well-being and spiritual life. At San Ildefonso, New Mexico, a stair rather than the usual ladder eases the way to a rooftop entry hole.
Photograph by Ira Block

*I*n time the pit-house people emerged to build, above-ground, rectangular house blocks, but they retained the basic shape of their pit house by building kivas, or cere-monial chambers, one of which was always attached to each house block. These were built underground and to the southeast. The kiva was no longer entered through a sloping ramp but through a hole in the roof. The old rampway was now repre-sented by a deeply recessed wall, still located in the southeast part of the kiva. This new structure resembled an old-fashioned keyhole so much that it is called a keyhole-shaped kiva by archaeologists.

Southeast of the kiva was the refuse depositing place, where the dead were buried. The positioning of the dead closest to the direction of the sunrise reflects a recognition by the Pueblo people that the sun father is both the giver and the taker of life. What he gives he also takes back, eventually. The three parts—house block, kiva, and refuse dump/cemetery—became standard.

And the kiva, in its central position, came to mediate between the living and the dead. Here the living may perform rituals addressed to the dead and, hence, communicate with them. In later

347

times there were great dramatic performances in which the living personified the spirits of the dead in these kivas.

Finally the villages became multistoried house blocks resembling fortresses. This presented a dilemma to the people: The buildings blocked the rising sun's rays from the dead buried outside. The old keyhole kiva must give way.

Today the kiva may be a rectangular room in the house block, but the old form is retained; an opening provides an unobstructed channel toward the sunrise, representing the lifeline into the village.

The people also took the shape of the pit house and old kiva to the mountaintops, creating a keyhole form with stones, with the lower end of the keyhole opened toward the sunrise. Only the form reminded one that it represented what was once an underground habitation and later a religious sanctum. The Tewa continue to make pilgrimages to the mountain earth navels, for these are places of great power: They provide the Tewa with a way of rediscovering who we are and of renewing our ties to our beginnings. They represent ongoing lifelines to sustain all creation. And—through the centuries when the Spanish and other peoples dominated the Tewa—these places have provided a tenacious symbol of survival.

Our genesis story establishes another vital aspect of our lives. Remember my naming ceremony: There were two women attending, two ears of corn offered with me to the sun. This duality is basic to understanding our behavior.

When the Tewa came onto land, the Hunt Chief took an ear of blue corn and handed it to one of the other men and said: "You are to lead and care for all the people during the summer." To another man he handed an ear of white corn and told him: "You shall lead and care for the people during the winter." This is how the Summer and Winter Chiefs were instituted.

The Hunt Chief then divided the people between the two chiefs. As they moved south down the Rio Grande, the Summer People traveled on the west side of the river, the Winter People on the east side.

The Summer People lived by agriculture, the Winter People by hunting.

From this time, the story tells us, the Tewa have been divided during their lives into moieties—Winter People, Summer People. Still today a Summer Chief guides us seven months of the year, during the agricultural cycle; a Winter Chief during the five months of hunting. There are special rituals, dances, costumes, and colors attached to each moiety. Everything that has symbolic significance to the Tewa is classified in dualities: Games, plants, and diseases are hot or cold, winter or summer. Some persons or things, like healers, are of the middle, mediating between the two. This gives order to our lives.

A child is incorporated into his moiety through the water-giving ceremony during his first year. The Winter Chief conducts his rite in October; the Summer Chief in late February or March. The ceremony is held in a sanctuary at the chief's home. There are an altar, a sand painting, and various symbols; the chief and his assistants dress in white buckskin. A final character appears, preceded by the call of a fox, as in the creation story. It is the Hunt Chief.

A female assistant holds the child; the moiety chief recites a short prayer and administers a drink of the sacred medicinal water from an abalone shell, thereby welcoming the child into the moiety.

The third rite in a child's life—water pouring—comes between the ages of six and ten and is held within the moiety. It marks the transition from the carefree, innocent state of early childhood to the status of adult, one of the Dry Food People. For four days the boys are made to carry a load of firewood they have chopped themselves, and the girls a basket of cornmeal they have ground themselves, to the homes of their sponsors.

A sponsor instructs each child in the beliefs and practices of the village. On the fourth night, the deities come to the kiva, and the child may go watch. Afterward, the sponsor bathes the child, pouring water over him. From this time, the child is given duties judged proper for his sex.

A finishing ritual a few years later brings the girls and boys to adulthood. For the boys it is particularly meaningful, for they now become eligible to assist and participate in the coming of the gods in their moiety's kiva. Thus the bonds of the moiety are further strengthened.

*I*t is at death that the bond of moiety is broken and the solidarity of the whole society emphasized again. This echoes the genesis story, for after the people had divided into two for their journey from the lake, they came together again when they arrived at their destination.

When a Tewa dies, relatives dress the corpse. The moccasins are reversed—for the Tewa believe everything in the afterlife is reversed from this life. There is a Spanish Catholic wake, a Requiem Mass, then the trip to the cemetery. There the priest completes the church's funeral rites: the sprinkling of holy water, a prayer, a handful of dirt thrown into the grave. Then all non-Indians leave.

A bag containing the clothing of the deceased is now placed under his head as a pillow, along with other personal possessions. When the grave is covered, a Tewa official tells the survivors that the deceased has gone to the place "of endless cicada singing," that he will be happy, and he admonishes them not to let the loss divide the home.

During the four days following death, the soul, or Dry Food Who Is No Longer, is believed to wander about in this world in the company of the ancestors. These four days produce a time of unease. There is the fear among relatives that the soul may become lonely and return to take one of them for company. Children are deemed most susceptible. The house itself must not be left unoccupied.

The uneasiness ends on the fourth night, when relatives gather again to perform the releasing rite. There are rituals with tobacco, a piece of charcoal, a series of four lines drawn on the floor. A pottery bowl, used in his naming ceremony long ago and cherished by him all his life, is broken, or "killed." Then a prayer reveals the purpose of the symbols:

> *We have muddied the waters for you [the smoke]. We have cast shadows between us [the charcoal]. We have made steep gullies between us [the lines]. Do not, therefore, reach for even a hair on our heads. Rather, help us attain that which we are always seeking: Long life, that our children may grow, abundant game, the raising of crops .... Now you must go, for you are now free.*

After their emergence the Tewa journey south, with planters, the Summer People, traveling on the west side of the Rio Grande, and hunters, the Winter People, on the east. At the 12th stop, the groups merge to found the pueblo of Posi. In the cardinal directions, each associated with a color, lie sacred mountains, mesas, and stone shrines. Here live the ancestors and other spirits. Ceremonies on the plaza, like this basket dance, mark the four seasons and provide a sense of renewal.

351

With the soul released, all breathe a sigh of relief. They wash their hands. As each finishes, he says, "May you have life." The others respond, "Let it be so." Everyone now eats.

The Tewa begin and end life as one people; we call the life cycle *poeh,* or emergence path. As a Tewa elder told me:

"In the beginning we were one. Then we divided into Summer People and Winter People; in the end we came together again as we are today."

This is the path of our lives.

Reader's Response ～ In what ways is your world different from the author's Tewa world? In what ways is it similar?

Library Link ～ *If you're interested in finding out more about Native American heritage, look for the October 1991 edition of* National Geographic *in your local library.*

# THE POTTERY OF
# San Ildefonso

San Ildefonso, just northeast of Santa Fe, New Mexico, is a Tewa Pueblo known for its beautiful pottery. Pueblo pottery making, a tradition among the Tewa, is one of the oldest known crafts of any North American Indian group. Prior to 1920 the Tewa at San Ildefonso made pottery for ceremonial or household use only, but in the mid-1920s many Tewa women began selling their pottery to tourists and collectors. The popularity of the pottery helped to establish the Pueblo as a center of Indian arts.

San Ildefonso
Black-on-Black Jar
1919.

The San Ildefonso Tewa make their pottery in various shapes and styles. Most use a variety of designs and techniques to create their pots and jars. Many potters at the Pueblo work in the black-on-black style originated by Maria Montoya Martinez and her husband Julian. By decorating polished pottery with wet clay (called slip) and then leaving the wet clay unpolished before firing, or baking, Martinez and her husband created two shades of black—one dull and plain, the other highly polished. This simple shading technique produces a dark contrast that is both beautiful and unique.

San Ildefonso potters also make polychrome pottery, which involves baking two or more colors onto the same pot or jar, though not necessarily on the same surface. The rich colors and intricate designs of polychrome pottery result in bowls and jars that reflect the varied colors of the southwestern desert.

San Ildefonso
Polychrome Jar
1925-1935.

The black-on-black and polychrome styles represent the diverse beauty of Pueblo pottery. And although new techniques have been developed, the potters at San Ildefonso continue to uphold the age-old tradition of their Tewa elders.

NOVELLA

# A CROWN OF WILD OLIVE

## BY ROSEMARY SUTCLIFF

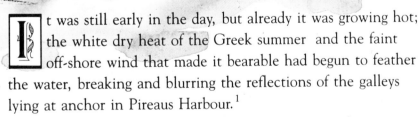

It was still early in the day, but already it was growing hot;
the white dry heat of the Greek summer and the faint
off-shore wind that made it bearable had begun to feather
the water, breaking and blurring the reflections of the galleys
lying at anchor in Pireaus Harbour.[1]

Half Athens, it seemed, had crowded down to the port to
watch the *Paralos*, the State Galley, sail for the Isthmus, taking
their finest athletes on the first stage of their journey to Olympia.

---

[1]Some words in this selection are spelled in the British style.

Every fourth summer it happened; every fourth summer for
more than three hundred years. Nothing was allowed to stand in
the way, earthquake or pestilence or even war—even the long and
weary war which, after a while of uneasy peace, had broken out
again last year between Athens and Sparta.

Back in the spring the Herald had come, proclaiming the
Truce of the Games; safe conduct through all lands and across all
seas, both for the athletes and those who went to watch them
compete. And now, from every Greek state and from colonies and
settlements all round the Mediterranean, the athletes would be
gathering. . . .

Aboard the *Paralos* was all the ordered bustle of departure,
ropes being cast off, rowers in their places at the oars. The Athenian athletes and their trainers with them had gathered on the
afterdeck. Amyntas, son of Ariston, had drawn a little apart from
the rest. He was the youngest there, still several months from his
eighteenth birthday and somewhat conscious that he had not yet
sacrificed his boy's long hair to Apollo, while the rest, even of
those entered for the boys' events—you counted as a boy at Olympia until you were twenty—were already short-haired and doing
their Military Service. A few of them even had scars gained in
border clashes with the Spartans, to prove that their real place,
whatever it might be on the race track or in the wrestling pit, was
with the men. Amyntas envied them. He was proud that he had
been picked so young to run for Athens in the Boys' Double
Stade,[2] the Four Hundred Yards. But he was lonely. He was bound
in with all the others by their shared training; but they were
bound together by something else, by another kind of life, other
loyalties and shared experiences and private jokes, from which he
was still shut out.

The last ropes holding ship to shore were being cast off now.
Fathers and brothers and friends on the jetty were calling last
moment advice and good luck wishes. Nobody called to Amyntas,
but he turned and looked back to where his father stood among
the crowd. Ariston had been a runner too in his day, before a
Spartan spear wound had stiffened his left knee and spoiled his

[2]Stade (stāde): a foot race the length of the stadium

own hopes of an Olympic Olive Crown. Everyone said that he and Amyntas were very alike, and looking back now at the slight dark man who still held himself like a runner, Amyntas hoped with a warm rush of pride, that they were right. He wished he had said so, before he came aboard; there were so many things he would have liked to have said, but he was even more tongue-tied with his father than he was with the rest of the world, when it came to saying the things that mattered. Now, as the last ropes fell away, he flung up his hand in salute, and tried to put them all into one wordless message. "I'll run the best race that's in me, Father—and if the Gods let me win it, I'll remember that I'm winning for us both."

Among the waving crowd, his father flung up an answering hand, as though he had somehow received the message. The water was widening between ship and shore; the Bos'n struck up the rowing time on his flute, and the rowers bent to their oars, sending the *Paralos* through the water towards the harbor mouth. Soon the crowd on shore was only a shingle of dark and coloured and white along the waterfront. But far off beyond the roofs of the warehouses and the covered docks, a flake of light showed where high over Athens the sunlight flashed back from the upraised spear-blade of the great Athene of the Citadel, four miles away.

They were out round the mole now, the one sail broke out from the mast, and they headed for the open gulf.

That night they beached the *Paralos* and made camp on the easternmost point of the long island of Salamis; and not long past noon the next day they went ashore at the Isthmus and took horse for Corinth on the far side, where a second galley was waiting to take them down the coast. At evening on the fifth day they rode down into the shallow valley where Olympian Zeus the Father of Gods and men had his sanctuary, and where the Sacred Games were celebrated in his honour.

What with the long journey and the strangeness of everything, Amyntas took in very little of that first evening. They were met and greeted by the Council of the Games, whose president made them a speech of welcome, after which the Chief Herald

read them the rules. And afterwards they ate the evening meal in the athletes' mess; food that seemed to have no more taste nor substance than the food one eats in a dream. Then the dream blended away into a dark nothingness of sleep that took Amyntas almost before he had lain down on the narrow stretcher bed in the athletes' lodging, which would be his for the next month.

He woke to the first dappled fingers of sunlight shafting in through the doorway of his cell. They wavered and danced a little, as though broken by the shadow of tree branches. Somewhere further down the valley a cuckoo was calling, and the world was real again, and his, and new as though it had been born that morning. He rolled over, and lay for a few moments, his hands behind his head, looking up at the bare rafters; then shot off the bed and through the doorway in one swallow-dive of movement, to sluice his head and shoulders in the icy water trickling from the mouth of a stone bull into a basin just outside. He came up for air, spluttering and shaking the water out of his eyes. For a moment he saw the colonnaded court and the plane tree arching over the basin through a splintered brightness of flying droplets. And then suddenly, in the brightness, there stood a boy of about his own age, who must have come out of the lodging close behind him. A boy with a lean angular body, and a dark, bony face under a shock of hair like the crest of an ill-groomed pony. For a long moment they stood looking at each other. Then Amyntas moved aside to let the other come to the conduit.

As the stranger ducked his head and shoulders under the falling water, Amyntas saw his back. From shoulder to flank it was criss-crossed with scars, past the purple stage but not yet faded to the silvery white that they would be in a few years' time; pinkish scars that looked as though the skin was still drawn uncomfortably tight over them.

He must have made some betraying sound or movement, because the other boy ducked out from under the water, thrusting the wet russet hair back out of his eyes, and demanded curtly,

"Have you never seen a Spartan back before?"

So that was it. Amyntas, like everyone else, had heard dark stories of Spartan boys flogged, sometimes to death, in a ritual test of courage, before the shrine of Artemis Orthia, the Lady of the Beasts.

"No," he said, "I am Athenian." And did not add that he hoped to see plenty of Spartan backs when once he had started his military service. It was odd, the cheap jibe came neatly into his head, and yet he did not even want to speak it. It was as though here at Olympia, the Truce of the Games was not just a rule of conduct, but something in one's heart. Instead, he added, "And my name is Amyntas."

They seemed to stand confronting each other for a long time. The Spartan boy had the look of a dog sniffing at a stranger's fist and taking his own time to make sure whether it was friendly. Then he smiled; a slow, rather grave smile, but unexpectedly warm. "And mine is Leon."

"And you're a runner." Amyntas was taking in his build and the way he stood.

"I am entered for the Double Stade."

"Then we race against each other."

Leon said in the same curt tone, "May we both run a good race."

"And meanwhile,—when did you arrive, Leon?"

"Last night, the same as you."

Amyntas, who usually found it nearly as difficult to talk to strangers as he did to his own father, was surprised to hear himself saying, "Then you'll have seen no more of Olympia than I have. Shall we go and get some clothes on and have a look around?"

But by that time more men and boys were coming out into the early sunshine, yawning and stretching the sleep out of their muscles. And Amyntas felt a hand clamp down on his shoulder, and heard the voice of Hippias his trainer, "Oh no you don't, my lad! Five days' break in training is long enough, and I've work for you before you do any sightseeing!"

After that, they were kept hard at it, on the practice track

and in the wrestling school that had the names of past Olympic victors carved on the colonnade walls. For the last month's training for the Games had to be done at Olympia itself; and the last month's training was hard, in the old style that did not allow for rest days in the modern fashion that most of the Athenian trainers favoured. Everything at Olympia had to be done the old way, even to clearing the stadium of its four years' growth of grass and weeds and spreading it with fresh sand. At other Crown Games, the work was done by paid labourers, but here, the contending athletes must do it themselves, to the glory of the Gods, as they had done it in the far-off days when the Games were new. Some of them grumbled a good deal and thought it was time that the Priests of Zeus and the Council of the Games brought their ideas up to date; but to Amyntas there seemed to be a sort of rightness about the thing as it was.

His training time was passed among boys from Corinth and Epidauros, Rhodes and Samos and Macedon. At first they were just figures in outline, like people seen too far off to have faces, whom he watched with interest at track work, at javelin or discus throwing or in the wrestling pit, trying to judge their form as he knew they were trying to judge his and each other's. But gradually as the early days went by, they changed into people with faces, with personal habits, and likes and dislikes, suffering from all the strains and stresses of the last weeks before the Games. But even before those first few days were over, he and the Spartan boy had drifted into a companionable pattern of doing things together. They would sluice each other down, squatting in the stone hip-baths in the washing room after practice, and scrape the mess of rubbing oil and sand off each other's backs—it took Amyntas a little while to learn to scrape the bronze blade of the strigil straight over the scars on Leon's back as though they were not there—and when they took their turn at scraping up the four years' growth of grass and sun-dried herbs from the stadium, they generally worked together, sharing one of the big rush carrying-baskets between them. And in the evenings, after the day's train-ing was over, or in the hot noonday break when most people stretched themselves out in the shade of the plane trees for sleep or quiet talk, they seemed, more often than not, to drift into each other's company.

Once or twice they went to have a look at the town of tents and booths that was beginning to spring up all round the Sacred Enclosure and the Gymnasium buildings—for a Games Festival drew many people beside those who came to compete or to watch; merchants and wine sellers and fortune tellers, poets determined to get poems heard, horse dealers from Corinth and Cyrene, gold-smiths and leather-workers, philosophers gathering for the pleasure of arguing with each other, sword and fire swallowers, and acrobats who could dance on their hands to the soft notes of Phrygian pipes. But Leon did not much like the crowded noisy tent-ground; and most often they wandered down to the river that flung its loop about the south side of Olympia. It had shrunk now in the summer heat, to little more than a chain of pools in the middle of its pale dried-out pebbly bed; but there was shade under the oleander trees, and generally a whisper of moving air. And lying on the bank in the shade was free. It had dawned on Amyntas quite early that the reason Leon did not like the fairground was that he had no money. The Spartans did not use money, or at least, having decided that it was a bad thing, they had no coinage but iron bars so big and heavy that nobody could carry them about, or even keep a store at home that was worth enough to be any use. They were very proud of their freedom from wealth, but it made life difficult at a gathering such as this, when they had to mix with people from other states. Leon covered up by being extremely scornful of the gay and foolish things for sale in the merchants' booths, and the acrobats who passed the bowl round for contributions after their performance; but he was just that shade too scornful to be convincing. And anyway, Amyntas had none too much money himself, to get him through the month.

So they went to the river. They were down there one hot noontide something over a week after they had first arrived at Olympia; Amyntas lying on his back, his hands behind his head, squinting up into the dark shadow-shapes of the oleander branches against the sky; Leon sitting beside him with his arms round his updrawn knees, staring out in the dazzle of sunlight over the open riverbed. They had been talking runners' talk, and suddenly Amyntas said, "I was watching the Corinthian making his practice run this morning. I don't *think* we have either of us much to fear from him."

"The Rhodian runs well," said Leon, not bringing back his gaze from the white dance of sunlight beyond the oleanders.

"But he uses himself up too quickly. He's the kind that makes all the front running at first, and has nothing left for the home stretch. Myself, I'd say that red-headed barbarian from Macedon had the better chance."

"He's well enough for speed; and he knows how and when to use it. . . . What do you give for Nikomedes' chances?"

"Nikomedes?—The boy from Megara? It's hard to say. Not

much, from the form he's shown so far; but we've only seen him at practice, and he's the sort that sometimes catches fire when it comes to the real thing. . . ."

There was a long silence between them, and they heard the churring of the grasshoppers, like the heat-shimmer turned to sound. And then Amyntas said, "I think you are the one I have most to fear."

And Leon turned his head slowly and looked down at him, and said, "Have you only just woken to that? I knew the same thing of *you*, three days ago."

And they were both silent again, and suddenly a little shocked. You might think that kind of thing, but it was best not to put it into words.

Leon made a quick sign with his fingers to avert ill luck; and Amyntas scrambled to his feet. "Come on, it's time we were getting back." They were both laughing, but a little breathlessly. Leon dived to his feet also, and shot ahead as they went up through the

riverside scrub. But next instant, between one flying leap and the next, he stumbled slightly, and checked; then turned back, stooping to search for something among the dusty root-tangle of dry grass and camomile. Amyntas, swerving just in time to avoid him, checked also.

"What is it?"

"Something sharp. . . ." Leon pulled out from where it had lain half-buried, the broken end of a sickle blade that looked as though it might have lain there since the last Games. "Seems it's not only the Stadium that needs clearing up." He began to walk on, carrying the jagged fragment in his hand. But Amyntas saw the blood on the dry ground where he had been standing.

"You have cut your foot."

"I know," Leon said, and went on walking.

"Yes, I *know* you know. Let me look at it."

"It's only a scratch."

"All the same—show me."

Leon stood on one leg, steadying himself with a hand on Amyntas' shoulder, and turned up the sole of his foot. "Look then. You can hardly see it."

There was a cut on the hard brown sole, not long, but deep, with the blood welling slowly. Amyntas said in sudden exasperation, "Haven't you *any* sense? Oh we all know about the Spartan boy with the fox under his cloak, and nobody but you Spartans thinks it's a particularly clever or praiseworthy story; but if you get dirt into that cut, you'll like enough have to scratch from the race!"

Leon suddenly grinned. "Nobody but we Spartans understand that story. But about the dirt, you could be right."

"I could. And that bit of iron is dirty enough for a start. Best get the wound cleaned up, in the river before we go back to the Gymnasium. Then your trainer can take over."

So with Leon sitting on a boulder at the edge of the shrunken river, Amyntas set to work with ruthless thoroughness to clean the cut. He pulled it open, the cool water running over his hands, and a thin thread of crimson fronded away downstream. It would help clean the wound to let it bleed a little; but after a few moments the bleeding almost stopped. No harm in making sure; he ducked his head to the place, sucked hard and spat crimson into the water. Then he tore a strip from the skirt of his tunic; he would have commandeered Leon's own—after all it was Leon's foot—but he knew that the Spartan boys were only allowed to own one tunic at a time; if he did that, Leon would be left without a respectable tunic to wear at the Sacrifices. He lashed the thin brown foot tightly. "Now—put your arm over my shoulder and try to keep your weight off the cut as much as you can."

"Cluck, cluck, cluck!" said Leon, but he did as Amyntas said.

As they skirted the great open space of the Hippodrome, where the chariot races would be held on the second day of the Games, they came up with a couple of the Athenian contingent, strolling under the plane trees. Eudorus the wrestler looked round and his face quickened with concern, "Run into trouble?"

"Ran into the remains of a sickle blade someone left in the

long grass," Amyntas said, touching the rusty bit of metal he had taken from Leon and stuck in his own belt. "It's near the tendon, but it's all right, so long as there's no dirt left in it."

"Near the tendon, eh? Then we'd best be taking no chances." Eudorus looked at Leon. "You are Spartan, I think?—Amyntas, go and find the Spartan trainer; I'll take over here." And then to Leon again, "Will you allow me to carry you up to the lodging? It seems the simplest way."

Amyntas caught one parting glimpse of Leon's rigid face as Eudorus lifted him, lightly as a ten-year-old, and set off towards the gymnasium buildings; and laughter caught at his stomach; but mixed with the laughter was sympathy. He knew he would have been just as furious in Leon's place. All this fuss and to-do over a cut that would have been nothing in itself—if the Games had not been only three weeks off.

He set off in search of the trainer.

In the middle of that night, Amyntas woke up with a thought already shaped and complete in his mind. It was an ugly thought, and it sat on his chest and mouthed at him slyly. "Leon is the one you have most to fear. If Leon is out of the race. . . ."

He looked at it in the darkness, feeling a little sick. Then he pushed it away, and rolled over on to his face with his head in his arms, and after a while he managed to go back to sleep again.

Next day, as soon as he could slip away between training sessions, he went out into the growing town of tents and booths, and found a seller of images and votive offerings, and bought a little bronze bull with silvered horns. It cost nearly all the money that he had to spare, so that he would not now be able to buy the hunting knife with silver inlay on the hilt that had caught his fancy a day or two since. With the little figure in his hand, he went to the Sacred Enclosure, where, among altars shaded by plane trees, and statues of Gods and Olympic heroes, the great Temple of Zeus faced the older and darker house of Hera his wife.

Before the Temple of Zeus, the ancient wild olive trees from which the victors' crowns were made cast dapple-shade across the lower steps of the vast portico. He spoke to the attendant priest in the deep threshold shadows beyond.

"I ask leave to enter and make an offering."

"Enter then, and make the offering," the man said.

And he went through into the vastness of the Temple itself, where the sunlight sifting through under the acanthus roof tiles made a honeycomb glow that hung high in the upper spaces and flowed down the gigantic columns, but scarcely touched the pavement under foot, so that he seemed to wade in cool shadows. At the far end, sheathed in gold and ivory, his feet half lost in shadows, his head gloried with the dim radiance of the upper air, stern and serene above the affairs of mortal men, stood the mighty statue of the God himself. Olympian Zeus, in whose honour the Sacred Games had been held for more than three hundred years. Three hundred years, such a little while; looking up at the heart-

369

stilling face above him, Amyntas wondered if the God had even noticed, yet, that they were begun. Everything in the God's House was so huge, even time. . . . For a moment his head swam, and he had no means of judging the size of anything, even himself, here where all the known landmarks of the world of men were left behind. Only one thing, when he looked at it, remained constant in size; the tiny bronze bull with the silvered horns that he held in his hand.

He went forward to the first of the Offering Tables before the feet of the gigantic statue, and set it down. Now, the tables were empty and waiting, but by the end of the festival they would be piled with offerings; small humble ones like his own, and silver cups and tripods of gilded bronze to be taken away and housed in the Temple treasury. On the eve of the Games they would begin to fill up, with votive offerings made for the most part by the athletes themselves, for their own victory, or the victory of a friend taking part in a different event. Amyntas was not making the offering for his own victory, nor for Leon's. He was not quite sure why he was making it, but it was for something much more complicated than victory in the Double Stade. With one finger still resting on the back of the little bronze bull, he sent up the best prayer he could sort out from the tangle of thoughts and feelings within himself. "Father of all things, Lord of these Sacred Games, let me keep a clean heart in this, let me run the best race that is in me, and think of nothing more."

Outside again, beyond the dapple-shade of the olive trees, the white sunlight fell dazzling across his eyes, and the world of men, in which things had returned to their normal size, received him back; and he knew that Hippias was going to be loudly angry with him for having missed a training session. But unaccountably, everything, including Hippias' anger, seemed surprisingly small.

Leon had to break training for three days, at least so far as track-work was concerned; and it was several more before he could get back into full training; so for a while it was doubtful whether he would be able to take his place in the race. But with still more than a week to go, both his trainer and the Doctor-Priest of

Asklepius[3] declared him fit, and his name remained on the list of entrants for the Double Stade.

And then it was the first day of the Festival; the day of solemn dedication, when each competitor must go before the Council to be looked over and identified, and take the Oath of the Games before the great bronze statue of Zeus of the Thunderbolts.

The day passed. And next morning before it was light, Amyntas woke to hear the unmistakable, unforgettable voice of the crowds gathering in the Stadium. A shapeless surf of sound, pricked by the sharper cries of the jugglers and acrobats, and the sellers of water and honeycakes, myrtle, and victors' ribbons calling their wares.

This was the day of the Sacred Procession; the Priests and Officials, the beasts garlanded for sacrifice, the athletes marching into the waiting Stadium, while the Herald proclaimed the name and state of each one as he passed the rostrum. Amyntas, marching in with the Athenians, heard his own name called, and Leon's, among names from Samos and Cyrene, Crete and Corinth, and Argos and Megara. And he smelled the incense on the morning air, and felt for the first time, under his swelling pride in being Athenian, the thread of his own Greekness interwoven with the Greekness of all those others. This must have been, a little, the thing their Great Grandfathers had felt when they stood together, shield to shield, to hurl back the whole strength of invading Persia, so that they might remain free. That had been in a Games year, too. . . .

The rest of that day was given over to the chariot and horse races; and that night Amyntas went to his sleeping cell with the thunder of hooves and wheels still sounding somewhere behind his ears. He seemed to hear it in his dreams all night, but when he woke in the morning, it had turned into the sound that he had woken to yesterday, the surf-sound of the gathering crowd. But this morning it had a new note for him, for this was the Day, and the crowd that was gathering out there round the Stadium was his crowd, and his belly tightened and the skin prickled at the back of his neck as he heard it.

[3]Asklepius (ăs klē′ pē əs): the Greek god of medicine

371

He lay for a few moments, listening, then got up and went out to the conduit. Leon came out after him as he had done that first morning of all, and they sluiced down as best they could. The water barely dribbled from the mouth of the stone bull now, for with the vast gathering of people, and the usual end-of-summer drought, the water shortage was getting desperate, as it always did by the time the Festival days arrived.

"How is the foot?" Amyntas asked.

"I can't remember where the cut was, unless I look for it."

They stood looking at each other, the friendship that they had never put into words trying to find some way to reach across from one to the other.

"We cannot even wish each other luck," Amyntas said at last, helplessly.

And Leon said, almost exactly as he had said it at their first meeting, "May both of us run a good race."

They reached out and touched hands quickly and went their separate ways.

The next time they saw each other, they were waiting oiled and naked for the track, with the rest of the Double Stade boys just outside the arched way into the Stadium. The Dolichus, the long distance race, and the Stade had been run, each with its boys' race immediately after. Now the trumpet was sounding to start the Double Stade. Amyntas' eyes went to meet Leon's, and found the Spartan boy's slightly frowning gaze waiting for him. He heard the sudden roar of the crowd, and his belly lifted and tightened. A little stir ran through the waiting boys; the next time the starting trumpet sounded, the next time the crowd gave that roar, it would be for them. Hippias was murmuring last-minute advice into Amyntas' ear, but he did not hear a word of it. . . . He was going out there before all those thousands upon thousands of staring eyes and yelling mouths, and he was going to fail. Not just fail to win the race, but *fail*. His belly was churning now, his heart banging away right up in his throat so that it almost choked him. His mouth was dry and the palms of his hands were wet; and the beginnings of panic were whimpering up in him. He looked again at Leon, and saw him run the tip of his tongue over his lips as though they were suddenly dry. It was the first time he had ever known the Spartan boy to betray anything of what was going on inside him; and the sight gave him a sense of companionship that somehow steadied him. He began to take deep quiet breaths, as he had been taught, and the rising panic quietened and sank away.

The voice of the crowd was rising, rising to a great roar; the Men's Double Stade was over. He heard the Herald crying the name of the winner, and another roar from the crowd; and then the runners were coming out through the arched entrance; and the boys pressed back to let them past, filthy with sweat and sand and oil. Amyntas looked at the face of the man with the victor's ribbons knotted round his head and arms, and saw that it was grey and spent and oddly peaceful.

"Now it's us!" someone said; and the boys were sprinting down the covered way, out into the open sun-drenched space of the Stadium.

The turf banks on either side of the broad track, and the lower slopes of the Kronon Hill that looked down upon it were packed with a vast multitude of onlookers. Half-way down on the right-hand side, raised above the tawny grass on which everybody else sat, were the benches for the Council, looking across to the white marble seat opposite, where the Priestess of Demeter, the only woman allowed at the Games, sat as still as though she herself were carved from marble, among all the jostling, swaying, noisy throng. Men were raking over the silver sand on the track. The trumpeter stood ready.

They had taken their places now behind the long white limestone curbs of the starting line. The Umpire was calling: "Runners! Feet to the lines!"

Amyntas felt the scorching heat of the limestone as he braced the ball of his right foot into the shaped groove. All the panic of a while back had left him, he felt light, and clear headed, and master of himself. He had drawn the sixth place, with Leon on his left and the boy from Megara on his right. Before him the track stretched white in the sunlight, an infinity of emptiness and distance.

The starting trumpet yelped; and the line of runners sprang forward like a wave of hunting dogs slipped from the leash.

Amyntas was running smoothly and without hurry. Let the green front-runners push on ahead. In this heat they would have burned themselves out before they reached the turning post. He and Leon were running neck and neck with the red-headed Macedonian. The Rhodian had gone ahead now after the front-runners, the rest were still bunched. Then the Corinthian made a sprint and passed the boy from Rhodes, but fell back almost at once. The white track was reeling back underfoot, the turning post racing towards them. The bunch had thinned out, the front-runners beginning to drop back already; and as they came up towards the turning post, first the boy from Macedon, and then Nikomedes catching fire at last, slid into the lead, with Amyntas and Leon close behind them. Rounding the post, Amyntas skidded on the loose sand and Leon went ahead; and it was then, seeing the lean scarred back ahead of him, that Amyntas lengthened his stride, knowing that the time had come to run. They were a quarter of the way down the home lap when they passed Nikomedes; the Megaran boy had taken fire too late. They were beginning to overhaul the redhead; and Amyntas knew in his bursting heart that unless something unexpected happened, the race must be between himself and Leon. Spartan and Macedonian were going neck and neck now; the position held for a few paces, and then the redhead gradually fell behind. Amyntas was going all out, there was pain in his breast and belly and in the backs of his legs, and he did not know where his next breath was coming from; but still the thin scarred back was just ahead. The crowd were beginning to give tongue, seeing the two come through to the front; a solid roar of sound that would go on rising now until they passed the finishing post. And then suddenly Amyntas knew that something was wrong; Leon was labouring a little, beginning to lose the first keen edge of his speed. Snatching a glance downward, he saw a fleck of crimson in the sand. The cut had re-opened.

His body went on running, but for a sort of splinter of time his head seemed quite apart from the rest of him, and filled with

an unmanageable swirl of thoughts and feelings. Leon might have passed the top of his speed anyway, it might be nothing to do with his foot—But the cut *had* re-opened. . . . To lose the race because of a cut foot. . . . It would be so easy not to make that final desperate effort that his whole body was crying out against. Then Leon would keep his lead. . . . And at the same time another part of himself was remembering his father standing on the quayside at Piraeus as the *Paralos* drew away—crying out that he was not run-

ning only for himself but for Athens, his City and his people. . . .
A crown of wild olive would be the greatest thing that anyone
could give to his friend. . . . It would be to insult Leon to let him
win . . . you could not do that to your friend. . . . And then, like
a clean cold sword of light cutting through the swirling tangle of
his thoughts, came the knowledge that greater than any of these
things were the Gods. These were the Sacred Games, not some
mere struggle between boys in the gymnasium. For one fleeting

instant of time he remembered himself standing in the Temple
before the great statue of Zeus, holding the tiny bronze bull with
the silvered horns. "Let me run the best race that is in me, and
think of nothing more."

He drove himself forward in one last agonizing burst of speed,
he was breathing against knives, and the roar of the blood in his
ears drowned the roar of the crowd. He was level with Leon—and
then there was nothing ahead of him but the winning post.

The onlookers had crowded right down towards it; even above
the howl of the blood in his head he heard them now, roar on
solid roar of sound, shouting him in to victory. And then Hippias
had caught him as he plunged past the post; and he was bending
over the trainer's arm, bending over the pain in his belly, snatching at his breath and trying not to be sick. People were throwing
sprigs of myrtle, he felt them flicking and falling on his head and
shoulders. The sickness eased a little and his head was clearing; he
began to hear friendly voices congratulating him; and Eudorus
came shouldering through the crowd with a coloured ribbon to tie
round his head. But when he looked round for Leon, the Spartan
boy had been swept away by his trainer. And a queer desolation
rose in Amyntas and robbed his moment of its glory.

Afterwards in the changing room, some of the other boys
came up to congratulate him. Leon did not come; but
when they had cleaned off the sand and oil and sweat, and
sluiced down with the little water that was allowed them, Amyntas
hung about, sitting on the well kerb outside while the trainer finished
seeing to his friend's foot. And when Leon came out at last, he came
straight across to the well, as though they had arranged to meet there.
His face was as unreadable as usual.

"You will have cooled off enough by now, do you want to
drink?" Amyntas said, mainly because somebody had to say something; and dipped the bronze cup that always stood on the well kerb
in the pail that he had drawn.

Leon took the cup from him and drank, and sat down on the

well kerb beside him. As Amyntas dipped the cup again and bent his head to drink in his turn, the ends of the victor's ribbon fell forward against his cheek, and he pulled it off impatiently, and dropped it beside the well.

"Why did you do that?" Leon said.

"I shall never be sure whether I won that race."

"The judges are not often mistaken, and I never heard yet of folk tying victors' ribbons on the wrong man."

Amyntas flicked a thumb at Leon's bandaged foot. "You know well enough what I mean. I'll never be sure whether I'd have come first past the post, if that hadn't opened up again."

Leon looked at him a moment in silence, then flung up his head and laughed. "Do you really think that could make any difference? It would take more than a cut foot to slow me up, Athenian!—You ran the better race, that's all."

It was said on such a harsh, bragging note that in the first moment Amyntas felt as though he had been struck in the face. Then he wondered if it was the overwhelming Spartan pride giving tongue, or simply Leon, hurt and angry and speaking the truth. Either way, he was too tired to be angry back again. And whichever it was, it seemed that Leon had shaken it off already. The noon break was over, and the trumpets were sounding for the Pentathlon.

"Up!" Leon said, when Amyntas did not move at once. "Are you going to let it be said that your own event is the only one that interests you?"

They went, quickly and together, while the trainer's eye was off them, for Leon was under order to keep off his foot. And the people cheered them both when they appeared in the Stadium. They seldom cared much for a good loser, but Leon had come in a close second, and they had seen the blood in the sand.

The next day the heavyweight events were held; and then it was the last day of all, the Crowning Day. Ever after, Amyntas remembered that day as a quietness after great stress and turmoil. It was not, in truth, much less noisy than the days that had gone before. The roaring of the Stadium crowds was gone; but in the town of tents the crowds milled to and fro. The jugglers with knives and the eaters of fire shouted for an audience and the merchants cried their wares; and within the Sacred Enclosure where the winners received their crowns and made their sacrifices before the Temples of Zeus and Hera, there were the flutes and the songs in praise of the victors, and the deep-voiced invocations to the Gods.

But in Amyntas himself, there was the quiet. He remembered the Herald crying his name, and the light springy coolness of the wild olive crown as it was pressed down on his head; and later, the spitting light of pine torches under the plane trees, where the officials and athletes were feasting. And he remembered most, looking up out of the torchlight, and seeing, high and remote above it all, the winged tripods on the roof of the great Temple, outlined against the light of a moon two days past the full.

The boys left before the feasting was over; and in his sleeping cell Amyntas heard the poets singing in praise of some chariot team, and the applause, while he gathered his few belongings together, ready for tomorrow's early start, and stowed his olive crown among them. Already the leaves were beginning to wilt after the heat of the day. The room that had seemed so strange the first night was familiar now; part of himself; and after tonight it would not know him anymore.

Next morning in all the hustle of departure, he and Leon contrived to meet and slip off for a little on their own.

The whole valley of Olympia was a chaos of tents and booths being taken down, merchants as well as athletes and onlookers making ready for the road. But the Sacred Enclosure itself was quiet, and the gates stood open. They went through, into the shade of the olive trees before the Temple of Zeus. A priest making the morning offering at a side altar looked at them; but they seemed to be doing no harm, and to want nothing, so he let them alone. There was a smell of frankincense in the air, and the early morning smell of last night's heavy dew on parched ground. They stood among the twisted trunks and low-hanging branches, and looked at each other and did not know what to say. Already they were remembering that there was war between Athens and Sparta, that the Truce of the Games would last them back to their own states, but no further; and the longer the silence lasted, the more they remembered.

From beyond the quiet of the Enclosure came all the sounds of the great concourse breaking up; voices calling, the stamping of impatient horses. "By this time tomorrow everyone will be gone," Amyntas said at last. "It will be just as it was before we came, for another four years."

"The Corinthians are off already."

"Catching the cool of the morning for those fine chariot horses," Amyntas said, and thought, There's so little time, why do we have to waste it like this?

"One of the charioteers had that hunting knife with the silver inlay. The one you took a fancy to. Why didn't you buy it after all?"

"I spent the money on something else." For a moment Amyntas was afraid that Leon would ask what. But the other boy only nodded and let it go.

He wished suddenly that he could give Leon something, but there was nothing among his few belongings that would make sense in the Spartan's world. It was a world so far off from his own. Too far to reach out, too far to call. Already they seemed to be drifting away from each other, drifting back to a month ago, before they had even met. He put out a hand quickly, as though to hold the other boy back for one more moment, and Leon's hand came to meet it.

"It has been good. All this month it has been good," Leon said.

"It has been good," Amyntas agreed. He wanted to say, "Until the next Games, then." But manhood and military service were only a few months away for both of them; if they did meet at another Games, there would be the faces of dead comrades, Spartan and Athenian, between them; and like enough, for one of them or both, there might be no other Games. Far more likely, if they ever saw each other again, it would be over the tops of their shields.

He had noticed before how, despite their different worlds, he

and Leon sometimes thought the same thing at the same time, and answered each other as though the thought had been spoken. Leon said in his abrupt, dead-level voice, "The Gods be with you Amyntas, and grant that we never meet again."

They put their arms round each other's necks and strained fiercely close for a moment, hard cheekbone against hard cheekbone.

"The Gods be with you, Leon."

And then Eudorus was calling, "Amyntas! Amyntas! We're all waiting!"

And Amyntas turned and ran—out through the gateway of the Sacred Enclosure, towards where the Athenian party were ready to start, and Eudorus was already coming back to look for him.

As they rode up from the Valley of Olympia and took the tracks towards the coast, Amyntas did not look back. The horses' legs brushed the dry dust-grey scrub beside the track, and loosed the hot aromatic scents of wild lavender and camomile and lentisk upon the air. A yellow butterfly hovered past, and watching it out of sight, it came to him suddenly, that he and Leon had exchanged gifts of a sort, after all. It was hard to give them a name, but they were real enough. And the outward and visible sign of his gift to Leon was in the little bronze bull with the silvered horns that he had left on the Offering Table before the feet of Olympian Zeus. And Leon's gift to him. . . . That had been made with the Spartan's boast that it would take more than a cut foot to slow him up. He had thought at the time that it was either the harsh Spartan pride, or the truth spoken in anger. But he understood now, quite suddenly, that it had been Leon giving up his own private and inward claim to the olive crown, so that he, Amyntas, might believe that he had rightfully won it. Amyntas knew that he would never be sure of that, never in all his life. But it made no difference to the gift.

The track had begun to run downhill, and the pale dust-cloud was rising behind them. He knew that if he looked back now, there would be nothing to see.

Reader's Response ⮎ In your opinion, are the Olympic games as important to peace among nations today as they were in the time of Amyntas?

# GLOSSARY

**Full pronunciation key*** The pronunciation of each word is shown just after the word, in this way:
**abbreviate** (ə brē′vē āt).

The letters and signs used are pronounced as in the words below.

The mark ′ is placed after a syllable with a primary or heavy accent as in the example above.

The mark ′ after a syllable shows a secondary or lighter accent, as in **abbreviation** (ə brē′vē ā′shən).

| SYMBOL | KEY WORDS | SYMBOL | KEY WORDS |
|---|---|---|---|
| a | ask, fat | b | bed, dub |
| ā | ape, date | d | did, had |
| ä | car, father | f | fall, off |
| | | g | get, dog |
| e | elf, ten | h | he, ahead |
| er | berry, care | j | joy, jump |
| ē | even, meet | k | kill, bake |
| | | l | let, ball |
| i | is, hit | m | met, trim |
| ir | mirror, here | n | not, ton |
| ī | ice, fire | p | put, tap |
| | | r | red, dear |
| o | lot, pond | s | sell, pass |
| ō | open, go | t | top, hat |
| ô | law, horn | v | vat, have |
| oi | oil, point | w | will, always |
| oo | look, pull | y | yet, yard |
| o͞o | ooze, tool | z | zebra, haze |
| yoo | unite, cure | | |
| yo͞o | cute, few | ch | chin, arch |
| ou | out, crowd | n̂g | ring, singer |
| | | sh | she, dash |
| u | up, cut | th | thin, truth |
| ur | fur, fern | *th* | then, father |
| | | zh | s in pleasure |
| ə | a in ago | | |
| | e in agent | ′ | as in (ā′b′l) |
| | e in father | | |
| | i in unity | | |
| | o in collect | | |
| | u in focus | | |

*Pronunciation key and respellings adapted from *Webster's New World Dictionary, Basic School Edition,* Copyright © 1983 by Simon & Schuster, Inc. Reprinted by permission.

# A

**ab·a·lo·ne** (ab'ə lō'nē) *noun.* a large, ear-shaped, edible shellfish. Its shell has a colorful pearly interior, often used for making ornaments.

**ab·hor·rence** (əb hôr'əns) *noun.* a feeling of hatred: He felt an *abhorrence* for the cruelty of their actions.

**a·bun·dant** (ə bun'dənt) *adjective.* **1.** plentiful; more than necessary. **2.** well supplied.

**ac·cen·tu·ate** (ak sen'choo wāt) *verb.* **1.** to emphasize or heighten the effect of: The room was very pretty, with red pillows *accentuating* the red in the wallpaper. **2.** to pronounce or mark by accenting or stressing. **accentuating.**

**ac·com·pa·ni·ment** (ə kum'pə ni mənt) *noun.* something that goes along with something else; especially, music played along with a solo part.

**aer·o·dy·nam·ics** (er'ō dī nam'iks) *noun.* the branch of mechanics that studies the relationship of atmospheric conditions, gravity, and flight.

**aes·thet·ic** (es thet'ik) *adjective.* relating to beauty and what is beautiful; artistic: The *aesthetic* quality of the scene inspired the painter.

**a·gen·da** (ə jen'də) *noun.* a list of things to be done; especially business to be conducted at a meeting.

**ag·gres·sive** (ə gres'iv) *adjective.* **1.** showing readiness to start fights or trouble: He was too *aggressive* to be an effective leader. **2.** bold, forceful, sometimes pushy.

**a·gil·i·ty** (ə jil'ə tē) *noun.* the ability to move with quickness and ease.

**air·borne** (er'bôrn) *adjective.* **1.** supported by or carried through the air. **2.** in flight; flying.

**al·a·bas·ter** (al'ə bas'tər) *noun.* a smooth, usually white stone used for statues, vases, and ornaments. —*adjective.* any substance that is like alabaster in color or texture.

**al·pha** (al'fə) *noun.* **1.** the first letter of the Greek alphabet. **2.** the first or the beginning of anything. —*adjective.* first in order of importance.

**al·ter** (ôl'tər) *noun.* to change; to make or become different.

**al·tim·e·ter** (al tim'ə tər) *noun.* any instrument used for determining altitude, especially in an aircraft.

**am·big·u·ous** (am big'yoo wəs) *adjective.* **1.** something that can be understood in more than one way; having two or more possible meanings. **2.** uncertain or indistinct.

**am·i·ca·ble** (am'i kə b'l) *adjective.* friendly; peaceable: They had an *amicable* discussion about dividing the work.

**a·nach·ro·nism** (ə nak'rə niz'm) *noun.* **1.** something not belonging to a particular time. **2.** something out of its proper place in time.

**an·te·cham·ber** (an'ti chām'bər) *noun.* a small room serving as an entrance way to a larger, more important room.

**ap·pre·hen·sion** (ap'rə hen'shən) *noun.* **1.** the arrest or capture of someone such as a criminal. **2.** the power of understanding. **3.** a feeling of fear or anxiety about the future: The thought of going to the doctor filled him with *apprehension*.

**ar·chae·ol·o·gist** *or* **ar·che·ol·o·gist** (är'kē ol'ə jist) *noun.* one who studies history by excavating the remains of ancient civilizations.

**ar·ti·fact** (är'tə fakt) *noun.* any object produced by human art or skill. **artifacts.**

**a·scend** (ə send') *verb.* to move upward; to climb. **ascends.**

**as·phyx·i·ate** (as fik'sē āt) *verb.* to cause a person or animal to lose consciousness or die by cutting off the normal intake of oxygen. **asphyxiated.**

**au·di·tion** (ô dish'ən) *noun.* a trial performance by which an actor, musician, singer, or dancer may be chosen for a job. —*verb.* to test or try out in an audition.

**aus·ter·i·ty** (ô ster'ə tē) *noun.* **1.** a harsh or stern action or manner. **2.** plainness; lack of luxury.

Aesthetic comes from a Greek word that means "perceptible by the senses." Many English words that begin with *ae* are Greek in origin. In recent years, there has been a trend toward dropping the initial *a* from words like *aesthetic*, but the original spelling is still preferred.

altimeter

# B

**ba·rom·e·ter** (bə rom'ə tər) *noun.* **1.** an instrument that measures air pressure and is useful for predicting changes in the weather. **2.** anything that indicates or predicts change.

**ba·zaar** (bə zär') *noun.* **1.** an outdoor market or a street of shops. **2.** a sale of miscellaneous items in which the profits benefit a club, church, or charity. **bazaars.**

**be·drag·gled** (bi drag''ld) *adjective.* wet, dirty, messy, as something that has been dragged through the mud: She came in from the storm, *bedraggled* and miserable.

**bell** (bel) *noun.* **1.** a hollow object, usually cuplike, made of metal or other hard material that makes a ringing sound when it is struck. **2.** the sound made by a bell. **3.** on shipboard, the stroke or strokes of a bell marking every half-hour. —*verb.* to cry out, as an animal in fear or flight. **bells.**

**bi·as** (bī'əs) *noun.* **1.** a line running diagonally across the weave of a fabric. **2.** a tendency to feel favorably or unfavorably about someone or something.

**black·out** (blak'out) *noun.* **1.** the act of putting out lights and covering windows at night, especially as protection against enemy air raids. **2.** loss of consciousness or vision. **3.** loss of electric power for a certain time.

**blight** (blīt) *noun.* **1.** a plant disease that causes plants to wither and die. **2.** anything that injures, withers, or destroys.

**bliss** (blis) *noun.* supreme happiness or delight. —**blissful** *adjective.* —**blissfully** *adverb.*

**brit·tle** (brit''l) *adjective.* **1.** hard, but easy to snap or break; inflexible. **2.** having a sharp, hard quality.

**broach** (brōch) *verb.* **1.** to introduce a subject for conversation. **2.** to make a hole in.

**brusque** (brusk) *adjective.* rude or abrupt in speaking; reticent or cool in manner: He liked his teacher, in spite of her *brusque* personality.

**bul·ly** (bo͝ol'ē) *noun.* an aggressive person who teases or hurts weaker people. —*verb.* **1.** to act like a bully toward; to intimidate. **2.** to force someone to do something by using threats. **bullied.**

# C

**cache** (kash) *noun.* **1.** a place used for hiding, storing, or preserving treasure or supplies. **2.** something hidden or stored in a cache.

**ca·ma·ra·de·rie** (käm'ə räd'ər ē) *noun.* warm feeling of friendship between two people or among members of a group: A feeling of *camaraderie* developed between the two girls as they worked together.

**cam·e·o** (kam'ē ō) *noun.* a carved gem or shell with differently colored layers. The top layer may have a portrait or some other figure carved into it.

**ca·pit·u·la·tion** (kə pich'ə lā'shən) *noun.* a surrender or giving up on certain conditions; yielding: The commander's *capitulation* before the battle was lost angered the surviving soldiers.

**cap·u·chin** (kap'yo͝o chin') *noun.* **1.** a woman's hooded cloak. **2.** a genus of long-tailed South American monkey.

**cat·a·log** *or* **cat·a·logue** (kat''l ôg) *noun.* **1.** a list of names, titles, or items listed by some system, especially alphabetical. **2.** a book or file containing systematic listings. —*verb.* to enter an item into such a list. **cataloged** *or* **catalogued, cataloging** *or* **cataloguing.**

**cav·ern·ous** (kav'ər nəs) *adjective.* **1.** full of caves or caverns. **2.** something that is like a cave, in that it is large and hollow.

**cer·e·mo·ni·al** (ser'ə mō'nē əl) *adjective.* having to do with ceremony or formal ritual: The *ceremonial* goblet was only used once a year.

**ces·sa·tion** (se sā'shən) *noun.* ceasing or stopping; to discontinue, either temporarily or for a long time: There was a *cessation* in activity when the teacher left the room.

**Bazaar** is one of few words that have come into English from the Persian language, in which it meant "market." It is believed that the word first made its way from Persian into Italian as *bazarra,* where it referred to an Oriental marketplace. The word then moved into English.

cameo

**cha·ot·ic** (kā ot′ik) *adjective.* disordered and confused.

**chat·tel** (chat″l) *noun.* a movable piece of property, such as furniture, livestock, etc.

**check·ered** (chek′ərd) *adjective.* **1.** divided into squares. **2.** having light and dark patches. **3.** full of ups and downs, some unpleasant or unsavory.

**ci·ca·da** (si kā′də) *noun.* an insect that looks like a fly with transparent wings. The male has an organ on its underside that makes a loud, shrill noise.

**cinch** (sinch) *noun.* **1.** a strap for a pack or saddle. **2.** *(slang)* something easy to do. It was a *cinch* to follow the recipe. —*verb.* **1.** to tighten a strap, as on a horse's saddle. **2.** *(informal language)* to make sure of: They *cinched* their place on the team with their performance.

**cir·cum·spect** (sur′kəm spekt) *adjective.* cautious; wary; very careful before acting or making a decision.

**cir·cum·vent** (sur′kəm vent′) *verb.* **1.** to get the better of; avoid; outwit. **2.** to go around. **circumvented.**

**clime** (klīm) *noun.* a region, country, or climate. **climes.**

**clum·sy** (klum′zē) *adjective.* **1.** awkward, not having good control. **2.** poorly made or done. **clumsier, clumsiest.** —**clumsily** *adverb.* in an awkward manner: He *clumsily* asked her for a date.

**coax** (kōks) *verb.* to persuade or influence by flattery, tact, or gentle persistence. **coaxed.**

**co·coon** (kə kōōn′) *noun.* the case that certain worms and caterpillars spin around themselves for protection as they change into moths or butterflies.

**com·pas·sion·ate** (kəm pash′ən it) *adjective.* feeling pity or a desire to help another; sympathetic.

**com·rade** (kom′rad) *noun.* a companion or friend.

**con·de·scend** (kon də send′) *verb.* **1.** to lower oneself. **2.** to grant a favor while making it clear that one is better than others; to patronize. —**condescension** *noun.* actions in a snobbish or superior manner: Although he was polite to us, his *condescension* was obvious and insulting.

**con·fis·cate** (kon′fə skāt) *verb.* to seize with authority. —**confiscated.**

**con·fron·ta·tion** (kon′frən tā′shən) *noun.* **1.** a face-to-face meeting. **2.** a crisis or conflict between two opposing groups.

**con·sec·u·tive** (kən sek′yə tiv) *adjective.* coming in order with no break in between. —**consecutively** *adverb.*

**con·spic·u·ous** (kən spik′yōō wəs) *adjective.* **1.** easily seen. **2.** attracting attention.

**con·spir·a·tor** (kən spir′ə tər) *noun.* a person who is involved in a conspiracy, or secret plan; plotter. —**conspiratorially** *adverb.* in a secretive manner: He glanced at me *conspiratorially* as we tiptoed out of the house.

**con·tem·plate** (kon′təm plāt) *verb.* **1.** to look at carefully. **2.** to consider thoughtfully. **3.** to intend or plan.

**con·trap·tion** (kən trap′shən) *noun.* a gadget or strange-looking mechanical device. **contraptions.**

**con·trive** (kən trīv′) *verb.* **1.** to plot or plan. **2.** to build or make in a clever or skillful manner. **3.** to manage to bring about, as with a clever plan. **contrived.**

**con·viv·i·al** (kən viv′ē əl) *adjective.* fond of people and socializing; fun-loving: People liked him because he was so *convivial.*

**con·vul·sion** (kən vul′shən) *noun.* **1.** an attack of sudden, involuntary tightening or twitching of the muscles. **2.** any strong or violent disturbance, such as an earthquake. **convulsions.**

**cool** (kōōl) *adjective.* **1.** somewhat cold. **2.** not too hot; comfortable. **3.** calm and deliberate in action. **4.** lacking enthusiasm or interest. **5.** *(slang)* very good.

**cor·rupt** (kə rupt′) *verb.* **1.** to cause to change from good to bad: The dream of easy money had *corrupted* the young man. **2.** to influence something in an improper way. **corrupted.**

**cringe** (krinj) *verb.* **1.** to shrink back in fear. **2.** to behave in a very humble way. **cringed.**

**croon** (krōōn) *verb.* to hum or sing softly and gently.

**cull** (kul) *verb.* **1.** to pick over; select; choose. **2.** to look over in order to find what is wanted. **culling.**

**cyn·i·cal** (sin′i k'l) *adjective.* **1.** doubting that anyone can be sincere, good, or trustworthy. **2.** sarcastic; bitter; gloomy.

| a fat | oi oil | ch chin |
|---|---|---|
| ā ape | oo look | sh she |
| ä car, father | ōō tool | th thin |
| e ten | ou out | th then |
| er care | u up | zh leisure |
| ē even | ur fur | n̄g ring |
| i hit | | |
| ir here | ə = a *in* ago | |
| ī bite, fire | e *in* agent | |
| o lot | i *in* unity | |
| ō go | o *in* collect | |
| ô law, horn | u *in* focus | |

Cool in its slang use has been with us since about 1950. It originated with jazz musicians who developed a style of music that they labeled *cool jazz.* Cool jazz was considered unemotional and intellectual in contrast with the bop music that came before it.

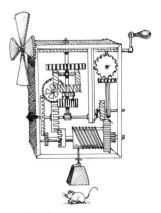

**contraption**

# D

**death·watch** (deth′woch) *noun.* a vigil or a watching at the side of one who is dying or has recently died.

**de·but** (di byōō′ *or* dā′byōō) *noun.* **1.** a first appearance before the public, as of an actor on the stage. **2.** the formal presentation of a girl into high society.

**dec·ade** (dek′ād) *noun.* a period of ten years.

**de·ceased** (di sēst′) *adjective.* dead. —**the deceased** *noun.* the dead person or persons.

**de·ci·pher** (di sī′fər) *verb.* **1.** to translate from code or secret writing; decode. **2.** to interpret or determine the meaning of: We tried to *decipher* the complicated map.

**de·file** (di fīl′) *verb.* **1.** to make dirty or foul. **2.** to corrupt. **3.** to violate the purity of. —**defiled** *adjective.* made impure; corrupted.

**de·mean** (di mēn′) *verb.* to degrade; to lower or cheapen: He *demeaned* himself by copying his friend's paper. **demeaning.**

**de·men·ted** (di men′tid) *adjective.* crazy; emotionally disturbed.

**de·par·ture** (di pär′chər) *noun.* **1.** the act of going away. **2.** a turning away from the usual way, or a changing to something new.

**des·o·late** (des′ə lit) *adjective.* **1.** deserted; abandoned; lonely. **2.** ruined or destroyed. **3.** gloomy; dreary; miserable.

**dex·ter·i·ty** (dek ster′ə tē) *noun.* skill in using one's hands, body, or mind. The saxophone player showed great *dexterity* on his instrument.

**di·a·met·ri·cal** (dī′ə met′ri k′l) *adjective.* **1.** having to do with a diameter. **2.** directly opposite. —**diametrically** *adverb.*

**di·he·dral** (dī hē′drəl) *adjective.* **1.** two-sided. **2.** in aeronautics, the upward or downward slope of an airplane's supporting surfaces.

**eaves**

**din·ette** (dī net′) *noun.* **1.** an alcove or small room used for dining. **2.** a set of table and chairs for such a room.

**dis·a·ble** (dis ā′b′l) *verb.* to make unable; to prevent normal movement or action. —**disabled, disabling.**

**dis·creet** (dis krēt′) *adjective.* careful not to say or do the wrong thing; prudent.

**dis·may** (dis mā′) *verb.* to make unable to act because of fear or confusion. —*noun.* a sudden feeling of fear or loss of courage; discouragement.

**drench** (drench) *verb.* to make thoroughly wet; soak. **drenched.**

**du·al·i·ty** (dōō al′ə tē *or* dyōō al′ə tē) *noun.* the quality of having two parts.

**du·el** (dōō′əl *or* dyōō′əl) *noun.* **1.** a fight with set rules between two people. **2.** any similar contest, as a debate. **duels.**

**dwin·dle** (dwin′d′l) *verb.* to make or become less or smaller. **dwindled.**

**dy·nas·ty** (dī′nəs tē) *noun.* **1.** a series of rulers from the same family or group. **2.** period of time during which a family or group reigns.

# E

**eaves** (ēvz) *plural noun.* the lower part of a sloped roof that hangs over the edge of a building.

**ec·stat·ic** (ek stat′ik) *adjective.* showing very great happiness; extreme delight.

**ef·face** (i fās′) *verb.* **1.** to rub out; erase. **2.** to obliterate or destroy. **3.** to make (oneself) less important.

**eight ball** (āt bal) *noun.* a black pool ball bearing the number eight. In one popular game, he who pockets the eight ball while other balls remain on the table loses the game.

**e·lim·in·ate** (i lim′ə nāt) *verb.* **1.** to get rid of; to do away with. **2.** to ignore. **3.** to remove from further competition by defeating.

e•merge (i murj′) *verb.* **1.** to come out and be seen; appear. **2.** to become known. **3.** to develop as something better.

em•i•grate (em′ə grāt) *verb.* to move from one country or part of a country to another. **emigrated.**

e•mit (i mit′) *verb.* to send forth or give out: The radio *emitted* some very strange sounds. **emitted.**

em•phy•se•ma (em′fə sē′mə) *noun.* a lung disease causing difficulty in breathing.

e•nig•ma (ə nig′mə) *noun.* anything or anyone that is puzzling or hard to understand.

ep•i•lep•sy (ep′ə lep′sē) *noun.* a disorder of the central nervous system that can cause fainting and convulsions.

e•rup•tion (i rup′shən) *noun.* **1.** a breaking or bursting forth with violent force. **2.** a throwing forth of lava, water, etc. **3.** a breaking out, as in a rash. **eruptions.**

es•sen•tial (ə sen′shəl) *adjective.* **1.** the most typical or basic part. **2.** most important; necessary; vital. —*noun.* something that is necessary.

etch (ech) *verb.* **1.** to produce a figure or design on metal or glass by means of lines eaten into the surface by acid. **2.** to outline. **etched.**

eth•nic (eth′nik) *adjective.* of or related to a distinctive racial, cultural, or language group.

ex•ca•va•tion (eks′kə vā′shən) *noun.* a hole or hollow made by digging.

ex•ert (ig zurt′) *verb.* **1.** to put forth or put into action: He tried to *exert* his authority over me, but I resisted. **2.** to put (oneself) into action or tiring effort.

ex•ile (eg′zīl *or* ek′sīl) *verb.* to cause a person or persons to leave their homeland or country and live somewhere else. **exiled.** —*noun.* **1.** the condition of being exiled. **2.** a person who has been banished.

ex•trem•i•ty (ik strem′ə tē) *noun.* **1.** the farthest point, end, or edge. **2.** an extreme condition of distress, need or danger.

ex•ult•ant (ig zult′′nt) *adjective.* full of triumph; expressing great joy. —**exultantly** *adverb.*

# F

fac•sim•i•le (fak sim′ə lē) *noun.* an exact copy or reproduction.

fas•tid•i•ous (fas tid′ē əs) *adjective.* hard to please; delicate or refined; squeamish.

flat•ter•y (flat′ər ē) *noun.* praise or a compliment that is too much or not really meant.

fore•run•ner (fôr′run′ər) *noun.* **1.** a person or thing that precedes someone or something. **2.** an advance sign of something or someone to follow.

forge (fôrj) *noun.* a furnace where metal is shaped and worked. —*verb.* **1.** to produce an imitation of something for the purpose of deceiving. **2.** to move slowly but steadily forward. **forged.**

for•lorn (fər lôrn′) *adjective.* sad; cheerless; lonely; left alone. —**forlornly** *adverb.*

frac•ture (frak′chər) *noun.* **1.** a break, rapture or crack. **2.** the act of breaking. —*verb.* to break or crack. **fractured.**

frig•id (frij′id) *adjective.* **1.** freezing cold. **2.** not friendly; stiff.

fu•ner•ar•y (fyoo′nə rer′ē) *adjective.* designed for, or part of, a funeral.

fu•tile (fyoot′′l) *adjective.* having no result or effect; done in vain; useless.

**forge**

# G

gaud•y (gôd′ē) *adjective.* showy and colorful in a cheap way; garish; tasteless. —**gaudier, gaudiest.**

gawk•y (gô′kē) *adjective.* tall and awkward.

gen•e•sis (jen′ə sis) *noun.* an origin; beginning.

ger•min•ate (jur′mə nāt) *verb.* to sprout or make sprout, as from a seed; to start growing. **germinating.**

glint (glint) *noun.* a sparkle or flash of light.

| a fat | oi oil | ch chin |
|---|---|---|
| ā ape | oo look | sh she |
| ä car, father | oo tool | th thin |
| e ten | ou out | th then |
| er care | u up | zh leisure |
| ē even | ur fur | nĝ ring |
| i hit | | |
| ir here | ə = a *in* ago | |
| ī bite, fire | e *in* agent | |
| o lot | i *in* unity | |
| ō go | o *in* collect | |
| ô law, horn | u *in* focus | |

**glyph** (glif) *noun.* a raised or carved figure or form that represents an idea or word; hieroglyph. **glyphs.**

**gnash** (nash) *verb.* to strike or grind the teeth together, as in a rage: It is frightening when he's so angry that he *gnashes* his teeth. **gnashes.**

**gorge** (gôrj) *noun.* a narrow, deep valley, often with a river running through it. —*verb.* to overeat or stuff greedily with food. **gorges.**

**grap·ple** (grap′l) *verb.* **1.** to struggle or wrestle with. **2.** to grip, seize.

**grim·y** (gri′me) *adjective.* covered with dirt and grime; filthy.

**glyph**

# H

**hal·low** (hal′ō) *verb.* to treat as sacred; to make or keep holy. —**hallowed** *adjective.* sacred; holy; revered.

**hap·haz·ard** (hap′haz′ərd) *adjective.* happening by chance; without a plan; accidental. —**haphazardly** *adverb.*

**har·mon·ics** (här mon′iks) *noun.* overtones; the higher pitches contained in a musical note.

**he·ral·dic** (hə ral′dik) *adjective.* having to do with heraldry, or the symbolism of royalty.

**he·red·i·tar·y** (hə red′ə ter′ē) *adjective.* **1.** derived from ancestors; inherited. **2.** of something that can be passed on from a plant or animal to its offspring.

**here·to·fore** (hir′tə fôr′) *adverb.* before now.

**hi·er·o·glyph·ic** (hī′ər ə glif′ik) *noun.* a picture or symbol representing a sound, word, object, or idea, as in the writing of the ancient Egyptians. —**hieroglyphics**

**hos·pi·tal·i·ty** (hos′pə tal′ə tē) *noun.* friendly and generous treatment of guests.

**hum·ble** (hum′b′l) *adjective.* **1.** modest and meek; knowing one's own faults; not proud: He *humbly* asked her forgiveness. **2.** plain and simple; lowly. —**humbly** *adverb.*

**Humble** comes to us from two Latin words: *humilis,* meaning "low or lowly;" and *humus,* meaning "ground or soil." While these meanings are literal, *humble* as it is used today applies to a person's character, behavior, or position in society.

# I

**i·dol·ize** (ī′d′l īz) *verb.* **1.** to love or admire very much or too much. **2.** to make an idol of. **idolized.**

**ig·no·min·i·ous** (ig′nə min′ē əs) *adjective.* **1.** indicating disgrace; dishonorable. **2.** humiliating. —**ignominiously** *adverb.*

**im·per·cep·ti·ble** (im′pər sep′tə b′l) *adjective.* so small as not to be able to be perceived or noticed. —**imperceptibly** *adverb.*

**in·con·gru·ous** (in kong′grōō wəs) *adjective.* out of place; not suitable or reasonable: The pretty daisies were *incongruous* growing in the junkyard.

**in·dis·pen·sa·ble** (in′dis pen′sə b′l) *adjective.* essential; that which cannot be done without: When she was ill, her friend's help was *indispensable.*

**in·ef·fec·tu·al** (in′i fek′chōō wəl) *adjective.* not able to produce the expected or usual effect. —**ineffectually** *adverb.*

**in·fe·ri·or·i·ty** (in fir′ē ôr′ə tē) *noun.* **1.** the condition of being lower in worth or quality. **2.** the state of being lower in position or rank.

**in·fil·trate** (in fil′trāt *or* in′fil trāt) *verb.* **1.** to filter into or move through. **2.** to join a group or organization for the secret purpose of spying, or to gain control.

**in·fin·it·y** (in fin′e tē) *noun.* **1.** the fact of being infinite or without beginning or end. **2.** unbounded space, time, or number. **3.** a great number; a great extent.

**in·gen·ious** (in jēn′yəs) *adjective.* **1.** showing cleverness or skill. **2.** doing something in an especially original or clever way.

**in·her·ent** (in hir′ənt *or* in her′ənt) *adjective.* being a permanent part of the nature of a person or thing.

**in·su·la·tion** (in′sə lā′shən) *noun.* **1.** keeping apart; protection. **2.** any material used for preventing electricity, heat, or sound from escaping.

**in·te·grate** (in′tə grāt) *verb.* **1.** to unify; to bring together. **2.** to do away with the segregating of people by race. **integrated.**

**in•ter•act** (in tər akt′) *verb.* to act upon one another. —**interaction** *noun.* action on each other.

**in•tri•cate** (in′tri kit) *adjective.*
**1.** complicated; involved. **2.** difficult to understand.

**in•vec•tive** (in vek′tiv) *noun.* violent attack in words; strong criticism; abuse; insults.

**in•ven•tive** (in ven′tiv) *adjective.* **1.** creative. **2.** skillful at invention.

**ir•rev•o•ca•ble** (i rev′ə kə b′l) *adjective.*
**1.** impossible to undo or take away.
**2.** incapable of being brought back or changed. —**irrevocably** *adverb.*

---

# J

**jim•my** (jim′ē) *noun.* a burglar's crowbar.
—*verb.* to break or pry open a lock, door, or window: They had lost their key, so she *jimmied* the lock. **jimmied.**

---

# K

**keen** (kēn) *noun.* a wailing cry for someone who has died. **keening** —*verb.* to wail loudly.

**kin•ship** (kin′ship′) *noun.* the state of being closely related, especially as in a family.

**knell** (nel) *noun.* **1.** the slow tolling of a bell, especially one announcing death.
**2.** a warning of the end or failure of something. **3.** any sad or doleful sound.

**knoll** (nōl) *noun.* a small, round hill.

**knot** (not) *noun.* **1.** an intertwining of string, ribbon, etc. **2.** a small group or cluster of people or things. **3.** the hard lump on a tree where a branch joins the trunk. **4.** a difficulty; problem. **5.** a nautical mile. **6.** a growth on or enlargement of a gland or muscle.

---

# L

**lab•y•rinth** (lab′ə rinth) *noun.* **1.** a place that consists of winding passages and dead ends, designed to confuse whoever tries to go through; maze. **2.** any intricate, confusing set of difficulties.

**la•ser** (lā′zər) *noun.* a device that produces a narrow, powerful beam of light in which all the waves are vibrating in the same direction at the same time.

**lat•er•al** (lat′ər əl) *adjective.* being on or directed toward the side.

**leave•tak•ing** (lēv′tāk′ing) *noun.* an act of departure; farewell.

**lib•er•ate** (lib′ə rāt) *verb.* to set free; release, as from captivity or slavery. **liberated.**

**loathe** (lōth) *verb.* to feel great hatred or disgust for; to detest.

**lo•tus** (lōt′əs) *noun.* a kind of waterlily noted for its large leaves and showy, often fragrant, flowers.

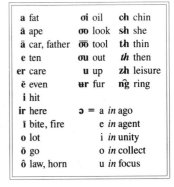

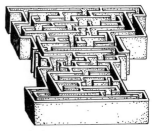

**labyrinth**

---

# M

**mag•ne•to** (mag nēt′ō) *noun.* a small electric generator, often used to produce the ignition spark for certain kinds of gasoline engines. **magnetos.**

**mal•func•tion** (mal fungk′shen) *verb.* failure to work properly. —*noun.* an instance of such failure.

**ma•nip•u•late** (mə nip′yə lāt) *verb.* **1.** to control by skilled use of the hands. **2.** to control in an unfair way. **3.** to change figures and accounts in bookkeeping for dishonest reasons.

**ma•te•ri•al•ize** (mə tir′ē ə līz) *verb.* **1.** to become actual fact. **2.** to assume material or visible form; to appear: He was afraid the ghost was going to *materialize* right there in his room. **3.** to appear suddenly or unexpectedly.

**me·di·o·cre** (mē′dē ō′kər) *adjective*. **1.** of only average quality, neither good nor bad. **2.** not good enough. —**mediocrity** *noun*. the quality of being ordinary.

**med·i·tate** (med′ə tāt) *verb*. **1.** to spend time in continuous quiet thinking; to reflect. **2.** to think about doing; plan. —**meditation** *noun*. act of being in deep thought.

**met·a·mor·pho·sis** (met′ə môr′fə sis) *noun*. **1.** change from one form, shape, or substance into another. **2.** complete change of character. **3.** in biology, an animal's change in form in its development from embryo to adult.

**min·is·tra·tion** (min′is trā′shən) *noun*. the act of helping or serving. **ministrations.**

**mis·chie·vous** (mis′chi vəs) *adjective*. **1.** naughty; causing annoyance or mild harm, often in fun. **2.** full of tricks and pranks. **3.** causing harm or damage to property or possessions.

**mis·er·y** (miz′ər ē) *noun*. **1.** a state of unhappiness and suffering. **2.** something that causes such suffering, as poverty or illness. **miseries.**

**moi·e·ty** (moi′ə tē) *noun*. **1.** a half. **2.** a part, portion or share. **moieties.**

**mol·ten** (mōl′t′n) *adjective* **1.** made liquid, especially by heat. **2.** formed by casting in a mold.

**mo·men·tum** (mō men′təm) *noun*. **1.** in physics, the force with which a body moves, which is the product of its mass multiplied by its speed. **2.** a strength or force that keeps growing.

**mon·i·tor** (mon′ə tər) *noun*. **1.** in school, a person chosen to help the teacher with certain tasks. **2.** a person or device that warns or reminds. **3.** a radio or TV set adapted for use in a studio. **4.** a unit that displays computer readouts.

**mon·soon** (mon sōōn′) *noun*. **1.** a seasonal wind that blows in the Indian Ocean and southern Asia, in the winter from the northeast and the summer from the southwest. **2.** the rains which are brought by the summer wind.

**mor·tal** (môr′t′l) *adjective*. **1.** sure to die at some time. **2.** relating to this life before death. **3.** likely to cause death. **4.** ending in death. **5.** very great; extreme.

**muse** (myōōz) *verb*. to consider quietly; to meditate on. —*adverb*. **musingly.**

**Pandemonium** was coined by poet John Milton in 1667 in his poem "Paradise Lost" to describe the capital of hell. He created it from two Greek words, *pan,* which means "all," and *daimōn,* which means "demon."

**pantomime**

# N

**nav·i·ga·tion** (nav′ə ga′shən) *noun*. **1.** the act or practice of navigating. **2.** the art or science of planning the direction or course of an airplane or ship.

**ne·crop·o·lis** (nə krop′ə lis) *noun*. a large burial area for the dead, especially in ancient times.

**niche** (nich) *noun*. **1.** a recessed space or hollow, usually in a wall, for the placement of an object. **2.** a place or position that is perfectly suited to a person. **niches.**

# O

**ob·sess** (əb ses′) *verb*. to occupy the mind completely, to an excessive degree; to haunt one's thoughts. **obsessed.**

# P

**pan·de·mo·ni·um** (pan′də mō′nē əm) *noun*. wild disorder, noise, uproar, or confusion.

**pan·to·mime** (pan′tē mīm) *noun*. **1.** a show in which the actors use only physical gestures and do not speak. **2.** the indication of something by use of gestures. —*verb*. to express something without using the voice.

**par·a·lyze** (par′ə līz) *verb*. **1.** to cause the loss of power to move or feel in any part of the body. **2.** to make powerless or inactive. **paralyzed.**

**pas·sive** (pas′iv) *adjective*. **1.** acted upon by something external. **2.** submitting or yielding without resistance. **3.** in grammar, having the verb in the form that shows that the subject was acted upon, rather than acting.

**pass·port** (pas′pôrt) *noun.* **1.** a government document that states the nationality of the person who carries it. **2.** anything that allows a person to go or get in somewhere, or do something.

**pa·thol·o·gist** (pə thol′ə jist) *noun.* an expert in the origins, causes, and development of disease.

**pe·cul·iar** (pi kyo͞ol′yər) *adjective.* **1.** unusual, odd; strange. **2.** distinctive to a particular group, thing, or person.

**pent** (pent) *adjective.* penned in or shut in.

**per·fo·rate** (pur′fə rāt) *verb.* **1.** to make a hole through. **2.** to make many small holes in a row. —**perforations** *plural noun.* the holes used to make something easy to tear.

**per·spire** (pər spīr′) *verb.* to sweat. **perspired.**

**per·sua·sive** (pər swā′siv) *adjective.* likely to be able to persuade or convince.

**plain·tive** (plān′tiv) *adjective.* expressing sadness; mournful.

**plea** (plē) *noun.* **1.** an appeal or request for help. **2.** an argument in defense of oneself. **3.** the legal response of a defendant in a law case.

**pon·der** (pon′dər) *verb.* to think over or consider carefully. —**pondering** *noun.* state of being in deep thought.

**pred·e·ces·sor** (pred′ə ses′ər) *noun.* **1.** one who has gone before another in time, as in a job or position. **2.** a thing followed by something else. **predecessors.**

**pre·mo·ni·tion** (prē′mə nish′ən) *noun.* a forewarning; a feeling that something will happen, especially something bad.

**pri·mor·di·al** (prī môr′dē əl) *adjective.* **1.** being or happening first in time; original.

**probe** (prōb) *noun.* **1.** an instrument used by a doctor to examine the inside of a wound. **2.** a careful investigation. —*verb.* **1.** to examine with a probe. **2.** to investigate thoroughly. **probed.**

**prof·fer** (prof′ər) *verb.* to offer: They *proffered* their friendship to the new classmate. **proffered.**

**prom·e·nade** (prom′ə nād′ *or* prom′ə näd′) *noun.* **1.** a walk taken for pleasure, exercise, or to be seen. **2.** a public place for walking: The *promenade* along the beach was crowded with people. —*verb.* to take a promenade.

**pros·trate** (pras′trat) *adjective.* **1.** lying face down. **2.** lying flat on one's back or face down. **3.** exhausted; weak; overcome. —*verb.* **1.** to lay in a prostrate position. **2.** to overcome.

**pro·to·col** (prōt′e kol) *noun.* the manners and forms of ceremony observed by diplomats of different countries.

**pro·to·type** (prōt′e tīp) *noun.* the first one of its kind; an original that serves as a model on which others are based.

**prov·erb** (prov′ərb) *noun.* **1.** a short saying, especially one that contains a wise thought. **2.** something that has become a typical example.

**pum·ice** (pum′is) *noun.* a light, porous volcanic rock, used in powder form as an abrasive or polishing agent. *Also called* **pumice stones.**

**pu·ny** (pyo͞o′nē) *adjective.* weak and feeble in importance; small in size and power.

# Q

**quad·ri·ple·gic** (kwo′dri plē′jik) *noun.* a person who is paralyzed from the neck down.

**quar·rel** (kwôr′əl) *noun.* an unfriendly or violent disagreement; dispute.

# R

**ra·tion** (rash′ən *or* rā′shən) *noun.* **1.** a portion or share. **2.** in times of scarcity, the amount of food, fuel, etc., each person is allowed to have. —*verb.* to divide into portions, for the purpose of distributing evenly.

**ra·tion·al·ize** (rash′ən ə līz′) *verb.* to make excuses for something, usually one's conduct.

**re·af·firm** (rē′ə furm′) *verb.* to declare again, as for emphasis: He wanted to *reaffirm* that he would never cheat on a test.

| a fat | oi oil | ch chin |
|---|---|---|
| ā ape | o͝o look | sh she |
| ä car, father | o͞o tool | th thin |
| e ten | ou out | *th* then |
| er care | u up | zh leisure |
| ē even | ur fur | n͡g ring |
| i hit | | |
| ir here | ə = a *in* ago | |
| ī bite, fire | e *in* agent | |
| o lot | i *in* unity | |
| ō go | o *in* collect | |
| ô law, horn | u *in* focus | |

**pumice**

**Puny** is taken from the old French word *puisné*, which means "younger." In a system in which first-born sons inherited any family wealth, those born after were necessarily weaker in power. The word eventually also meant smaller in size.

**re·cede** (ri′sēd′) *verb.* **1.** to move back; withdraw. **2.** to move or fade away. **receded.**

**reek** (rēk) *verb.* to give off a strong, unpleasant odor. —*noun.* a strong, bad smell; stench.

**re·ha·bil·i·tate** (rē′hə bil′ə tāt) *verb.* **1.** to make good or whole again. **2.** to restore to a former, better condition. —**rehabilitation** *noun.* the state of being brought back to good condition.

**re·hearse** (ri hʉrs′) *verb.* **1.** to prepare for a public performance by practicing beforehand. **2.** to repeat over and over again. **3.** to tell or relate. **rehearsing.**

**rem·i·nis·cent** (rem′ə nis″nt) *adjective.* **1.** remebering the past. **2.** causing one to remember: The blosoms were *reminiscent* of a flower that grew around her childhood home.

**re·morse** (ri môrs′) *noun.* a hopeless feeling of guilt or sorrow over a wrong one has done: She felt great *remorse* after she stole the money.

**re·nown** (ri noun′) *noun.* great fame; celebrity. —**renowned** *adjective.* well known.

**rep·er·toire** (rep′ər twär) *noun.* all the plays, songs, operas, etc., that a company or person knows and is prepared to perform.

**re·put·ed** (ri pyoot′id) *adjective.* supposed; usually thought of. —**reputedly** *adverb.* according to popular belief.

**re·sound** (ri zound′) *verb.* **1.** to cause to be filled with sound; echo. **2.** to sound loudly. —**resounding** *adjective.* making a loud echoing sound.

**re·tract** (ri trakt′) *verb.* **1.** to withdraw. **2.** to take back. —**retractable** *adjective.* able to be pulled in or drawn back: This knife has a *retractable* blade.

**rite** (rīt) *noun.* **1.** a ceremony that is performed in an established manner. **2.** any formal ceremony or act.

**rit·u·al** (rich′oo wəl) *noun.* **1.** an established form for a solemn rite or ceremony. **2.** anything performed at regular intervals. —**ritualistic** *adjective.* of, like, or done as a rite.

**rue·ful** (roo′fel) *adjective.* causing, feeling or expressing regret. —**ruefully** *adverb.*

Sarcophagus is made up of two Greek words, which translate as "flesh eating." It originally meant a kind of stone that the Greeks thought consumed the flesh of the dead, thereby making it a good material for coffins.

**sarong**

# S

**sac·ri·lege** (sak′rə lij) *noun.* an action showing disrespect for something sacred.

**sar·coph·a·gus** (sär kof′ə gəs) *noun.* **1.** any stone coffin or tomb. **2.** an ornamental, carved stone coffin, usually exposed to view.

**sa·rong** (sə rông′) *noun.* a skirtlike garment made of silk or cotton. **sarongs.**

**sa·vor** (sā′vər) *noun.* **1.** the special taste, odor, or flavor of a thing. **2.** relish; zest. —*verb.* **1.** to have a special flavor or taste. **2.** to taste or enjoy with great pleasure.

**scant** (skant) *adjective.* **1.** barely enough: They tried to feed all the men from their *scant* supplies. **2.** just short of full.

**scent** (sent) *noun.* **1.** an odor; smell. **2.** the sense of smell. **3.** the odor left by an animal. **4.** perfume. —*verb.* **1.** to smell. **2.** to get a hint of. **3.** to put perfume on.

**schol·ar·ship** (skol′ər ship) *noun.* **1.** the knowledge of one who studies; learning. **2.** money given to help a student pay for his or her education.

**scoff** (skôf *or* skof) *noun.* to make fun of; to jeer or mock.

**scorn** (skôrn) *noun.* **1.** contempt; the feeling one has toward something thought of as low or evil. **2.** the showing of such a feeling. **3.** someone or something treated with scorn. —*verb.* **1.** to think of and treat someone or something as low and evil; to show contempt. **2.** to refuse to do something deemed wrong. **scorned.**

**scraw·ny** (skrô′nē) *adjective.* skinny; boney; very thin.

**scribe** (skrīb) *noun.* **1.** one who writes out or copies books, or documents, usually before the invention of printing. **2.** a writer. **3.** a teacher of Jewish law. **scribes.**

**scrim·mage** (skrim′ij) *noun.* **1.** a rough-and-tumble struggle. **2.** a game played among members of the same team for practice.

**scru·ti·ny** (skroot″n ē) *noun.* a close examination: His *scrutiny* did not reveal any new problems.

**scul•ler•y** (skul′ər ē) *noun.* a room next to the kitchen where dirty kitchen work is done and things are stored.
**se•er** (sir) *noun.* a person who is believed to have the ability to see the future.
**seg•re•gate** (seg′rə gāt) *verb.* to set one apart from another; to keep different races separate, as in public schools. —**segregation** *noun.* the act of keeping people separate or segregated.
**seize** (sēz) *verb.* **1.** to take hold of suddenly; to grasp. **2.** to arrest. **3.** to take over with force. **4.** to attack suddenly. **seized.**
**se•mes•ter** (sə mes′tər) *noun.* one of the two terms, or instructional periods, that make up a school year.
**sham** (sham) *noun.* an imitation, fake, or counterfeit. —*adjective.* not real; false. —*verb.* to act in a deceptive way; to fake.
**shuf•fle** (shuf′′l) *verb.* **1.** to drag the feet along the floor when walking or dancing. **2.** to mix together playing cards to change their order. **3.** to mix together or handle in a disorganized fashion. **4.** to shift things around from place to place.
**sig•na•ture** (sig′nə chər) *noun.* **1.** the name of a person, written by that person: I needed my mother's *signature* on my report card. **2.** in music, the symbol used at the beginning of a piece that gives the key or time.
**sim•i•an** (sim′ē ən) *adjective.* of or like apes and monkeys. —*noun.* an ape or monkey.
**si•mul•ta•ne•ous** (sī′m′l tā′nē əs) *adjective.* happening at the same time, being done together. **simultaneously.**
**skep•ti•cal** (skep′ti k′l) *adjective.* not easily believing something; having or expressing doubt about something.
**som•ber** (som′bər) *adjective.* **1.** dark and dull; gloomy. **2.** serious and sad.
**so•phis•ti•ca•ted** (sə fis′tə kāt′id) *adjective.* **1.** experienced in the ways of the world; not innocent. **2.** technology or techniques based on the latest ideas.
**sound•proof** (sound′pro͞of) *adjective.* capable of keeping sound from entering or spreading. —**soundproofing** *noun.* material used to deaden or reduce sound.
**sou•ve•nir** (so͞o və nir′) *noun.* an object that is kept as a reminder of something.
**span** (span) *noun.* **1.** the distance of approximately 9 inches that is the distance between the tips of the thumb and little finger when the hand is spread. **2.** the part of a beam, bridge, arch, etc. between two supports. **3.** a certain period of time. **4.** a pair of animals used together. —*verb.* to stretch across: His term as principal *spanned* 10 years. **spanned.**
**spasm** (spaz′′m) *noun.* **1.** a sudden, involuntary contraction of muscles. **2.** any sudden, short burst of activity or feeling.
**spon•sor** (spon′sər) *noun.* **1.** a person who is responsible for another person. **2.** a person or business that advertises on radio or TV and thereby helps pay the cost of programming. —*verb.* to be a sponsor for. **sponsors.**
**sta•lac•tite** (stə lak′tīt) *noun.* a lime deposit, shaped like an icicle, hanging down from the roof of a cave. **stalactites.**
**stealth•y** (stel′thē) *adjective.* moving or acting quietly, secretly, and furtively. —**stealthily** *adverb.* in a manner not seen or heard: She was sneaking *stealthily* along behind the bushes.
**stern** (sturn) *noun.* the back end of a boat or ship.
**stodg•y** (stoj′ē) *adjective.* dull; stuffy; uninteresting: He felt bored while spending the day with his *stodgy* uncle.
**sto•ic** (stō′ik) *noun.* a person who remains calm and self-controlled and does not appear to respond to pleasure or pain. —*adjective.* not responsive to pleasure or pain.
**stren•u•ous** (stren′yo͞o wəs) *adjective.* **1.** requiring much energy or effort. **2.** very active or energetic.
**sub•merge** (səb murj′) *verb.* **1.** to put or go under water. **2.** to cover or hide. **submerged.**
**sub•mis•sion** (səb mish′ən) *noun.* **1.** the act of submitting to the power or authority of another. **2.** the state of being humble or obedient. **3.** the act of giving, or submitting, something to someone for decision or consideration.
**sub•ti•tle** (sub′tīt′′l) *noun.* in movies, words that appear at the bottom of the screen, translating the words the actors speak into another language. **subtitles.**

| | | |
|---|---|---|
| **a** fat | **oi** oil | **ch** chin |
| **ā** ape | **oo** look | **sh** she |
| **ä** car, father | **o͞o** tool | **th** thin |
| **e** ten | **ou** out | ***th*** then |
| **er** care | **u** up | **zh** leisure |
| **ē** even | **ur** fur | **ng** ring |
| **i** hit | | |
| **ir** here | **ə** = a *in* ago | |
| **ī** bite, fire | e *in* agent | |
| **o** lot | i *in* unity | |
| **ō** go | o *in* collect | |
| **ô** law, horn | u *in* focus | |

**Skeptical** comes to us from the ancient Greek word *skeptikos*, meaning "thoughtful or inquiring." When followers of one school of Greek philosophy began questioning all assumptions, they found they could not arrive at any real knowledge. These philosophers were called *Skeptics.*

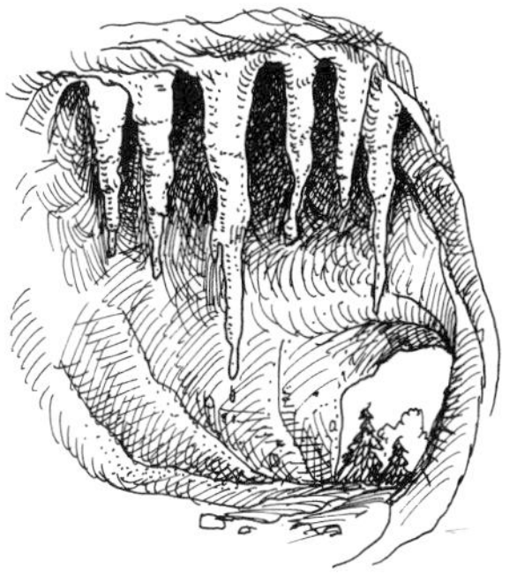

**stalactites**

**sub·tle** (sut"l) *adjective*. **1.** having a keen awareness of small differences in effect or meaning. **2.** hard to understand or recognize. **3.** crafty; clever; sly. **4.** having or showing delicate skill.

**suc·cumb** (sə kum′) *verb*. **1.** to give in or yield to: He *succumbed* to the temptation to eat a hot-fudge sundae. **2.** to die. **succumbed.**

**suf·fo·cate** (suf′ə kāt) *verb*. **1.** to kill by depriving of air; smother. **2.** to die from lack of oxygen. **3.** to have a feeling of smothering. **4.** to have difficulty breathing. **suffocating.**

**su·per·sti·tion** (soo′per stish′en) *noun*. **1.** a belief that something can influence something else, with no real proof that it can, as in the childhood rhyme "don't step on the crack or you'll break your mother's back." **2.** any belief or practice based on magic or chance.

**sus·cep·ti·ble** (sə sep′tə b'l) *adjective*. easily influenced by; open to; sensitive: He is very *susceptible* to catching cold.

**sus·tain** (sə stān′) *verb*. **1.** to hold up the weight of. **2.** to keep up. **3.** to keep up the courage or spirits of. **4.** to undergo or endure. **sustaining.**

---

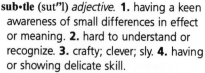

# T

**ta·ble** (tā b'l) *noun*. **1.** a piece of furniture with a flat top and supporting legs. **2.** food being served. **3.** the people seated at a table. **4.** a short list. **5.** a systematic arrangement of information, often involving numbers, usually arranged in parallel columns. **tables.**

**tact** (takt) *noun*. the ability to say or do the right thing, especially without causing anger or hurting feelings.

**ta·per** (tā′pər) *verb*. **1.** to make or become narrower a little at a time. **2.** to lessen little by little: The mother heard the baby's cry *taper* off as she fell asleep. —*noun*. **1.** the fact of becoming gradually thinner. **2.** a small or very slender candle. **tapers.**

**tax·i** (tak′sē) *noun*. an automobile that carries passengers for payment; taxicab. —*verb*. **1.** to ride in a taxicab. **2.** in aviation, to move slowly along the ground or water before takeoff or after landing. **taxied.**

**tech·ni·cian** (tek nish′ən) *noun*. a person who is skilled in performing the tasks in a particular field of art or science. **technicians.**

**te·di·ous** (tē′dē əs *or* tē′jəs) *adjective*. long and boring: Pulling weeds is *tedious* work.

**te·na·cious** (tə nā′shəs) *adjective*. **1.** holding or tending to hold firmly or tightly. **2.** stubborn; holding fast. **3.** keeping or holding on to something for a long time: The child had a *tenacious* memory.

**terse** (tʉrs) *adjective*. short and to the point; concise. —**tersely** *adverb*. in a clear manner using few words.

**the·sis** (thē′sis) *noun*. **1.** a statement or an idea to be defended in an argument. **2.** a long piece of writing based on research done to fulfill the requirements for a university degree.

**thim·ble** (thim′b'l) *noun*. a plastic, metal, or wooden cap worn over the finger, to protect it while sewing. —**thimbleful. 1.** an amount that would fit into a thimble. **2.** a very small quantity.

**to·ga** (to′gə) *noun*. a loose garment worn in public by the citizens of ancient Rome.

**trans·lu·cent** (trans loo′s'nt) *adjective*. allowing light to pass through, but not allowing a clear view of what is on the other side, such as frosted glass.

**trea·dle** (tred"l) *noun*. a lever worked by the foot to drive a machine. —*verb*. to work with a treadle. **treadles.**

**trek** (trek) *verb*. **1.** to make one's way slowly and with difficulty. **2.** to go on foot. —*noun*. a long, difficult trip: Jon and Tracy like to go on *treks* in the Himalayas. **treks.**

**trow·el** (trou′əl) *noun*. **1.** a small, flat-bladed tool, used for smoothing plaster, mortar, etc. **2.** a small hand tool used by gardeners for digging.

**trun·dle** (trun′d'l) *verb*. **1.** to transport in a wheeled vehicle. **2.** to roll along. **trundled.**

**Tact** is derived from the Latin word *tactus*, which means "touch." In modern language, *tact* is defined as the ability to understand the delicacy of a particular situation and behave accordingly.

**taper**

# U

**un·a·bashed** (un ə basht′) *adjective.* not embarrassed; unashamed: He cried with *unabashed* emotion when his dog died.

**un·bid·den** (un bid″n) *adjective.*
**1.** uninvited; without having been asked.
**2.** spontaneous.

**un·flinch·ing** (un flin′ching) *adjective.* not giving in or yielding; not showing fear or indecision.

**un·heed·ing** (un hēd′iñg) *adjective.* without paying attention.

**un·scru·pu·lous** (un skrōō′pyə ləs) *adjective.* without regard for what is the right or moral thing to do; not honest.

**un·stint·ed** (un stint′əd) *adjective.* unlimited; generous.

# V

**vac·u·um** (vak′yōō wəm *or* vak′yōōm) *noun.* **1.** space that is absolutely free of matter. **2.** a contained space from which almost all air and gas has been removed. —*verb.* to clean with a vacuum cleaner.

**van·dal·ize** (van′d′l īz) *verb.* to destroy or deface property maliciously, especially anything artistic or beautiful.

**van·tage** (van′tij) *noun.* **1.** advantage or superiority over a competitor. **2.** a position that gives one a clear view, also called **vantage point.**

**vec·tor path** (vek′ter path) *noun.* the path a rocket takes to reach its destination.

**ve·ran·da** (və ran′də) *noun.* an open porch, usually roofed, along the outside of a building.

**ver·dict** (vur′dikt) *noun.* **1.** a decision reached by a jury in a trial. **2.** conclusion; judgment; decision: The *verdict* was that the meal was a huge success.

**vi·a** (vī′ə *or* vē′ə) *preposition.* **1.** by way of: They went to Frankfurt *via* London. **2.** by means of: They sent the parcel *via* next-day service.

**vil·la** (vil′ə) *noun.* a large, impressive house in the country or outside a city.

**vis·i·bil·i·ty** (viz′ə bil′ə tē) *adjective.* **1.** the quality of being visible or able to be seen. **2.** the degree of clearness in the atmosphere.

**vi·sion·ar·y** (vizh′ən er′ē) *adjective.* **1.** not based on fact. **2.** dreamy, impractical. **3.** idealistic. —*noun.* **1.** a person who has visions. **2.** a person who attempts to reach visionary goals; idealist.

**viv·id** (viv′id) *adjective.* **1.** brilliant and strong, as in *vivid* color. **2.** having a clear picture in the mind as if real. **3.** full of vigor and freshness; lively. **vividly.**

| | | | |
|---|---|---|---|
| a fat | oi oil | ch chin | |
| ā ape | ōō look | sh she | |
| ä car, father | ōō tool | th thin | |
| e ten | ou out | th then | |
| er care | u up | zh leisure | |
| ē even | ur fur | ñg ring | |
| i hit | | | |
| ir here | ə = a *in* ago | | |
| ī bite, fire | e *in* agent | | |
| o lot | i *in* unity | | |
| ō go | o *in* collect | | |
| ô law, horn | u *in* focus | | |

# W

**wa·ry** (wer′e) *adjective.* **1.** cautious; watchful; on one's guard. **2.** showing caution.

**wind·lass** (wind′ləs) *noun.* a winch for hauling and lifting, especially one that has a core or drum around which the hoisting rope winds and that is turned by a crank.

**wrench** (rench) *noun.* **1.** a violent twist to one side. **2.** an injury caused by twisting. **3.** sudden strong emotion. **4.** a small tool, used for turning nuts and bolts. —*verb.* **1.** to twist or pull violently. **2.** to injure by a sudden sharp twisting. **3.** to strain meaning. **4.** to force a reply or expression of feelings: His hidden rage was *wrenched* from him by the skillful lawyer. **wrenched.**

# Z

**zo·di·ac** (zō′də ak′) *noun.* an imaginary belt that goes across the sky and that includes the paths of most of the planets. It is divided into twelve constellations or signs. In astrology, the sign under which one is born is believed to affect one's personality and fate.

**Vandalize** is taken from the ancient Germanic tribes of Vandals who ransacked Rome in the year A.D. 455. They destroyed many precious cultural objects as they destroyed the city. It is probably from that event that the word derives its current meaning, although it wasn't used in this sense until the end of the eighteenth century.

zodiac

# ABOUT THE
# Authors

### ARNOLD ADOFF

✳ Born in New York in 1935, Arnold Adoff began his career as a teacher in the Harlem district of New York City. Although he enjoyed teaching, Adoff became concerned about the lack of black literature available for his students. His solution was to compile his own anthologies of black literature. Among his most well-known anthologies are *Black Out Loud: An Anthology of Modern Poems of Black Americans* and *The Poetry of Black America: An Anthology of the 20th Century.*

### SAMUEL ALLEN

▲ Samuel Allen, born in 1917, has also written under the pseudonym *Paul Vesey.* While living in Europe, Allen was "inspired to write a poetry grounded in the fusion of African and Afro-American culture." His collections of poetry include *Ivory Tusks and Other Poems, Paul Vesey's Ledger,* and *Every Round and Other Poems.*

### JUDIE ANGELL

■ Judie Angell, who was born in New York City in 1937, thinks that "growing up heads the list of The Hardest Things To Do In Life. It's so hard, in fact, that some of us never get there. But even if the world changes as rapidly as it does, the feelings that we have while we're coping with those changes don't. I take a lot of those feelings, hug them, wrap them carefully in some words, and present them in a book with an invisible card that says, maybe this'll help a little—make you laugh—make you feel you're not alone."

## BRENT ASHABRANNER

❋ Brent Ashabranner, born in 1921, grew up in Shawnee, Oklahoma and graduated from Oklahoma State University in 1948. He began writing full-time in 1980, drawing on his experiences with various cultures. These experiences led him to write about people "who are not considered part of mainstream culture." He has won numerous awards for his writing, including the *School Library Journal* Best Book of the Year award and the ALA Notable Book award.

## HILARY BECKETT

▲ Hilary Beckett, who lives in New York City, has written short stories, poems, articles, and reviews of books by other authors. She has also written books of her own. One of her books, *Street Fair Summer*, reflects her love of street fairs. Two other books she has written are *My Brother, Angel* and *Rafael and the Raiders*.

## WENDELL BERRY

▨ Wendell Berry was born in Kentucky in 1934, and has spent most of his life there. A poet, novelist, and essayist, Wendell Berry's work expresses his concern for his native Kentucky. He has received the National Institute of Arts and Letters Literary Award and the Bess Hokin Prize for poetry.

## RAY BRADBURY

❋ When Ray Bradbury was in high school, he founded and edited a mimeographed quarterly called *Futurai Fantasia*. Since then he has had more than 400 short stories published. His work appears in over 700 anthologies, and he has written and adapted several movies, including *It Came from Outer Space* and *The Beast from 20,000 Fathoms*. Bradbury has also written numerous television plays, including eight shows for "Alfred Hitchcock Presents."

## SHEILA BURNFORD

✳ Sheila Burnford was born in Scotland in 1918. She has said, "Communication between animals has always fascinated me, not just instinctive means, but day to day, individual and original communication." For her book *The Incredible Journey,* she won the Canadian Library Association Book of the Year medal and the American Library Association Aurianne Award.

## ARTHUR C. CLARKE

▲ Arthur C. Clarke was born in England in 1917. He became interested in astronomy when he was about eleven, and he spent many nights mapping the moon. "Before long," he says, "I knew the lunar landscape much better than my native Somerset." He became a science fiction fan when he was a teenager, and in the 1950s he developed a keen interest in skin diving. Many of his stories reflect his interest in science fiction and the sea.

## ROBIN COOK

■ Robin Cook, born in 1940, is a physician. He is also the author of several very popular novels. When his first book, *The Year of the Intern,* did not make the best-seller lists, Cook set out to learn why. He read best-selling books and paid careful attention to how other novelists create suspense. His next book, *Coma,* was not only a best-selling novel, but was also made into a popular movie.

## WILLIAM CORBIN

▲ Willam Corbin was born in Des Moines, Iowa in 1916. After a long career in the newspaper business as a reporter, daily columnist, and feature writer, Corbin decided to try his hand at fiction for young adults. *Deadline,* his first book for teen-age readers, was published in 1952. Since then, he has written a great deal of fiction for young adults, and two of his books, *Smoke* and *Horse in the House,* were produced for television.

## T. S. ELIOT

✳ T. S. (Thomas Stearns) Eliot was born in 1888 and grew up in St. Louis, Missouri. After he graduated from Harvard, he went to England to attend Oxford University. He became a British citizen and never returned to the United States to live. Considered one of the major poets of the twentieth century, T. S. Eliot was also a well-known critic and playwright. He won many awards and honors, including the prestigious Nobel Prize for literature. He is one of two Americans honored at Westminster Abbey: a memorial stone was placed near the bust of Henry Wadsworth Longfellow.

## PENELOPE FARMER

■ Penelope Farmer was born in England in 1939. As a child she enjoyed reading and writing stories. She said, "I don't write a book for children. I write a book; and this is a big distinction, I think." She also said, "When you are a writer, you work very much by yourself, shut up in a little room. Being a writer can be incredibly lonely sometimes." One of her books, *The Summer Birds,* received a Carnegie Medal commendation.

## ROBERT FROST

▲ Robert Frost was born in San Francisco in 1874 but spent most of his adult life in New England. He wrote his first poem, in ballad form, when he was fourteen years old. Frost, whose poems are noted for their straightforward language and graceful style, loved nature and the outdoors. Many of his finest poems were inspired by the natural environment of New Hampshire and Vermont. In 1961, Frost participated in President John F. Kennedy's inauguration ceremonies by reading two of his poems: *Dedication* and *The Gift Outright.* He received many literary awards, including four Pulitzer Prizes for poetry.

## JEAN CRAIGHEAD GEORGE

✳ Jean Craighead George, born in 1919, has written many books for young people, including the Newbery medal winner *Julie of the Wolves* and *My Side of the Mountain,* which was made into a movie. She says she writes "about children in nature and their relationship to the complex web of life. I call my books 'documentary novels,' for the investigations into nature are scientific and carefully researched. Today a work for children must be accurate and faithful to the truth."

## FRED GIPSON

▦ Fred Gipson, born in Mason, Texas in 1908, has written hundreds of short stories and numerous magazine articles. He first learned to tell tales from his father, whom he describes as "an astute observer of nature along with being a wonderful storyteller." Growing up in the Hill Country of Texas, Gipson learned about the dogs, wild animals and great outdoors he would later write about in his stories, books and articles. *Old Yeller,* his most widely read work, is considered a classic of American fiction.

## VIRGINIA HAMILTON

▲ Virginia Hamilton, one of today's most highly acclaimed writers of fiction for children, received her education at Antioch College and Ohio State University. She also studied literature and the novel at the New School for Social Research. Hamilton's work has earned her numerous literary awards, including the Edgar Allan Poe Award for *The House of Dies Drear.* Two of her other books, *The Planet of Junior Brown* and *Sweet Whispers, Brother Rush,* were Newbery Honor Books. She and her husband, poet Arnold Adoff, live in Yellow Springs, Ohio with their two children.

## JAMES HERRIOT

* James Herriot, whose real name is James Alfred Wight, was born in Scotland in 1916. He was a veterinary surgeon in Yorkshire, England, for nearly 30 years before he wrote his first book at the age of 50. Darrowby, the setting for his books, is a made-up town that has features of two towns near Yorkshire. Herriot says about being a veterinarian: "It can be rough and dirty and the accident rate is high. If a horse kicks you, it can mean a broken leg. My daughter Rosemary was mad keen to be a country vet, but I talked her out of it. So she's a doctor instead, which is the next best thing."

## MINFONG HO

Minfong Ho was born in Rangoon, Burma in 1951, and grew up in Thailand. She now lives in Ithaca, New York. Her novel *Sing to the Dawn* won first prize from the Council of Interracial Books for Children. Minfong Ho said, "When I wrote *Sing to the Dawn,* it was in a moment of homesickness during the thick of winter in upstate New York, when Thailand seemed incredibly far away. Writing about the dappled sunlight and school children of home brought them closer to me; it aired on paper that part of me which couldn't find any place in America." She says, "I write to bring back what is gone, to relive what is lost, to make a mosaic out of fragments."

## LOUISE LAWRENCE

▲ Louise Lawrence was born in Surrey, England in 1945. Lawrence, who has written eight novels for young adults, says she had not intended to become a writer. But "one day, while I was washing dishes, an idea for a book simply dropped into my mind seemingly from nowhere. And so I wrote it down. And so I began." *Calling B for Butterfly* and *Children of the Dust* were both named Best Books for Young Adults by the American Library Association.

## BARRY HOLSTUN LOPEZ

✳ Born in 1945 in Port Chester, New York, Barry H. Lopez graduated from the University of Notre Dame, and later did graduate work in folklore at the University of Oregon. Lopez gained wide acclaim through his articles and books on nature and the environment. Lopez has also written three collections of short fiction, an anthology of Native American trickster stories, and a collection of essays—all of which reflect an affinity for nature and the people who live in close contact with it.

## DAVID MACAULAY

■ David Macaulay moved to the U.S. from England in 1957, when he was eleven years old. An author and illustrator, Macaulay said he spent a lot of time drawing when he was in high school. "I must have copied every photograph ever taken of the Beatles." After high school he studied architecture at the Rhode Island School of Design. He liked illustrating books and began to ask his friends to write books so that he could illustrate them. Then he wrote his own book and illustrated it. He said his first book "was difficult in the beginning since I am not a 'natural' writer." Now he finds that "writing is as much fun and as much of a challenge as making the pictures for the book."

## BERYL MARKHAM

▲ Beryl Markham was born in England in 1902, but was taken to North Africa by her father when she was four years old. As an adult she trained and bred race horses, then she became an aviator. She carried mail, passengers, and supplies to remote corners of the Sudan, Tanzania, Kenya, Zambia, and Zimbabwe. In 1936 she became the first woman to fly solo across the Atlantic from east to west. Her book *West with the Night* was first published in 1942. It was republished in 1987, one year after her death, and has been a best seller ever since.

## SCOTT O'DELL

✳ Scott O'Dell (1903-1989) grew up in California in the early 1900s. He said, "Los Angeles was a frontier town with more horses than automobiles and more jack rabbits than people. That is why, I suppose, the feel of the frontier and the sound of the sea are in my books."

## DANIEL OKRENT

◼ Daniel Okrent, who was born in 1948 in Detroit, Michigan, never intended to become a writer. "I began to write by accident—I had always loved baseball, and devoted rather more time to it than was reasonable for a grown man. Editor friends, bemused by my passion, threw a little money at me to share it with a magazine public." His friends had invested wisely, as Okrent went on to contribute to such periodicals as *Sports Illustrated, Esquire,* and *Inside Sports.*

## ALFONSO ORTIZ

▲ Alfonso Ortiz was born in San Juan Pueblo, New Mexico in 1939. After graduating from the University of New Mexico in 1961, Ortiz received his Ph. D. at the University of Chicago in 1967. He is now Professor of Anthropology at the University of New Mexico, Albuquerque. In addition to contributing to numerous anthropology journals, Ortiz has written a number of books about American Indian heritage, including *The Tewa World: Space, Time, Being, and Becoming in a Pueblo Society* and *New Perspectives on the Pueblos.*

## ANN PETRY

✳ Born in Old Saybrook, Connecticut in 1912, Ann Petry studied pharmacy before devoting herself to writing. She eventually developed a keen interest in writing about slaves and slavery. After writing a biography of Harriet Tubman, Petry portrayed another slave, the title character of *Tituba of Salem Village,* who became a central figure in the Massachusetts witchcraft trials of the seventeenth century.

## MAY SARTON

☀ May Sarton, who was born in Belgium in 1912, moved to Cambridge, Massachusetts when she was four years old. She said that she began to write poetry in the ninth grade. When she finished high school, she wanted to become an actress, so she went to New York City. After a few years she gave up acting and concentrated on writing. She has won many awards for her poetry, and she has also written fiction and nonfiction.

## LUZ NUNCIO SCHICK

■ Luz Nuncio Schick was born in Mexico City. When she was two years old her family immigrated to the United States, eventually settling in Chicago. She feels it is crucial for young people, especially those who want to write, to become aware of the music and power of language. Schick received a Master of Philosophy in French from Yale University and works as a freelance writer, editor, and translator. She lives in Lisle, Illinois, with her husband and two children.

## ROD SERLING

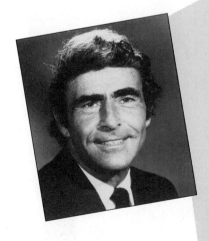

▲ Rod Serling began his journey into the dimension of sight, sound and mind on December 24, 1924 in Syracuse, New York. Despite his success with such television programs as *The Twilight Zone, Rod Serling's Night Gallery,* and many dramatic teleplays, Serling frequently criticized the networks for the medium's mediocrity and commercialism. Serling complained about the futility of presenting "a drama or documentary that is adult, incisive, probing, when every fifteen minutes the proceedings are interrupted by twelve dancing rabbits with toilet paper." Despite his disputes with network television, Serling managed to win virtually every TV award available, including six Emmys. In the years leading up to his death in 1975, Serling taught courses and lectured at many universities.

## KARL SHAPIRO

✳ Karl Shapiro, born in 1913, is both a poet and a literary
critic. He won many awards for his early poetry, including the
Pulitzer Prize for poetry. His early poems, which were
influenced by the work of the poet W. H. Auden, were of a
traditional nature. Later, Shapiro began to experiment with his
poetry. He said he felt that the restrictions of traditional poetry
stifled the poet's creativity. Many of his later poems are free
verse, a style of poetry made famous by Walt Whitman.

## PERCY BYSSHE SHELLEY

■ Percy Bysshe Shelley (1792-1822) is considered one of the
great lyric poets of the English language. He was born in
England but left there when he was twenty-four. Shelley, who
died when he was thirty years old, spent the last six years of his
life in Italy. He was drowned while sailing off the coast of
Naples. Among his best known poems are "To a Skylark" and
"Ozymandias."

## ROBERT LOUIS STEVENSON

▲ Robert Louis Stevenson was born in Scotland in 1850. He
was a sickly child and often had to stay in bed instead of going
out to play with other children. When he grew up, he wrote
many poems based on his childhood. He also wrote exciting
adventure stories, one of which is *Treasure Island.* Stevenson
said that the idea for the book came after he drew a map of an
island: "I made the map of an island; it was elaborately colored;
the shape of it took my fancy beyond expression." He said that
when he looked at the map, the "characters of the book began
to appear among imaginary woods."

### ROSEMARY SUTCLIFF

✳ Rosemary Sutcliff was born in Surrey, England in 1920. Her interest in writing began when her mother read aloud to her *Peter Rabbit, Winnie-the-Pooh,* and the books of Charles Dickens and Anthony Trollope. She has won numerous awards for her writing, including the Boston Globe–Horn Book Award and the Carnegie Medal Award.

### GLENNETTE TILLEY TURNER

■ When she was growing up, Glennette Tilley Turner enjoyed reading biographies. Having taught for almost twenty-five years, she discovered that the young adults in her classes also liked to read about real people. As a teacher she was named Outstanding Woman Educator in Dupage County, Illinois. Turner is the author of *Surprise for Mrs. Burns, The Underground Railroad in Dupage County, Illinois.*

### LOUIS UNTERMEYER

▲ Louis Untermeyer (1885-1977) was born in New York City. As the oldest of three children, it was often his job to entertain the younger children. Untermeyer wrote in his autobiography, "Fantasy was the most important part of my boyhood." When he was older, he continued to entertain young people by writing and editing books of stories and poetry.

### JAY WILLIAMS

✳ Jay Williams (1914-1978) has written many books, both fiction and nonfiction, for young people. He said, "At the age of twelve I won a prize (it was a book) for the best original ghost story told 'round the campfire in a boys' camp. The experience went to my head and I have been telling stories to children ever since."

## WILLIAM CARLOS WILLIAMS

※ William Carlos Williams (1883-1963) had a double career—he was a medical doctor as well as a poet. He felt that a poet should "write, as a physician works, upon the things before him." He was interested in capturing the details of everyday life and he felt that poetry should reflect the lives and experiences of ordinary people. He received the Pulitzer Prize for poetry in 1963.

## WILLIAM BUTLER YEATS

■ William Butler Yeats, Irish poet and dramatist, was born near Dublin in 1865. Although his family moved to London when he was still a boy, Yeats spent much of his youth with his grandparents in County Sligo, Ireland. There he absorbed the Irish myths and legends that would have such a great influence on his writing. He and several other young writers sparked what became known as the Irish Literary Revival. Yeats was active in Irish politics and he was made a senator of the Irish Free State in 1922. On his seven-tieth birthday he was honored by his countrymen as "the greatest living Irishman."

## LAURENCE YEP

▲ Laurence Yep, born in 1948, is well known for his science fiction writing for both children and adults. Yep said of children's writers that they "are still in touch with the magical power of words and pictures to capture the world in a way that many who write for adults are not."

## JIM YOSHIDA

※ Jim Yoshida was born in Seattle, Washington in 1921, where he grew up and attended high school. Visiting in Japan when World War II broke out, Yoshida was captured and conscripted by the Japanese Imperial Army. As a result, the United States government revoked Yoshida's citizenship after the war. He sued the government for reinstatement and finally regained his citizenship in 1954. He published the story of his life in 1972.

# GENRE INDEX

# AUTHOR INDEX